ALSO BY FRANCES WILSON

Literary Seductions

The Courtesan's Revenge

THE BALLAD OF DOROTHY WORDSWORTH

THE BALLAD OF Dorothy Wordsworth

A LIFE

FRANCES WILSON

FARRAR, STRAUS AND GIROUX
NEW YORK

Farrar, Straus and Giroux
18 West 18th Street, New York 10011

Printed in the United States of America
Originally published in 2008 by Faber and Faber Limited, Great Britain
Published in the United States by Farrar, Straus and Giroux
First American edition, 2009

Owing to limitations of space, illustration credits appear on page 317.

Library of Congress Cataloging-in-Publication Data
Wilson, Frances, 1964–
The ballad of Dorothy Wordsworth : a life / Frances Wilson. — 1st American ed.
p. cm.
Includes bibliographical references and index.
"Originally published in 2008 by Faber and Faber Limited, Great Britain"—T.p. verso.
ISBN-13: 978-0-374-10867-0 (alk. paper)
ISBN-10: 0-374-10867-6 (alk. paper)
1. Wordsworth, Dorothy, 1771–1855. 2. Wordsworth, William, 1770–1850—Family. 3. Authors, English—19th century—Biography. 4. Women and literature—England—History—19th century. I. Title.

PR5849.W55 2009
828'.703—dc22
[B]

2008041263

Designed by Michelle McMillian

www.fsgbooks.com

1 3 5 7 9 10 8 6 4 2

In memory of my own aunt Dorothy,

and of my grandmother Margery

. . . Mine eyes did ne'er
Rest on a lovely object, nor my mind
Take pleasure in the midst of happy thoughts,
But either She whom now I have, who now
Divides with me this loved abode, was there,
Or not far off. Where'er my footsteps turned,
Her Voice was like a hidden Bird that sang;
The thought of her was like a flash of light
Or an unseen companionship, a breath
Or fragrance independent of the wind;
In all my goings, in the new and old
Of all my meditations, and in this
Favourite of all, in this the most of all.

—WILLIAM WORDSWORTH, *Home at Grasmere*

CONTENTS

ILLUSTRATIONS

A NOTE ON THE TEXT

In order to distinguish Dorothy Wordsworth's writing in the Grasmere Journals from that of her other journals or her letters, and so as not to crowd the text with too many quotation marks, I have italicized the words, passages, and entries I quote from this source.

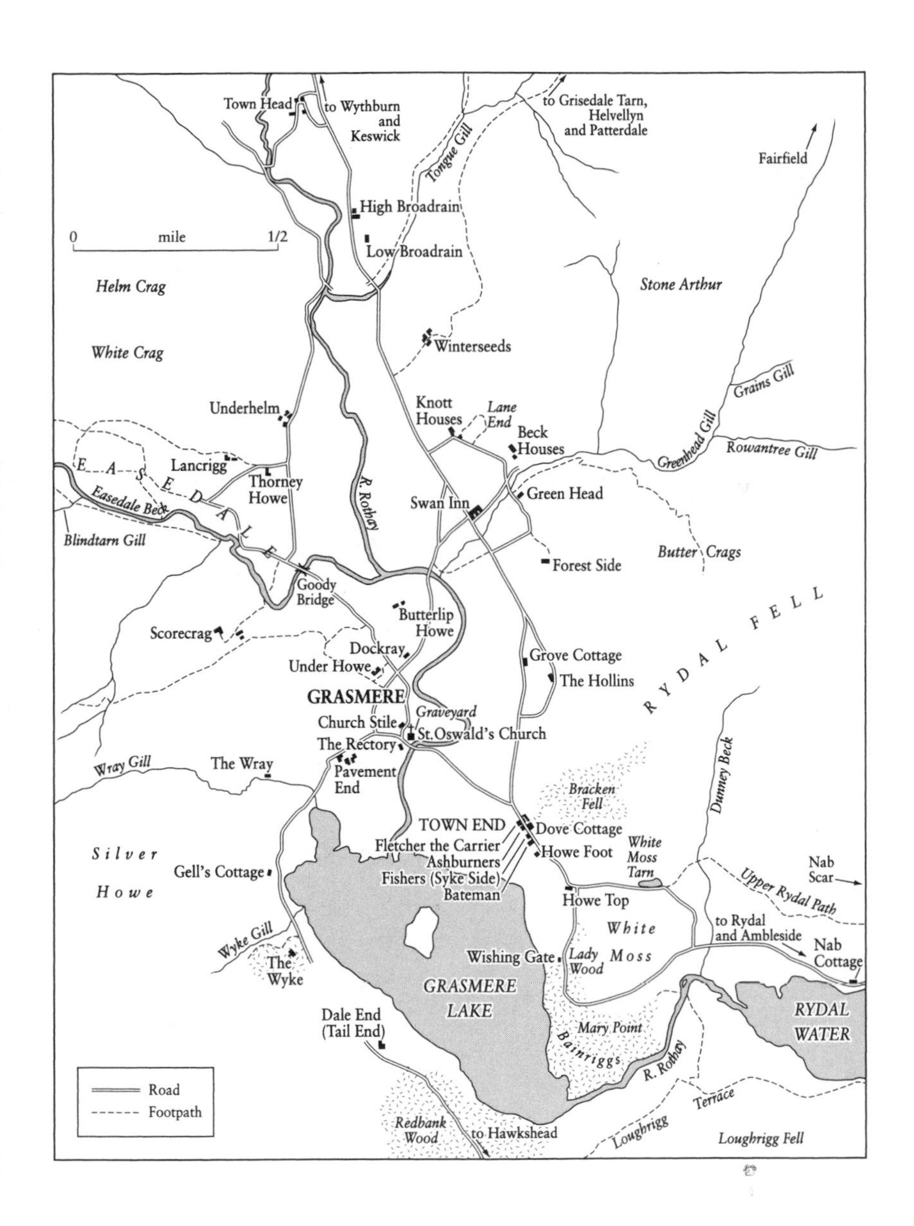

Town Head
to Wythburn and Keswick
to Grisedale Tarn, Helvellyn and Patterdale
Tongue Gill
Fairfield
High Broadrain
0 mile 1/2
Low Broadrain
Helm Crag
Stone Arthur
White Crag
Winterseeds
Grains Gill
Underhelm
Knott Houses
Lane End
Beck Houses
Greenhead Gill
Rowantree Gill
Lancrigg
E A S E D A L E
Thorney Howe
Easedale Beck
R. Rothay
Swan Inn
Green Head
Blindtarn Gill
Butter Crags
Forest Side
Goody Bridge
Butterlip Howe
R Y D A L F E L L
Scorecrag
Dockray
Grove Cottage
Under Howe
The Hollins
GRASMERE
Graveyard
Church Stile
St. Oswald's Church
The Rectory
Wray Gill
The Wray
Pavement End
Dunney Beck
Bracken Fell
TOWN END
Dove Cottage
Fletcher the Carrier
Ashburners
Howe Foot
White Moss Tarn
Silver Howe
Gell's Cottage
Fishers (Syke Side)
Bateman
Nab Scar
Upper Rydal Path
Howe Top
White Moss
to Rydal and Ambleside
Wyke Gill
Nab Cottage
Wishing Gate
Lady Wood
The Wyke
GRASMERE LAKE
RYDAL WATER
Dale End (Tail End)
Mary Point
Bainriggs
R. Rothay
Road
Footpath
Terrace
Loughrigg
Redbank Wood
to Hawkshead
Loughrigg Fell

THE BALLAD OF
DOROTHY WORDSWORTH

Introduction

CROSSING THE THRESHOLD

A wedding or a festival,
A mourning or a funeral.

—WILLIAM WORDSWORTH, "Ode: Intimations of Immortality"

. . . in *our* life alone does Nature live—
Our's is her Wedding-garment, our's her Shroud!

—SAMUEL TAYLOR COLERIDGE, "Dejection: An Ode"

She can stand it no longer. When she looks from her window at the two men running up the avenue to tell her that the wedding is over, she throws herself down on the bed, where she lies in a trance, neither hearing nor seeing. Earlier that morning the groom had entered her room and she had removed the ring, which she had been wearing all night, and handed it back to him with a blessing. He had then returned it to her finger, blessing it once more, before leaving for the church to bind himself to another. When she is told by the bride's sister that the newlyweds are coming, she somehow rises from her bed and finds herself flying down the stairs and out the front door, her body moving against her own volition, not stopping until she is in the arms of the groom. Together they cross the threshold of the house, where they wait to greet the bride.

Dorothy Wordsworth's journal entry for October 4, 1802, describes her brother William's marriage to Mary Hutchinson from the perspective of her bedroom at Gallow Hill, the Hutchinsons' Yorkshire farm, where she waited for the couple to return from the local church at Brompton. She was too distraught to attend the ceremony herself. For readers of her journals, Dorothy's account of William's wedding morning comes as a surprise, and not only because of the peculiar early-morning ceremony performed between the brother and the sister and the intensity of her physical response to the event. It strikes a new tone in her writing: after two and a half years of recording what she sees, she now records what she feels about something she has not seen, and it is typical of Dorothy Wordsworth that this long-awaited focus on herself comes just as she is going out of focus, slipping into a semiconscious state as one chapter of her life closes and the next begins.

Following her description of Wordsworth's wedding, Dorothy's journal seems to lose its purpose. One of her final entries, made a few months later in the new year not long after she had turned thirty-one, has her resolving to keep the project going in a fresh notebook bought during the summer in France: *I will take a nice Calais Book & will for the future write regularly &, if I can legibly, so much for this my resolution on Tuesday night, January 11 1803. Now I am going to take Tapioca for my supper, & Mary an Egg, William some cold mutton, his poor chest is tired.* Six days later, her final entry, headed *Monda[y],* is left blank. In many cases, people turn to their journals when there is nowhere else to turn, when they need to divide themselves into two in order to talk. But in the case of Dorothy Wordsworth, it was when her life alone with her brother was shattered that she stopped writing, as if writing and William were bound up with one another.

❧

This is the story of four small notebooks whose contents Dorothy Wordsworth never meant to be published, and which have become known as the Grasmere Journals. In tightly compressed entries that are mostly regular and mostly legible, they describe a routine of mutton and moonscapes, walking and headaches, watching and waiting, pie baking and poem making. Their style, at times pellucid, at times opaque, lies somewhere between the rapture of a love letter and the portentousness of a thriller; the tight, economical form they adopt is that of the lyric, but in the grandness of their emotions they are yearning toward the epic. The quickly scribbled pages catch the sights and sounds that other eyes and ears miss: the dancing and reeling of daffodils by the lakeside, the silence of winter frost on bare trees, and the glitter of light on a sheep's fleece. They record the love between a brother and a sister, and climax with Dorothy's "strange fits of passion," to use Wordsworth's enigmatic phrase, on the morning of his wedding.

The two and a half years covered by her Grasmere Journals would earn Dorothy Wordsworth the reputation of being, as Ernest de Selincourt, one of her earliest editors and biographers, puts it, "probably the most remarkable and the most distinguished of English prose writers who never wrote a line for the general public." The fact that she is one of our finest nature writers, that her phrases and descriptions were lifted and used by both Wordsworth and Coleridge, and that scholars refer to her for background material on her brother's most creative period directs us away from the startling originality of her voice and the strangeness of the story that reveals itself.

More than any other aspect of her character, it was Dorothy Wordsworth's responsiveness that was valued and praised by all who knew her. As a little girl she burst into tears when she first saw the sea, revealing the sensibility for which she was celebrated by her family. An old woman, she wept at the sight of her garden flowers after an illness had kept her indoors. In the readiness and accuracy of her responses, her taste was, Coleridge said, "a perfect electrometer—it bends, protrudes, and draws in, at subtlest beauties and most recondite faults." An electrometer was a recent invention, consisting of a fragile piece of gold, enclosed in glass, which responded to the most minute fluctuations of electrical charge, and Coleridge's metaphor bestowed on Dorothy his highest possible praise. For the writer and opium eater Thomas De Quincey, who became friends with the Wordsworths after William married, Dorothy was all nervous energy, rather, one imagines, like a highly tuned radio picking up waves. "The pulses of light," De Quincey said, "are not more quick or more inevitable in their flow and undulation, than were the answering and echoing movement of her sympathising attention." Dorothy's responses were immediate, but in her journals—a form of writing we associate with the recording of fresh reactions—she gives no response to the astonishing poems that were pouring out of Wordsworth, many of which she inspired herself and every word of which she stored inside her like charms in a magpie's nest. Nor did she record her response to the conversations she heard between Wordsworth and Coleridge as she wandered with them into the gloaming on the Quantock Hills, or lay with them beneath the shifting skies in Grasmere Vale. The poetic revolution going on around her, to which she contributed on a daily basis and which provides the backdrop to her journal, is the story she chose not to tell, rather as Louis XVI, filling in his diary for July 14, 1789—the day of the storming of the Bastille, following which his own days were numbered—simply wrote, "Rien."

The Grasmere Journals have taken on a curious status since their publication in full in 1958. They have never been out of print and they are regarded as an English national treasure, but their greatness as literature is agreed upon without anyone's being able to say what they are actually about or what type of woman it was who wrote them. In this sense they resemble Wordsworth's Lucy poems, whose poignancy and profundity are increased by the fact that we cannot agree on what their subject might be. Do Dorothy's journals describe her joy or dejection? Are her reflections, observations, and impressions a metaphor for her interior life, or is she simply documenting what she sees? Is her love for her brother that of a rejected mistress, or sisterly devotion of the kind that is hard for a contemporary reader to understand? Does Dorothy cast herself as the heroine of a tragedy or a comedy? Shakespearean comedies close, after all, on a pastoral wedding that anticipates a harmonious future, while the tragedies culminate in death and a new beginning. The Grasmere Journals offer both conclusions.

She was a small woman—under five feet tall—with a wiry frame. She was never beautiful, and the loss of her teeth by the time she was forty, together with her extreme thinness, her weathered skin, and the exhausting nature of her lifestyle, meant that she aged prematurely, looking twenty years older than she was. We have only two likenesses of Dorothy Wordsworth's face: a silhouette taken by an unknown artist in 1806, when the sitter was thirty-four and her lips had not yet begun to fold over her toothless gums, and a portrait painted by a Cumberland artist when Dorothy was sixty-two, showing a Victorian in a frilly cap busy at her writing. It is telling that she is depicted with pen and paper—she spent more time writing than she ever spent at her gardening or out walking. William hated the act of writing, and as his secretary and amanuensis Dorothy wrote out hundreds upon hundreds of his lines; she also kept up a voluminous correspondence with their relatives and friends and, when she found a spare moment, jotted down a few words of her own.

With her low forehead, strong nose, and pronounced chin, Dorothy had the same angular face as William, particularly as he is caught by Henry Edridge in the same year as her silhouette was cut. It seems appropriate that we have only a dark outline of the younger Dorothy, as the finer details of her appearance seem to have eluded her friends. Coleridge's description of Dorothy's face, when he first met her, tells us precisely nothing: "If you expected to see a pretty woman, you would think her ordinary—if you expected to find an ordinary woman, you would think her pretty." Nor have any who admired her talk left behind a memorable thing she might have said; we have no record of Dorothy's urgent, excitable voice with its round Yorkshire vowels and its nervous stammer. Dorothy Wordsworth tends to be described in abstract terms, leaving us only with a sense of her energy. Thomas De Quincey, who met her first when she was thirty-six, saw this energy as so overwhelming that it detracted from her sexuality. "Hurry mars and defeats even the most ordinary expression of the feminine character," he said. Her "abruptness and trepidation" came across to him as "rudeness" and lack of grace.

Those who knew Dorothy in her hot youth describe her as possessing all the wildness of the Brontë heroines she helped to inspire. It was the quality of her gaze they noticed first. For John Thelwall, the radical, she was "the maid of ardent eye"; Wordsworth, in "Tintern Abbey," famously praised "the shooting lights" of her "wild eyes," which were a clear and light gray-blue, and Coleridge, taking his cue, wrote of "the wild lights in her eyes." De Quincey described her eyes as "wild and startling" and Dorothy as "all fire, and . . . ardour," the "very wildest (in the sense of the most natural) person I have ever known." She had something of the "gipsy" to her, De Quincey said, which Coleridge catches in his description of the mysterious Christabel, the eponymous heroine of the ballad he wrote when he was at his most enamored of Dorothy.

Her wildness, meaning the unbridled, uncultivated, undomesticated side of her character, is not caught in Dorothy's journals. Despite her turning her back on a predictable life of churchgoing and charity in order to live with her wayward brother, there is nothing uninhibited in her journal entries. Dorothy is in fact markedly restrained in what she says, the very opposite of how she apparently was in her personal relations. In her journal she describes the Grasmere Vale as looking *very beautiful, in excessive simplicity yet at the same time in uncommon obscurity*, and it is the combination of excessive simplicity and uncommon obscurity that best describes Dorothy herself. She had a neurotic personality, and while we get a strong sense of her anxieties in her writing, she will rarely describe her state of mind. She never recorded an idea of her own, a reaction to a thought, or an explanation of her tears when she was unhappy or moved by a poem or play. What is striking about Dorothy as she appears in her journals, up to the point of the description of her brother's wedding, is how obedient she is, how she does not go beyond what is expected of her, in terms of either her gender or her relationship with William. Where was all this wildness? Her prose is defined by modesty and reserve, by the fear of what might happen were she to let herself go.

Today the name of Dorothy Wordsworth is more likely to inspire pity than to reignite the flash of her former power. Her reputation as one of the casualties of nineteenth-century femininity seems sealed. Dorothy Wordsworth has come down to us as the quintessential Victorian virgin, a little dotty but in general the perfect, selfless, and sexless complement to her self-absorbed and humorless sibling. It is her supposed sexlessness on which her biographers have focused. They have long been fascinated by the fact of her femininity—Dorothy is discussed as a remarkable woman, whereas Wordsworth is discussed as a remarkable person—but it is in relation to questions of her *sexuality* that the discussion stalls. It was appropriate, wrote De Quincey in 1839, that she was called "Dorothy" because it is a name we associate with maiden aunts; there is a hint in his description that he thought her a lesbian, but there is also a hint that he was half in love with her and that she rejected him. Addressing Dorothy directly in an essay he wrote about Wordsworth for *Tait's Edinburgh Magazine*, De Quincey admitted that he was not the only man to have "loved and admired you in your fervid prime," the term "admired" being the contemporary equivalent of what we might call "fancied." And yet Dorothy has been described as a "creature apart," an oddball who happily bypassed the needs with which the rest of us are burdened. It is William and not Dorothy who has to deal with the problem of physical desire: "Devoted as brother and sister were to one another, Dorothy seems to have been aware . . . that her brother's morbid moods and illnesses arose from sex-repression and that he should marry," wrote Amanda Ellis in *Rebels and Conservatives* in 1967, as if sexual repression were not something from which

Dorothy might suffer also. "Dorothy, if passionate, was essentially virginal," concludes Elizabeth Gunn in *A Passion for the Particular* (1981). A recent film, *Festival*, has as the butt of its joke an earnest actress performing every morning to an empty theater a play about Dorothy in which nothing happens. She looks out her window to admire the daffodils and the swallows; she wails at the mention of William's marriage. Edmund Lee, in the first biography of Dorothy to appear, *The Story of a Sister's Love*, published in 1886, praises her for the manner in which she "consecrated her life to her brother's good, relinquishing for herself everything outside him in such a way that she became absorbed in his own existence." Dorothy Wordsworth is famous for having lived her brother's life to the full and for being someone about whose independent existence there is precious little to say, and yet it is on the subject of absorption in her brother that Dorothy found, in her journals, so much to say herself.

In 1889, thirty-four years after Dorothy's death, Mrs. Henry Fawcett described her in *Some Eminent Women of Our Times* as someone who "did not know jealousy in love; her love was so perfect that she rejoiced in every addition to her brother's happiness, and did not, as a meaner woman might have done, wish his heart to be vacant of all affection save what he felt for herself." Mrs. Fawcett had only edited extracts of Dorothy's journals on which to form her judgments, but in their 1985 biography, *Dorothy Wordsworth*, based on all the sources there are available, both published and unpublished, Robert Gittings and Jo Manton reiterate this myth of Dorothy as not quite human:

> Yet, with all her lovable qualities, there is no sign that she ever aroused or experienced physical desire, nor

> that she felt this as a loss . . . From girlhood she seemed destined to be a creature apart, one of that distinctive company of nineteenth-century women, clinging like sterile buds to the family stem, tight-furled until November withered them.

Perhaps they are right, and Dorothy Wordsworth did go through her entire lifetime responding sensuously to every leaf and stream, falling to pieces with love for her loved ones, living at the mercy of her impulses and emotions, yet never once experienced or aroused physical desire or felt that this was a loss. But what is their evidence for supposing this? De Quincey believed that Dorothy had received "several offers," among them one from the young critic William Hazlitt, a suggestion generally dismissed as too unlikely to be taken seriously. And yet we know from his book *Liber Amoris* that Hazlitt, like De Quincey himself, was attracted to plain, hard-working women, and if Hazlitt did not go so far as to propose marriage, who is to say that he did not proposition the "wild" and "impassioned" Dorothy? All these "offers," De Quincey said, she "without a moment's hesitation . . . rejected decisively." Because a woman has not, so far as we know, had sexual intercourse does not mean she has never inspired or felt desire.

There is nothing in Dorothy's writing to suggest that from girlhood she seemed destined to live like "a sterile bud"; on the contrary, she comes across as someone who responds to her physical environment with open arms, someone acutely alert to the pleasures of the senses, who wants nothing more than to love and be loved in a home of her own. The problem with Dorothy Wordsworth is not, I suggest, that she did not experience or excite desire but that the idea of her doing so makes her readers so uncomfortable.

Journals, unlike autobiographies or memoirs, do not narrate a life, at least not intentionally so; they inscribe instead what the critic Donald Stauffer called the record of "an existence," the thoughts, feelings, and events of a regular series of days, which only with time begin to take on a specific direction, shape, or pattern. This, apart from her lack of ambition and his excess of it, is the main difference between Dorothy Wordsworth's writing and that of William. They both wrote autobiography, but she recorded the current goings-on in her own circumambient universe while he looked backward, rewriting his past to make sense of the present. They both explored consciousness, but his self is ever evolving, dependent on, yet increasingly distinguished from, the world around him, while hers gradually dissolves into its surroundings. When Dorothy refers to herself, it is usually to inscribe her own effacement: *My heart was so full that I could hardly speak.* At her most emotionally full, she is at her least expressive. Wordsworth wrote to see his life as a whole, as a grand narrative continuum; his great poem, *The Prelude*, reworked over fifty years, describes nothing less than the evolution of a poet's mind. He sees his life as a river, flowing from the source to the sea, but Dorothy's Grasmere Journals, like the stone on which she is sitting when they begin, are rocks, occasional, unexpected moments of pause and reflection around which the water eddies.

What purpose did Dorothy's journal serve? In her biography of the diarist Samuel Pepys, *The Unequalled Self*, Claire Tomalin quotes the politician Tony Benn, for whom writing a diary allows him to experience everything three times: first, as a lived experience; second, in the writing down of it; and third, in the rereading of the entry. Tomalin suggests that for Pepys there was a fourth reason, the offering of the self to posterity. For Dorothy Wordsworth, the case is rather different. Her journal was a way of making something out of nothing. She wrote not to preserve her memories but to give to William what he called in "Ode to Duty" "a repose that ever is the same." Her journal was less about recollecting her life than about collecting together some of its elements while editing the existence of others—such as Mary and Sara Hutchinson, Sarah Coleridge, and Annette Vallon. Dorothy wrote as a way of both pushing back the time when William was absent and holding it still when he was there. *The fire flutters, the watch ticks. I hear nothing save the breathing of my Beloved, as he now & then pushes his book forward, & turns over a leaf.* Her journal made motionless the world in which she lived, defending it from mutability and change. Daily life, in her hands, becomes elegy: *W sowed the Scarlet Beans in the orchard. I read Henry 5th there. W lay on his back on the seat. I wept, For names, sounds, faiths, delights & duties lost.* Dorothy fixed what was fluid and marked the passage of the present, writing not for posterity but for Wordsworth himself.

The Grasmere Journals describe a world that is not only still but also silent. The homeless who come to Dove Cottage, or those Dorothy and William meet on the road, have voices—*We met near Skelleth a pretty little Boy with a wallet over his shoulder . . . He spoke gently & without complaint*—but Dorothy and William do not speak, at least not in her journal. We hear William's voice only once, when Dorothy reports his comment that her tears over Coleridge's opium addiction, hopeless love for Sara Hutchinson, departure for London, and debilitating writer's block are *nervous blubbering*, and the crudeness of his remark smarts against the fragility of her prose. William and Dorothy talked to each other all the time, of course, as they worked the garden, ate their morning broth, or tramped the road to Ambleside to get their post, and she would stay up with her brother and Coleridge half the night talking. It is unlikely, given their flow of friends and neighbors, that Dove Cottage was ever quiet, but the clatter and sway of these exchanges are not what Dorothy wants to retain of their days. The only sound that breaks the silence of the sympathy she depicts between herself and William is the chanting of his poetry, which he preferred to compose as he walked. *William composing in the wood in the morning*, she writes; *Wm & I walked along the Cockermouth road—he was altering his poems*. She is so absorbed in William and his words that she has no sense of how comical these constitutionals appear to those who pass them by: William with what De Quincey described as his "cade"-like stride—"a cade being some sort of insect which advances by an oblique motion"—that would edge his companions off the road, Dorothy with what De Quincey called her "unsexual" gait, bent forward, hurried in her movements. "Mr. Wordsworth went bumming and booing about," one local recalled of Wordsworth's muttering as he paced up and down the path, "and she, Miss Dorothy, kept close behint him, and she picked up the bits as he let 'em fall, and tak 'em down, and put 'em on paper for him."

Her brother's marriage was to be Dorothy's funeral, but for Wordsworth it heralded a new beginning. The ceremony took place at the start of a day, the start of a week, the start of a month, the start of a century, and coincided with the end of a period of immense creativity. On Monday, October 4, 1802, he exchanged the "unchartered freedom" of his life with Dorothy for his next great concern: homage to duty. We might say that he moved from the state of childhood into adulthood. Wordsworth's marriage would last for nearly five contented and uneventful decades, a fact that astonished his friends. "The most interesting circumstance in this marriage," wrote De Quincey, "the one which perplexed us exceedingly, was the very possibility that it should ever have been brought to bear. For we could not conceive of Wordsworth as submitting his faculties to the humilities and devotion of courtship." He appeared emotionally cold, ascetic, almost holy in his reverence for his poetic calling. Wordsworth was now thirty-two, and his most exciting years had been lived: he had been in France during the early years of the Revolution, had fallen in love with a French Royalist and fathered her child, had suffered a profound crisis of self and belief, had built himself up again with the help of Dorothy; the poetry that would secure his reputation had been written; his days as a radical in both politics and literature were behind him; the intensity of his friendship with Coleridge had begun to wane; and he no longer required the receptiveness and recall of his sister's eyes and ears.

It is not unusual to think of this or that moment in the lives of ourselves or of others as representing a beginning, end, or turning point, or to see a certain experience as signaling either a high or a low mark, a peak or a trough. One of the advantages enjoyed by a biographer is the opportunity to plot the pattern of a life as if on a graph—to say with some certainty that this or that year represented either the best or the worst of times for the person being written about. In his poetry, William Wordsworth saw childhood as the highest point for us all; in biography, it is marriage that is usually regarded as a peak in the graph, following which—and this is famously the case with Wordsworth—there is a downward plunge and a plateau. In novels or stories marriage more often serves, as it does in Dorothy Wordsworth's Grasmere Journals, as an ending in itself. For the groom it betokens the end of restlessness, adventure, selfishness, and folly, while for the bride it is the reward that comes of waiting. So far as the reader is concerned, they lived happily ever after. For those close to the happy couple, the exclusivity enjoyed in marriage can be a violent, rejecting experience: after the wedding feast the front door is firmly closed.

The peak of Dorothy Wordsworth's own life was the time between the Christmas of 1799, when, as she put it, she and William *were left to ourselves & had turned our whole hearts to Grasmere*, and October 1802, when William married and they were left to themselves no longer. During these years, Dorothy never went farther than a day's journey from Dove Cottage. "A happier life, by far, was hers in youth," recalled De Quincey. "Amongst the loveliest scenes of sylvan England . . . her time fleeted away like some golden age." This period I call her threshold years, the golden age in which she was most happy and most aware of the fleeting temporality of that happiness, when she rested on the threshold between what Wordsworth called the "two natures in me, joy the one / The other melancholy." These were also the years in which, some believe, the relationship between Wordsworth and Dorothy crossed the threshold of brotherly and sisterly love. It was now that Dorothy was most alert to the corrosive effects of time; as William's impending marriage threatened to bring to an end the world they shared, she was positioned uneasily between the realization of paradise and the anticipation of its loss. Here, at the point of change, where one door closes and another opens, we experience life at its most intense, and it is on the threshold between one state and another that we can find Dorothy poised again and again. Whether she is observing the moon sailing along, lying on her bed in stillness, or simply gazing into her sublunary world until she can *see no longer*, she is endlessly ready to drift over the borders of vision. It was also here that Dorothy discovered that she had what Coleridge calls in *The Rime of the Ancient Mariner* "strange power of speech" and composed, in the form of her journal, a ballad of her own.

Ballads were everywhere in Dorothy's life. William filled the notebook he began in January 1800 with ballads, such as "The Romance of Robert the Devill" and "The Exile of Erin." This was the year he was putting together the poems for the second volume of his *Lyrical Ballads*. In the early weeks of keeping her Grasmere Journals Dorothy records spending her time reading ballads, noting on May 17, 1800, three days after her first entry, *Worked hard & Read Midsummer nights Dream, Ballads—sauntered a little in the garden*, on June 1, *Read Ballads, went to church,* and on June 4, *Walked to the lake side in the morning, took up plants & sat upon a stone reading Ballads*. Perhaps she is dipping into William's notebook, or else soaking up his edition of Percy's *Reliques of Ancient English Poetry*. It is typical of Dorothy that she does not say which ones she read or liked the best, but ballads, which form part of the content and structure of her day, also inform the content and structure of her journal. The voice that now emerges from her writing is different from the stylized, impersonal one of her earlier journal, kept when she lived with William in Alfoxden House in Somerset, or the rigid, conventional tone of the journal she had kept in Germany, or from the gossipy, garrulous voice of her many letters. As in a ballad, Dorothy lets her story unfold scene by scene, with structural simplicity and without commentary or authorial intrusion; contained in her accounts of quietness and stilltime lies a drama of turbulence and psychological tension.

The night before his friend's wedding, Coleridge had a dream. The marriage of Wordsworth and Mary Hutchinson was to take place on the seventh anniversary of his own, disastrous marriage, and he dreamed of William and Mary and the dramatic change their union would mean for himself and Dorothy. So great was to be the alteration of their small group that in his dream Dorothy was unrecognizable. She was no longer the small, slight, lithe, voluble creature he knew, with the gypsy brown face, ardent, fiery, darting eyes, and quick, nimble gestures. Her familiarity was gone, she was "altered in every feature . . . fat, thick-limbed & rather red-haired—[the woman in the dream bore] in short no resemblance to her at all—and I said, if I did not *know* you to be Dorothy, I never should *suppose* it. Why, says she, I have not a feature the same."

Nothing was ever again to be the same for Dorothy, whose love of her brother was, she wrote, "the building up of my being, the light of my path." Five days before the great event she confided to her closest friend, Jane Pollard, "I half dread that concentration of all tender feelings, past, present and future which will come upon me on the wedding morning." Dorothy often feels things by "halves." I began this book with a paraphrase of the concentration of feelings that came upon her on the wedding morning; here they are again, but this time in Dorothy's own words:

> *On Monday 4th October 1802, my Brother William was married to Mary Hutchinson. I slept a good deal of the night & rose fresh & well in the morning—at a little after 8 o'clock I saw them go down the avenue towards the Church. William had parted from me upstairs. I gave him the wedding ring—*

with how deep a blessing! I took it from my forefinger where I had worn it the whole of the night before—he slipped it again onto my finger & blessed me fervently. When they were absent my dear little Sara [Hutchinson, sister of the bride] prepared the breakfast. I kept myself as quiet as I could, but when I saw the two men running up the walk, coming to tell us it was over, I could stand it no longer & threw myself on the bed where I lay in stillness, neither hearing or seeing anything, till Sara came upstairs to me & said "They are coming." This forced me from the bed where I lay & I moved I knew not how straight forward, faster than my strength could carry me till I met my beloved William & fell upon his bosom. He & John Hutchinson led me to the house & there I stayed to welcome my dear Mary.

"Man survives earthquakes, epidemics, the horrors of disease, and all the agonies of the soul," said Tolstoy, "but for all time his most tormenting tragedy has been, is, and will be the tragedy of the bedroom." Dorothy sets her own tragedy in the bedroom, but the fact that we are peeping through the keyhole at this unhappy scene may make it seem more tragic and more shocking than it really is. There is a degree of suspense involved in the reading of anyone's private diary, but the particular tension that comes from reading Dorothy Wordsworth's journal is not only the result of taking pleasure in an illicit activity. It is born also of the friction between what she does and does not say, between the trauma she describes and the measured, restrained vocabulary in which she couches that description, between what she appears to know and not to know of herself, and the contrast between the self she believes herself to be and the curious creature she was described as being by others. In this sense, the tensions in her writing reflect the conflicts in her personality. The most perceptive account of Dorothy comes from De Quincey, who saw what others missed. Apart from observing that she stammered and stooped, had a clumsy gait, an "unsexual awkwardness," an "organic sensibility," and a twitching, "glancing quickness to her motions," he notes that she was perpetually subject to self-conflict—"the irresistible instincts of her temperament" were checked "in obedience to the decorum of her sex and age." The effect of this struggle was, he says, "distressing to witness." It is an apt comment: Dorothy Wordsworth is often distressing to witness.

Most of her journal entries were written on, or soon after, the day in question, but Dorothy described the occasion of her brother's wedding four days after the event, on Friday, October 8, when she had returned with the bride and groom to Dove Cottage from the honeymoon. It is part of a long entry that took in August and September as well, including a trip to Calais with William to meet his former lover, Annette Vallon, and his nine-year-old daughter. Perhaps Dorothy had been composing in her mind all week how she was going to describe to her journal the wedding day, making the above passage a well-crafted and considered piece of prose. Or perhaps she improvised, the words simply dropping from her pen without apparent thought. The passage might have taken her an hour to write, or it might have taken a matter of minutes. She might have exaggerated her distress, or she might have understated it. William and Mary might have been in the room with her, reading and sewing respectively as her quill scratched the paper, or she might have snatched time alone while they were sleeping or out walking. Whatever the circumstances of its composition, there is an important distance between Dorothy's original experience and her later representation of it here, a distance that Wordsworth described as the effect of "emotion recollected in tranquillity."

This is not the first picture of physical closeness between brother and sister that Dorothy has recorded—the journals are filled with examples of their strange love, depicted by her with tantalizing economy—but one of the most striking aspects of this tableau is what Dorothy holds back from saying. How much does she understand of the intimacy between William and Mary from which she is excluded, and how much do we understand of the intimacy between William and Dorothy? What do their actions actually mean? Is the gesture of the ring symbolic of Wordsworth's continued commitment to Dorothy despite the presence of Mary, or of what he calls elsewhere the "mighty gulf of separation" that is about to take place between himself and his "dear, dear sister"? Is it a marriage or a divorce taking place in the bedroom?

Dorothy's record of the wedding concludes with a picture of the bridegroom returning from the church not with his wife but with his sister on his arm. Walking to the house with her brother by her side, Dorothy is back where she belongs. On foot together they have covered hundreds of miles, she with her familiar "stooping attitude," he moving in his oblique fashion, with a wry and twisted gait that would eventually, as De Quincey said, "edge off his companion from the middle to the side of the highroad." Arriving thus back at the house and crossing the threshold with Dorothy by his side, Wordsworth confirms to her that both nothing and everything between them has changed.

What purpose did the recording of Wordsworth's wedding morning serve for Dorothy? "The thoughts of my heart . . . how could I bear to look on *them* after they were written?" wrote Elizabeth Barrett of her painful feelings for Hugh Stuart Boyd—married, blind, and twice her age. She confided to her journal: "Adam made fig leaves necessary for the mind, as well as for the body." "I can't read it over; and God knows what contradictions it may contain," wrote Byron of his own journal. "If I am sincere with myself (but I fear one lies more to one's self than to anyone else), every page should confute, refute, and utterly abjure its predecessor." We construct the self we can bear to face in our journal writing, but our entries also harbor abjection and shame. Did Dorothy ever reread this passage recalling the day that she was edged off by William, from the middle to the side of his life? Would she have then considered it a successful account of her feelings; would she remember other exchanges and experiences during that morning which she had not recorded; would she have recognized the wretched woman lying there on the bed as a portrait of herself?

It has been traditional, perhaps as a result of Wordsworth's description of her voice in *Home at Grasmere* as being "like a hidden bird that sang," to describe Dorothy's writing itself as birdlike. "The words themselves are as unobtrusive as sparrows," one critic says of the Grasmere Journals; "the writing is as natural and unforced as the singing of larks," says another. "We listen to her," says a third, "as we might listen to a thrush singing." William described himself and Dorothy as resembling two swans—birds who mate for life—and in her last, dark years the now inarticulate sounds she made were compared to those of "a partridge or a turkey." But the bird that comes most to mind when I read Dorothy's burdened journals is the albatross draped around the Ancient Mariner's neck in Coleridge's famous *Rime*. Dorothy Wordsworth emerges from her own ballad both as an image of the great seabird shot down in its prime and as a version of the voyager himself, with the "glittering eye." "I pass, like night, from land to land; / I have strange power of speech," the Mariner explains to the wedding guest. Dorothy, too, chose the day of a wedding on which to tell her tale of crossing the line, and then passed, like night, away.

Chapter One

FOR RICHER, FOR POORER: LONGING

"My life is dreary,
He cometh not," she said.

—ALFRED, LORD TENNYSON, "Mariana"

What voice console the incessant sigh,
And everlasting longings for the lost?

—JOHN LOGAN, "Ode: Written in a Visit to the Country in Autumn"

The soul of Romanticism was longing without goal
and boundary and object.

—FRITZ STRICH, *Deutsche Klassik und Romantik*

She is sitting on a stone when we first meet her, by the shore of Windermere. Dorothy and William have been living together in Grasmere since Christmastime 1799, five days before her twenty-eighth birthday. It is now an early afternoon in late spring, and Dorothy is crying. William and their younger brother John, who has been with them for four of the five months they have been at Dove Cottage, have set off over the Yorkshire Dales to Gallow Hill near Scarborough, in order to see Mary Hutchinson, leaving Dorothy alone in a house for the first time in her life.

She does not say why she is not included on this visit to her friend, but it is almost certainly because William has decided to marry Mary. Dorothy and William, who share everything together, have agreed that this visit is something William has to do without her. It is from William and not John that Dorothy cannot bear to part, and it is with William's name that the Grasmere Journals begin:

> *May 14th 1800. Wm & John set off into Yorkshire after dinner at ½ past 2 o'clock—cold pork in their pockets. I left them at the turning of the Low-wood bay under the trees. My heart was so full that I could hardly speak to W when I gave him a farewell kiss. I sate a long time upon a stone at the margin of the lake, & after a flood of tears my heart was easier. The lake looked to me I knew not why dull & melancholy, the weltering on the shores seemed a heavy sound.*

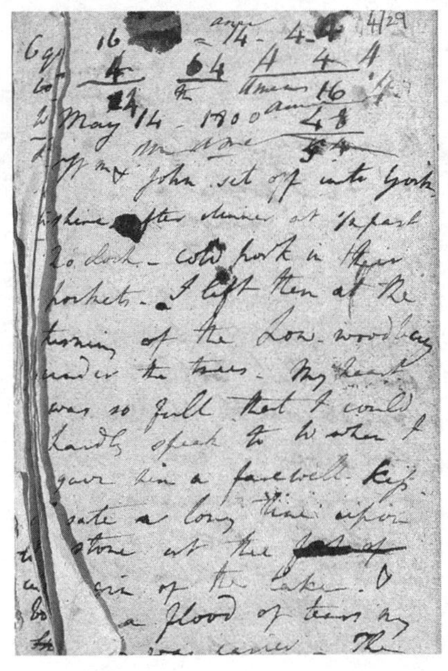
May 14 – 1800
Wm & John set off into York
shire after dinner at ½ past
2 o clock – cold pork in their
pockets – I left them at the
turning of the Low-wood bay
under the trees – My heart
was so full that I could
hardly speak to W when I
gave him a farewell kiss
sate a long time upon
stone at the
gin of the lake. &
a flood of tears my
was easier – The

The opening lines of the Grasmere Journals

Dorothy Wordsworth documents things rather than thoughts, but one of the hallmarks of her Grasmere Journals is the way in which, by blending factual accuracy with emotion, she gives new shapes to subjects and scenes. The world she draws, with Dove Cottage and its environs at the center and all that is out of her vision peripheral, is defined by edges and boundaries, separations, spaces, and oppositions. Dorothy's walks are all in the vale that encloses her home; walking out of Grasmere, William is stepping over the circumference. In his poem *Home at Grasmere*, Wordsworth describes "our dear vale" as a place that "received us . . . with a passionate welcoming," that "loves us now." Wrapping him up and folding him in, their valley is the perfect mother: "I feel your guardianship; I take it to my arms." This afternoon the vale is enclosing neither of them. The lake, which Dorothy loves, is now distant and comfortless, *dull & melancholy, the weltering on the shores seemed a heavy sound*. She weighs and measures her condition: her heart is *full*, she cries until it is lighter; her brothers are together, she is apart from them; they are walking, she is still; she leaves them *under* the trees, she sits *upon* a stone. Dorothy initially wrote that she sat upon a stone at "the foot of the lake" before changing "foot" to "margin," which gets in more her sense of frames, limits, borders. It is William who provides the contours of her life.

Her writing is praised for its simplicity and transparency, for being unaware of its own effects, but what is striking in the opening scene of the Grasmere Journals is how self-conscious Dorothy is. She appears, badger-like, when no one is looking; Dorothy is most vivid when William is not there. Her mind, as the critic William Hazlitt said of Wordsworth's, is assumed to be the reverse of the dramatic, but there is a great deal of drama in the way Dorothy sets the stage. She reviews her actions, surveys her own image, picturing herself to herself, envisaging what she looks like as she weeps by the lake at half past two, as though she were checking in the glass—as women often do—the effect of tears on her face. But at the same time as being conscious of the impression she makes, Dorothy is curiously egoless; the cold pork in William's and John's pockets has a more solid identity than she does. It is as if she were simply a path down the hillside, a channel through which perceptions pass, like streams.

John's absence is of no emotional consequence to her, even though Dorothy had not seen him for nearly eight years and he has been at Dove Cottage for almost the same amount of time as she and William have themselves. At sea with the East India Company from 1790, John was a sailor without a home on land. He considered himself a burden on other people: when he arrived at Dove Cottage in January, he was so overcome by shyness that he twice turned back from the front door, eventually sending a message from the local inn to tell his siblings he was there. Once united with Dorothy and William, he paced the slate floor of their cottage "exulting . . . that his Father's Children had once again a home together." John, ever practical and keen to earn his keep, helped in the house and garden and suited, in his temperament, Dorothy and William entirely. He was, they thought, a "silent poet." It was John, wrote Dorothy, who "was continually pointing out something which perhaps would have escaped our observation, for he had so fine an eye that no distinction was unnoticed by him." Herein lies another of the oddities of Dorothy's journal: not only does John, so harmonious a companion, go unmentioned, but for all her accounts of the life she shared with William as a couple, the two of them are almost never alone during the time she covers. In 1827 Dorothy would remember 1800 as the year in which they were isolated from the rest of the world. "W and I quite alone this evening as 27 years ago," she wrote in the journal she then kept. But throughout that year the tiny cottage had been filled to bursting point, with Mary Hutchinson arriving for a five-week stay the month after John's arrival and Coleridge appearing in April for four further weeks, returning with his wife and young child for another month at the end of June. Dorothy no doubt had to give the camp bed she slept in to the Coleridges and move into John's room, leaving John to double up with William. Because Coleridge arrived more unwell that June than he had been since a boy, making him bed-bound for two weeks, with William unwell himself, and with Sarah Coleridge and Dorothy not in sympathy with one another, the house would have seemed smaller still.

Then barely had Mary left before William was off seeing her again, at her brother's new farm in Gallow Hill, and this time without Dorothy. In mourning the loss of her life alone with William, Dorothy is mourning the loss of something she has never, except for their melancholic months in Goslar, really had.

Having poured out her grief on the shores of the lake, Dorothy sets off home. As she begins her five-mile journey back to the cottage, she does as she always does when she fades into melancholy: she looks and she lists. Looking, she reconnects, bit by bit, detail by detail, with outward things, and she and the world come back into color. She is in a micro-realm, a detective searching for clues. Listing, she itemizes her surroundings as if ticking off an inventory. As they do for Hamlet's Ophelia, flowers symbolize her sorrow:

> *I walked as long as I could amongst the stones of the shore. The wood rich in flowers. A beautiful yellow, palish yellow*

flower, that looked thick round & double, & smelt very sweet—I supposed it was a ranunculus—Crowfoot, the grassy-leaved Rabbit-toothed white flower, strawberries, Geranium—scentless violet, anemones two kinds, orchises, primroses. The heckberry very beautiful as a low shrub.

It is now that she determines to keep a journal until William's return: *I set about keeping my resolve because I will not quarrel with myself, & because I shall give Wm Pleasure by it when he comes home again.* Dorothy begins her journal when she fears the loss of her brother; her writing will serve as a reminder to him of what it is he values in her most—the purity of her observations, the richness of her sensibility, her alertness to "the sudden charm," as Coleridge put it, of light and shade on familiar things—and a reminder of how abandoned she feels when he is with Mary. Keeping a journal about the emptiness of their home without him, Dorothy conveys more than a hint of accusation in its origins. It seems that Dorothy is hoping to give William something rather more complicated than *pleasure*.

At nine o'clock that night, her face flame colored from the fire and her head dully aching from the strain of the day, she takes out a small mottled-brown notebook. It has been used before, during the freezing winter she and William spent in Goslar two years earlier, but six pages have been cut from the front and five from the back. She has already written inside the front cover, listing the clothes she would take to Germany (shirts, nightcaps, and handkerchiefs) and the groceries she bought there (bread, milk, sugar, rum). On the back cover is a doodled drawing, the size of one of Thomas Bewick's thumbnail illustrations, of two churches, one with a cemetery attached. Also already contained at the back of the book are five verses from Wordsworth's "Complaint of a

The back cover of the first notebook of the Grasmere Journals

Forsaken Indian Woman" and epigrams taken from the life of the American scientist and inventor of the lightning rod, Benjamin Franklin, who lived with his wife, Dorothy recorded, "together with reciprocal affection for fifty nine years / And without private fortune." It is in keeping with her character that she noted this down; Dorothy is a keen reader of biography, and Franklin provides a model of the life she and William want to lead: industrious, frugal, dedicated to work. In small, neat writing she pens her first line: *May 14th 1800. Wm & John set off into Yorkshire*, followed by some *amens* to test the nib of her quill. The Grasmere Journals have begun.

Many diarists write to make the bits and pieces of their daily selves seem continuous, but Dorothy appears among the flotsam and jetsam of her non sequiturs as episodic, fractured, and forensic. The first entry of her journal continues:

> *Arrived at home with a bad head-ach, set some slips of privet. This evening cold had a fire—my face now flame-coloured. It is nine o'clock, I shall soon go to bed. A young woman begged at the door—she had come from Manchester on Sunday morn with two shillings & a slip of paper which she supposed a Bank note—it was a cheat. She had buried her husband & three children within a year & a half—all in one grave—burying very dear—paupers all put in one place—20 shillings paid for as much ground as will bury a man—a gravestone to be put over it or the right will be lost—1 1/6 each time the ground is opened. Oh! That I had a letter from William!*

It is the fragmented style and its incompletion as well as the story it tells of the self as a perceiving subject that makes Dorothy's journal so identifiably Romantic, if we understand Romanticism at least in part to be, as the German poet Friedrich Schlegel said, an art that is eternally in the "process of becoming" and "can never be completed."

She meant it to seal her brother closer to her, but also to seal together her own discordant sides: *because I will not quarrel with myself* is the first reason Dorothy gives for starting a journal, and something of what she means by this striking phrase becomes more apparent as the months roll by. Perhaps this is what De Quincey called the distressing "self-conflict" that he felt resulted from the friction between her "excessive organic sensibility" and the demand for a certain "decorum of her sex and age." If writing for Dorothy is a way of avoiding conflict, she suggests that it is also a way of outwitting her demon: she sees writing as a pacifying, unifying activity that she hopes will bring the two sides of herself into harmony. As such, she makes it clear that she does not regard herself to be a writer in the way that her brother is a writer. Self-conflict was for him the basis of poetry, the battle between pain and pleasure making up the very stuff of Wordsworth's creativity, not least because writing, particularly rewriting, made him ill. The need to shed himself of words as a snake sheds its skin was his vocation. Wordsworth would never have turned to writing by way of avoiding self-conflict: it was there, on the page, that his self-conflict began.

Dorothy's unambitious approach to her journal is vital in understanding the kind of person she was: living among the most brilliant poets of the age, she saw that for Wordsworth and Coleridge their craft consisted in the pursuit of endlessness, of infinite complexity, that they found no security in the words by which they were tormented and struck down. She realized the full implications of becoming a writer and did not set out to achieve anything so vertiginous. "I should detest the idea of setting myself up as an author," she wrote to a friend. Instead, when she begins her journal, she identifies herself with the grieving woman who comes begging at the cottage door, whose entire family has been lost to her in a matter of a year and a half. Wishing, only seven hours after he leaves to see his future wife, that she could have a letter from William, Dorothy instead begins a letter to him. Recording the visit of the bereaved pauper is one of the ways by which she communicates her fears for her immediate future. Dorothy's record of the widow's visit also tells her brother something of her present state of mind: with the loss of him, she loses everything.

So far unmentioned in her journal is Mary Hutchinson, the reason behind the project's origin. Dorothy's prose is weighed down by what goes unsaid.

The Grasmere Journals were born of longing. Dorothy Wordsworth's theme, if journals can be said to have themes, is loss, which has also been, so far, the story of her life. She was first separated from William following the sudden death of their mother, Anne, in 1778. Dorothy was six, "a little Prattler among men"; William was seven, and they were playmates. It was apparently Anne Wordsworth's dying wish that her third child and only daughter be taken from home and raised by her second cousin Elizabeth Threlkeld in the Yorkshire town of Halifax. The four Wordsworth sons, Richard, William, John, and Christopher, stayed behind in the Cumberland market town of Cockermouth, but as they became old enough, they went off to boarding school at Hawkshead, in the heart of the Lake District.

The Wordsworths were genteel; John Wordsworth, the father Dorothy hardly knew, was an attorney to Lord Lowther, and the redbrick house she left, in which she was born on Christmas Day 1771, is still the grandest in Cockermouth. Situated on the main street, it is fronted by stone steps and a portico, with a terrace behind that overlooks the river Derwent. The place remained, in Dorothy's adult memory, "a spot which I remember as vividly as if I had been there just the other day." Anne Wordsworth read her children the tales of Robin Hood and Jack the Giant Killer, and sent them to play in fields of yellow ragwort. Her death was a devastation that determined the rest of Dorothy's life. She did not return to Cockermouth, not even for Christmas, which was also the time of her birthday. "I was never once at home," she recalled on her thirty-fourth birthday, "was never for a single moment under my father's roof after her death, which I cannot think of without regret." John Wordsworth's rejection of his daughter she never understood. "We at the same moment lost a father, a mother, a home," Dorothy later wrote to her childhood friend Jane Pollard. But Dorothy's brothers did not, initially, lose a father or a home. It was only Dorothy, as Wordsworth later wrote of his mother, who "lost a home in losing thee." Along with the loss of their mother the boys lost only a sister, but what was lost by Dorothy was a part of herself.

The Halifax household where Dorothy grew up was solid, cheerful, and devoted. Elizabeth Threlkeld, whom Dorothy would always call "Aunt," was also raising her deceased sister's five children, aged from ten to seventeen, while managing the haberdashery business that had belonged to her brother-in-law. Dorothy was the youngest and favorite of her new foster family, and due to the kindness of Aunt Threlkeld the years of her childhood seem to have passed smoothly enough for a child who had been deprived of her mother and home before being seemingly forgotten by her father and brothers. She spent her time hanging out of windows, "wandering wild" with Jane Pollard, searching for bilberries, black porringer in hand, bursting in and out of the boisterous Pollard family home, and picking up a checkered education in a variety of schools. Jane Pollard, the same age as Dorothy, would become part of the fabric of her life. The Pollards were a large, happy family of six girls, daughters of a well-to-do wood merchant, and Dorothy was treated as one of them. "Oh! How often has that Fire-place been surrounded by a party of happy children of whom I was not the least happy!" she recalled of Mrs. Pollard's parlor. None of Jane's letters to Dorothy survives, but Dorothy's letters to Jane show that the language of their friendship was organized around the stylized sentimentality employed by middle-class girls in the eighteenth century. Dorothy would always be influenced by literature, but her friendship with Jane Pollard reveals something more about her. When she loved, she never let go; attachment for Dorothy was a continuation of selfhood, and before William's reappearance it was with Jane that she constructed a happier world.

When Dorothy was twelve, her father died, leaving behind a financial mess: Lord Lowther, the despot to whom John Wordsworth had been agent, owed his former employee £4,500 in salary and expenses. His refusal to honor the debt meant that the Wordsworth children were left with nothing; from living in the grandest house in town, they were homeless and destitute, dependent on the kindness of others. Elizabeth Threlkeld, who had protected the girl from the gravity of her mother's loss—"the loss of a mother can only be made up by such a friend as my dear Aunt"—would now shelter her from the implications of John Wordsworth's death as well. It was only when she had left the Threlkeld fold that Dorothy began to "feel the loss I sustained when I was deprived of a father." Any dreams she might have harbored of one day returning home to Cockermouth to live together with him once again were over. Her father's dismissal of Dorothy from his life could now never be explained by him, or repaired.

As a young teenager, Dorothy went through the usual rites of passage for girls of her age, consuming the thick volumes of *Clarissa*, curling her hair, checking her weight, thinking about hats and high heels, and going to dances, but nothing erased for her the memory of her childhood home, "though I have never seen it in its neatness, as my Father and Mother used to keep it, since I was six years old." She grew up to have low self-esteem. "You will wonder at her taste," she remarked of a baby who liked her singing; "You [will] smile at my little skill," she said of her drawings; "I never took an infant in my arms," she said of her child-care skills, "that did not . . . beg to be removed"; "Wretched, wretched writing!" she said in 1803 of her *Recollections of a Tour Made in Scotland,* "I can hardly read it myself"; "I have no command of language, no power of expressing my ideas, and no one was ever so inept at moulding words into a regular metre," she said of her attempts at poetry. As for fiction, "I did try one story," she admitted, "but failed so sadly that I was completely discouraged." "I have nothing to recommend me to your regard," she concluded at an early age in a letter to Jane, "but a warm, honest and affectionate heart." Dorothy saw herself as someone whose only talent was her capacity for devotion. "I have not those powers which Coleridge thinks I have," she remarked in later years. "My only merits are my devotedness to those I love and I hope charity towards all mankind." Her stammer we can assume was a childhood predicament, a nervousness born from lack of confidence.

It is remarkable, in the light of the cataclysmic losses Dorothy sustained at six years old and the many remarks she would later make as to her general worthlessness, that biographers insist so heartily on her childhood happiness, but then she is rarely credited with having a psychological or unconscious life. "The tears of childhood," Ernest de Selincourt cheerfully declares, "are quickly dried." "During the happy years at Halifax," echo her most recent biographers, Robert Gittings and Jo Manton, "Dorothy had almost forgotten her father, since she never went home, even for Christmas, which was her own birthday." There is nothing to suggest that she forgot her father in these years—rather the reverse, in fact, as Christmas was a time she found hard to bear—and there is no real evidence that she was particularly happy as a child. This is not to say that Dorothy's intimacy with Jane Pollard was not significant, which it undoubtedly was, or that she did not feel what she called great "gratitude and affection" toward Elizabeth Threlkeld, whom she described as having been her "mother," but since being grateful and affectionate were what Dorothy did best, the gratitude and affection she felt toward her aunt and friend are not reliable indicators of her deep happiness, and Dorothy's future attitude toward homes and being happy suggests a complex relation to both. She had no choice in Halifax, with her father and siblings fading away from her, but to get on with things as they were, and Dorothy's practicality operated alongside a permanent sense of herself as unwanted and displaced. As it was, as soon as she had the chance, she would drop everything to be with her brother and make up for the time they had lost. Dorothy remained in touch with Elizabeth Threlkeld, who lived into her nineties, but after settling down with William, she ceased to visit her on any regular basis, which suggests that her aunt had not, in any substantial or permanent way, taken on the role of mother, while the Halifax cousins Dorothy grew up with hardly featured in her life at all.

The end of her childhood came, as with the other changes in her life, without warning. In May 1787, aged fifteen, Dorothy left Halifax and was summoned to live, like Fanny Price in Jane Austen's *Mansfield Park*, as a professional poor relation in the dismal house of her mother's parents, William and Dorothy Cookson. For the next eighteen months Dorothy can be found above the family draper's shop in the market square of Penrith. The bourgeois Cooksons considered the Wordsworths to have ideas above their station which it was their duty to correct, and Dorothy, who had spent the last nine years in a progressive, energetic, Dissenting household, loathed the joyless world of her grandparents, with their "petty" cares and foolish gossip, their relentless aspirations, accusations, condemnations, carping, criticism, and reminder of rank. "One would imagine," she wrote, "that a grandmother would feel for her grandchild all the tenderness of a mother, particularly when that Grandchild had no other parent, but there is so little tenderness in her manner or of anything affectionate, that whilst I am in her house I cannot at all consider myself as at home, I feel like a stranger." Dorothy compared "the cold insensibility" of her grandmother with the goodness of Aunt Threlkeld and yearned for the freedom of Halifax, "yet I am obliged to set upon the occasion as *notable* a face as if I was delighted with it and that nothing could be more agreeable to me." By "notable" she meant capable and housewifely. As for Dorothy, her grandmother found her "intractable and wild" rather than the "very *sedate, clever, notable* girl" she would have preferred, and the rare occasions when Grandfather Cookson spoke at all were in order to scold. Dorothy now went out only on Sundays and otherwise spent her time sewing, "for whole hours without saying anything . . . our only conversation is about *work, work,* or what sort of a servant such a one's is, who are her parents, what places she lived in, why she left them, etc etc."

A significant benefit of her new life was the opportunity of getting to know once more the brothers from whom she had been separated for the last nine years. William, John, and Christopher, although still at school in Hawkshead (Richard, the eldest, was now training nearby to be a lawyer), were taken in by the Cooksons for the duration of the holidays. Now that four of the siblings were reunited, there was the chance to recover some of the family life that had been stolen from them. John, shy to the point of silence (his father had likened him to an ibis, the shiest of the beasts), had "an excellent heart"; dull Richard, whom Dorothy would know the least well, was not, she insisted to Jane Pollard, dull at all; William and Christopher she recognized as being clever, while in William's temperament she also recognized something of her own. It was as if she were meeting them for the first time, and Dorothy's emotions were overwhelming:

> Christopher is steady and sincere in his attachments; William has both these virtues in an eminent degree; and a sort of violence of Affection if I may so term it which demonstrates itself every moment of the day when the Objects of his affection are present with him, in a thousand almost imperceptible attentions to their wishes, in a sort of restless watchfulness which I know not how to describe, a Tenderness that never sleeps, and at the same time such a delicacy of manners as I have observed in few men.

Dorothy now spent her brothers' times at school dragging through the dreariness of small-town life, waiting, on her wretched uncle Christopher's leisure, for the boys to return. "I was for a whole week kept in expectation of my brothers," Dorothy wrote despairingly to Jane Pollard of one particularly grim occasion, "who staid at school all that time after the vacation begun owing to the ill nature of my uncle who would not send horses for them because when they wrote they did not happen to mention them, and only said when they should break up which was always before sufficient."

The sense of responsibility felt by the brothers toward their intelligent and unhappy sister, cut out of their lives so inexplicably and orphaned at a much younger age, must have been considerable, but it was William rather than Richard, John, or Christopher who shared most urgently Dorothy's pain. They were reunited like two birds hearing one another's call: "Two of a scattered brood that could not bear / To live in loneliness." In "The Vale of Esthwaite," his earliest long poem, Wordsworth pays tribute to Dorothy by saying that she represents his dead mother. She is a revenant:

Sister for whom I feel a love
Which warms a brother far above,
On you, as sad she marks the scene,
Why does my heart so fondly lean?
Why but because in you is given
All, all, my soul would wish from Heaven?
Why but because I fondly view
All, all that Heav'n has claimed, in you.

Dorothy and William were united in misery. "We have been endeared to each other by early misfortune," she told Jane Pollard; their conversations always finished with "wishing we had a father and a home." It is only now that Dorothy began the belated process of mourning her parents' death: "Many a time have W[illiam], J[ohn], C[hristopher] and myself shed tears together, tears of the bitterest sorrow." The delay of her mourning perhaps explains the prematurity of the grief she later felt for the anticipated loss of William to Mary Hutchinson. Like the White Queen in *Through the Looking-Glass,* Dorothy had learned to weep before she pricked her finger.

The blunt directness of her correspondence with Jane Pollard, in which Dorothy's emotions are fashionably exaggerated, is so different from the sharpness, shyness, and indirection of her journal entries that it is sometimes hard to believe they are by the same woman. The self she refers to here is fuller and more present than it ever is in the journals, but there are moments when we get a foretaste of the nervous tension caught later in her diary writing, particularly around the prospect of parting. As ever, separation for Dorothy breaks down the boundary between joy and misery, making them collapse into one indeterminate emotion:

> I might perhaps have employed an hour or two in writing to you but I have so few, so very few to pass with my brothers that I could not leave them. You know not how happy I am in their company. I do not now want a friend who will share with me my distresses. I do not now pass half my time alone. I can bear the ill-nature of all my relations, for the affection of my Brothers consoles me in all my Griefs, but how soon alas! shall I be deprived of this consolation! And how soon shall I again become melancholy, even more melancholy than before.

And in anticipation of the morning of William's wedding, where she lies trancelike upon a bed, or the first entry of her journal, where she sits crying on a stone, Dorothy draws Jane a picture of how she appears in her abandonment: "Imagine me sitting in my bedgown, my hair out of curl and hanging about my face, with a small candle beside me, and my whole person the picture of poverty (as it always is in a bedgown) and you will then see your friend Dorothy." Even as a teenager, she stages her tragedy in the bedroom.

Initially it was the absence of her younger brothers as well as of William that brought on these black depressions. Dorothy was devoted equally to them all. "Neither absence nor distance nor time can ever break the chain that binds me to my brothers," she told Jane Pollard. When the boys returned to Hawkshead in the summer of 1787, she described having

> parted with the kindest and most affectionate of Brothers, I cannot paint to you my distress at their departure, I can only tell you that for a few hours I

> was absolutely miserable, a thousand tormenting fears rushed upon me, the approaching Winter, the ill nature of my grandfather and Uncle Christopher, the little probability there is of my soon again seeing my younger brother . . .

The younger brother she is preparing to miss is John, whose departure thirteen years later from the Low-wood turning, to walk with William into Yorkshire, was to be of minor significance to Dorothy.

But Dorothy was not completely alone during the Hawkshead terms. It was during her time in Penrith that she became friends with Mary Hutchinson. The two girls were as opposite in temperament as Wordsworth and Coleridge would be—Mary was quiet, self-contained, poised; Dorothy loquacious, intimate, highly strung—but their situations were identical: the Hutchinson children had also been orphaned and, as Dorothy liked to put it, "scattered abroad," and Mary was also living (along with her younger sister Peggy) at the mercy of unsympathetic relations. Aged eight, Mary had been removed from her family home to live with grandparents; when she returned four years later, her mother died giving birth to her tenth child. Aged thirteen, Mary became surrogate mother to the family, but when their father died two years after that, the brood was separated. Like the wild and motherless Earnshaw children of Wuthering Heights and the quiet and motherless Linton children of Thrushcross Grange, these two households were destined to form a family. The Wordsworth and Hutchinson mothers had been friends in Penrith; one of Mary's earliest memories was of her mother "weeping and warming herself by the kitchen fire upon the return from the funeral" of Anne Wordsworth. William and Mary had for a time been to the same dame school; now they spent the summers of 1787 and 1788 in the company of each other, and of Dorothy.

When William began his studies at Cambridge, Dorothy, Mary, and Peggy would "steal" out of their homes to each other's kitchen fires. In the warmth, cut off from the rest of the household, they could talk, after which, "to delay the moment of parting," they "paced up one street and down another by moon or starlight." This existence of stolen conversations and protracted partings would have been Dorothy's lot had not another, more sympathetic Cookson uncle stepped in. The Reverend William Cookson took an interest in the vulnerable sixteen-year-old girl living under his parents' roof and made it his business to tutor her in French and mathematics. When he became engaged to Dorothy Cowper, the couple invited his young niece to live with them in the rectory to which, as a fellow of St. John's College, Cambridge, he had been appointed in Norfolk. Dorothy Wordsworth's life was, once more, to change suddenly, but this time for the better. "To live in the country and with such kind friends! . . . I was almost mad with joy," she told Jane, adding, in a phrase that recalls De Quincey's description of her as fraught with inner conflict, "I cried and laughed alternately." So after the wedding in October 1788, she set forth with another William and Dorothy to a new and "happy home"; the journey to Norfolk was to double as the newlyweds' honeymoon, and Dorothy Wordsworth was to begin her life as the perpetual third party. Such was her excitement that when they stopped at Cambridge in order to see William, Dorothy was casual about her brother's company. "We only staid a day in Cambridge, as you may be sure we were anxious to see our destined abode," she explained to Jane.

The red-and-black-brick rectory of Forncett St. Peter, halfway between the towns of Norwich and Diss, is found at the end of a long and tree-lined gravel path. Set in an isolated spot beside the river Tas, it is a handsome, comfortable Queen Anne house complete with a Dutch gable. Next to it lies the church of St. Peter and St. Paul, with its spacious graveyard, its rooks and cowslips and striking Anglo-Saxon round tower built in flint. The light sandy loam of Forncett St. Peter is markedly different from the rocky terrains that Dorothy had been used to in Yorkshire and Cumberland. Entering East Anglia even from London, you feel the immediate strangeness of the place, the way in which the flatness of the land exaggerates perspectives and elongates the horizon, allowing long but disquietingly uneventful views, transforming the scale of things so that the spires and trees are given a squat appearance. It is a curious thought that it was here, under the ever-expanding East Anglian skies, that Dorothy and William, both northern to the core, would nurture their future relationship.

Dorothy was now to embrace a rectory life of evangelism, philanthropy, and self-improvement. The routine she describes looking forward to in her early letters from Forncett is very different from the irregularity she would for a moment enjoy at Dove Cottage, when she and Wordsworth rose on waking and positioned meals around writing and walks. "We have sketched out a plan of the manner in which we are to spend our time," Dorothy enthused to Jane. "We are to have prayers at nine o'clock (you will observe it is *winter*), after breakfast is over we are to read, write, and I am to improve myself in French until twelve o'clock, when we are to walk or visit our sick and poor neighbours till three, which is our dining hour." After supper, William Cookson was to read aloud to the two Dorothys. As for her own reading time, that would soon disappear with the arrival each year of a new Cookson baby, when Dorothy became indispensable as "head nurse, housekeeper, tutoress of the little ones or rather superintendent of the nursery," and was once more "stealing," as she put it, occasions to be by herself.

In 1790, when he should have been studying for exams, Wordsworth undertook his first extensive walk. With his friend Robert Jones, he trod a thousand miles across France and into the Alps of Rousseau's Republican Switzerland. It was at this point that he became a Romantic: he purposefully walked away from the contemporary culture of the Grand Tour, the more popular means of combining travel with self-improvement, and toward the greater wisdom of nature. Until now there are few signs in Dorothy of the woman who would become her brother's ears and eyes, so when, in September 1790, William writes to her alone of his siblings, and tells her that amid the sublimity and beauty, "I have thought of you perpetually; and never have my eyes burst upon a scene of particular loveliness but I have almost instantly wished that you could for a moment be transported to the place where I stood to enjoy it," it comes as something of a surprise. Scenes of loveliness have not entered Dorothy's epistolary world as yet, but neither have they entered in such a way her conversations with William. It is only after expressing how he longs to share with her the magnificent views that William explains to his sister the form now taken by his nature worship:

> I am a perfect Enthusiast in my admiration of Nature in all her various forms; and I have looked upon and as it were conversed with the objects which this country has presented to my view so long, and with such encreasing pleasure, that the idea of parting from them oppresses me with a sadness similar to what I have always felt in quitting a beloved friend.

Dorothy, who was at this stage spending her days dandling babies and teaching her Sunday school class, was flattered by her brother's inclusion of her in his magnificent journey and traced his route on a map, suggesting to Jane Pollard that she might like to do so, too. "You are right in supposing me partial to William," Dorothy confessed; he gave her more attention than did her other brothers. "He was never tired of comforting his sister, he never left her in anger, he always met her with joy, he preferred her society to every other pleasure."

In January 1790, William Wilberforce, William Cookson's old college friend, came to Forncett for the month. The charming, rich, and recently evangelized MP for Hull had already begun to make a name for himself. Eight months earlier he had moved in a brilliant speech twelve resolutions condemning the slave trade, winning the support of the house, including William Pitt, Edmund Burke, and Charles James Fox. To enable the planters to produce evidence at the bar, further debate was postponed until the next parliamentary session. Conversation at Forncett would have revolved around the case, for which Wilberforce was daily preparing the evidence. For Dorothy, who had loathed the poverty of her grandmother's conversation, listening to Wilberforce talk with her uncle would have been a thrilling experience, opening doors to her, engaging her imaginative sympathy on a grand scale. And as her brother had, Wilberforce made it clear that Dorothy had a part in his vision of a better world, giving her ten guineas a year "to distribute in what manner I think best to the poor." His gift was a mark not only of the high regard in which Wilberforce held this young woman but of a commitment of sorts, a desire to continue the relationship: Dorothy was to invest in the good of her community; he was to invest in the good of her. For someone who expressed the "painful idea that one's existence is of very little use" and who had been shoved from pillar to post at the convenience of others, these ten guineas would have been received as a sign of validation and belonging, and Dorothy cannot have failed to feel flattered at being singled out as virtuous by so greatly respected a figure. "I believe him to be one of the best of men," she told Jane, whose subsequent goading and teasing irritated her sensitive friend. In her letters to Jane, Dorothy neither admits to nor denies her attraction to Wilberforce, stating only that if he were ever to marry at all, which seemed unlikely, he would not look at an unaccomplished woman like herself. Besides, "No man I have seen has appeared to regard me with any degree of partiality; nor has anyone gained my affections, of this you can be in no doubt."

Would Wilberforce have been attracted to Dorothy Wordsworth? It is worth recalling the initial impression she made on De Quincey: "How noble a creature did she seem when I first knew her!" She was fiery, agitated, and embarrassed but also dutiful, energetic, and domestic, adored by her aunt and young cousins, a woman with a gift for friendship, a love of learning, a need to love, and a strong desire to be needed. She had the qualities of a satisfying companion, but would he have found her sexually attractive? De Quincey thought she had an asexual gait *when outside*, but remember that he also found the prospect of Wordsworth—who appears to have had a strong and dominating physical drive—paying court to Mary unimaginable. De Quincey is otherwise emphatic in his description of Dorothy as a sensuous physical being, someone over and above the ordinary woman: she had not just "organic sensibility" but an "*excessive* organic sensibility," and not just "sensibility" but a "*luxurious* sensibility." It is Wordsworth and not his sister who comes across as having never experienced or aroused a physical feeling. His poetry is startlingly without sexuality, his landscapes are peopled by children, old men, widows, and idiots; there is not a sexually active creature among them.

And why would Dorothy not have been attracted to Wilberforce? She was drawn to charismatic characters and intellectual stimulation, to men with a mission and men who regarded her well ("I hope you were an *immediate* abolitionist," she wrote to Jane Pollard, "and are angry with the House of Commons for continuing the traffic in human flesh so long as till 96"), and she had not yet pledged herself to her brother, whose drive, seriousness, and desire to effect change must have reminded her of Wilberforce. But she sharply—in a tone unlike any she had used to Jane Pollard before—terminated her discussions on the topic. "I cannot suppose you entertain any such improbable suspicions as you are pleased to hint. I shall think you unkind if you say anything more to me upon the subject."

At the end of 1790, William, now returned from his Swiss walking tour, spent six weeks at Forncett, during which time he and Dorothy laid the foundations of the companionship that would sustain them for the rest of their lives: "Oh Jane . . . he won my affection to a Degree which I cannot describe: his Attentions to me were such as the most insensible mortals must have been touched with, there was no Pleasure that he would not have given up with joy for half an hour's Conversation with me." It was in Norfolk that William and Dorothy began to walk together, and to distinguish between the pleasures of different types of walking. There was the aesthetic experience of "wandering," during which time the walker is alert to the intensity of smells, sights, and sounds; and there was "pacing," a cerebral exercise to encourage thought. This is best described by one of the locals in Grasmere, who remembered William pacing about, with Dorothy scuttling along behind:

> He would set his head a bit forrad and put his hands behint his back. And then he would start a bumming, and it was bum, bum, stop, then bum, bum, bum, reet down till t'other end, and then he's set down and git a bit o'paper and write a bit.

They walked every morning and evening for two hours, and paced in the garden from four every afternoon until half past six. "Unless you have accustomed yourself to this kind of walking," Dorothy explained to Jane, "you will have no idea that it can be pleasant, but I assure you it is most delightful." After he left Forncett, she would not see William again for three years, during which time Dorothy wrote:

> Often have I gone out when the keenest North wind has been whistling amongst the trees over our heads. I have paced that walk in the garden which will always be dear to me from remembrance of those long, long conversations I have had supported upon my brother's arm.

Wordsworth's relationship with Dorothy was, like the production of his poems, founded on movement, grounded in walking, and finally bum-bum-bummed into existence.

Following her brother's visit, Dorothy's days were now structured around her own, albeit restricted, walks, beginning at six o'clock in the morning. Walking had become a poetic experience:

"I walk alone as long as I can in the garden; I am particularly fond of a moon-light or twilight walk." But her routine was broken when, in 1792, William Cookson, who had been tutor to the royal children, became canon of Windsor and the Forncett household moved south for three months. It requires some leap of imagination to see the Dorothy of the Grasmere Journals taking her wild walks on the terraces of Windsor Castle and enjoying the patronage of King George III, but the appreciation of hierarchy and the idealization of family life were important parts of her makeup:

> I think it is impossible to see the king and his family at Windsor without loving them, even if you eye them with impartiality and consider them really as *man* and women not as King and Princesses, but I own I am too much of an aristocrat or what you please to call me, not to reverence him because he is a Monarch more than I should were he a private gentleman, and not to see with Pleasure his daughters treated with more respect than ordinary people.

At the same time as she was making these observations, William, now in revolutionary France, was becoming a Democrat and learning to "disapprove of monarchical and aristocratical governments, however modified. Hereditary distinctions and privileged orders of every species I think must necessarily counteract the progress of human improvement: hence it follows that I am not amongst the admirers of the British constitution."

William's failure to distinguish himself at Cambridge and the general lack of direction he had displayed since leaving the university had not endeared him to his Cookson uncles, who considered as undeserved Dorothy's attachment to her brother. William

Cookson believed that a study of Oriental languages when Wordsworth returned from whatever he was doing in France would help prepare his nephew for a life of letters, while Wordsworth himself hoped that his time abroad would raise his French to the standard required for a gentleman's traveling companion. He had considered for a moment joining the army, recognizing that he had a "talent for command," and there were thoughts of his being ordained (then "vegetating on a paltry curacy," William anticipated), which encouraged Dorothy to fantasize about a future sharing his parsonage. At this stage in their relationship she admired her brother's spirit, was excited by his energy, and loved his appreciation of her, but she had a moderate assessment of his talents and abilities. "[He] has a great attachment to poetry," she explained to Jane, "which is not the most likely thing to produce his advancement in the world; his pleasures are chiefly of the imagination, he is never so happy as when in a beautiful country."

In 1792 Dorothy had told Jane, "I am perfectly happy at Forncett," but by 1793 the pleasures of the rectory were wearing thin. Her uncle's company, now that he and Dorothy disagreed over William, was of limited value, and sharing a bedroom with her aunt, who went to sleep at nine and slept lightly, had become tiresome. Something else had changed: late in 1792, William, excelling in his role of rebel nephew, returned from France, leaving behind a Catholic mistress, Annette Vallon, and a child. Caroline, whom he had never seen, was born in Orléans in December 1792. He planned, so William told Dorothy, to reunite with mother and daughter once he had got some funds together, but he seemed to have little idea what he was doing and to be hurtling into an emotional crisis. The effect of his intense and rapid encounter with Annette was to renew his long-term commitment to Dorothy, as if the implications of his affair awoke a guilt about his sister's being excluded from another family home. Perhaps they could set up home together with his future wife and child? In a letter that Annette then sent to Dorothy anticipating such a happy event, the young mother's delight and relief are touching, and her description of the home William will indeed later share with his sister, wife, and daughter is uncannily accurate:

> When we are there, Oh sister, how happy we shall be! And you, my dear [William], do you desire that day as ardently as your Annette? When you are surrounded by your sister, your wife, your daughter, who will only breathe for you, we shall have but one feeling, one heart, one soul, and everything will depend on my dear Williams.

The letters William was now writing to Dorothy also express the idea of oneness; only he was dreaming of sharing his feelings, heart, and soul with Dorothy alone rather than in a triangular relationship involving Dorothy and Annette together. Dorothy was now more than William's compass and his polestar; she was fundamental to his whole being: "How much do I wish that each emotion of pleasure and pain that visits your heart should excite a similar pleasure or a similar pain within me, by that sympathy that will almost identify us when we have stolen to our little cottage!" The intensity of William's response to Dorothy implies that it was, as much as anything, his need for his sister that brought him back from France.

The Cookson uncles, when they heard about the addition to the Wordsworth family, were less delighted than Dorothy had been, and an invitation to visit Forncett was not received by the young Democrat. Dorothy was once more in a state of longing. "I have passed one and twenty years of my life and that the first six years only of this time was spent in the enjoyment of the same pleasures that were enjoyed by my brothers and that I was then too young to be sensible of the blessing." She was longing to make up lost time with William but also to be with Jane, and she seems at this point to have decided that she would not marry: "Love will never bind me closer to any human Being than Friendship binds me to you my earliest female Friend, and to William my earliest and my dearest Male Friend." She nonetheless wanted to live as a married couple and began to fantasize about the home she would one day share with William, into which she would welcome Jane as a guest:

> I look forward with full confidence to the Happiness of receiving you in my little Parsonage, I hope you will spend at least a year with me. I have laid the particular scheme of happiness for each season. When I think of Winter I hasten to furnish our little Parlour, I close the Shutters, set out the Tea-table, brighten the fire. When our Refreshment is ended I produce our Work, and William brings his book to our Table and contributes at once to our Instruction and amusement, and at Intervals we lay aside the Book and each hazard our observations upon what has been read without the fear of Ridicule or censure. We talk over past days, we do not sigh for any pleasures beyond our humble Habitation, "the central point of all our joys."

The ideal life she describes is strikingly similar to the ideal she planned for Forncett: William and Dorothy Cookson have simply been exchanged for William and Dorothy Wordsworth, and Jane is in the position of third party. It is Dorothy's home: for herself, her brother, and her chosen friend, and the friend she chooses to share it with is not her "sister," Annette. Wordsworth, meanwhile, in his first published poem, *An Evening Walk,* addressed to Dorothy, described "Gilding that cottage with her fondest ray / . . . Where we, my Friend, to golden days shall rise."

Dorothy's preoccupation is now not only with seeing Jane in Halifax, as soon as her aunt Cookson can spare her and Mr. Griffiths (a friend of her uncle's who is to act as escort) becomes available, but with secretly meeting there William as well, while pretending to her relatives that the siblings ran into each other by chance. "Oh count, count the days, my love," she writes to Jane, "I measure them with a lover's scale," but it is William and not Jane with whom Dorothy is acting as a lover. William, meanwhile, is writing, "Oh my dear, dear sister, with what transport shall I again meet you, with what rapture shall I again wear out the day in your sight. I assure you so eager is my desire to see you that all obstacles vanish. I see you in a moment, running or rather flying to my arms." The plotting required in order to pull off the rendezvous is arduous: Mr. Griffiths keeps changing his plans, and William is on a walking tour of Wales. "I cannot foresee the Day of my Felicity," Dorothy wrote in one of her many fits of despair, "the Day in which I am once more to find a Home under the same Roof with my Brother; all is still obscure and dark, and there is much Ground to fear that my scheme may prove a Shadow, a mere vision of happiness." The waiting makes her ill. "I am so very anxious that I know not how I shall support any further delay," she tells her aunt in Halifax. Meanwhile, she nervously forewarns Jane that William is something of an acquired taste, that you must be with him more than once before he will relax in your company, that he is not a handsome man—"his person is not in his favour"—but that his smile detracts from his plainness.

At the end of January 1793, Wordsworth's first published poems, *Descriptive Sketches* and *An Evening Walk*, appeared. Dorothy's comments on his early poetry reveal that somewhere between picking berries in Halifax, stitching sheets in Penrith, and bathing babies in Forncett she has developed a strong and independent poetic sense. Her critical voice is frank, certain, and sufficiently self-assured to suggest that William was then dependent on her finer sensibility. "The poems contain many Passages exquisitely beautiful," Dorothy told Jane,

> but they also contain many Faults, the chief of which are Obscurity, and a too frequent use of some particular expressions and uncommon words for instance *moveless*, which he applies in a sense if not new, at least different from its ordinary one; by moveless when applied to the Swan he means that sort of motion which is smooth without agitation; it is a very beautiful epithet but ought to have been cautiously used, he ought at any rate only to have hazarded it once, instead of which it occurs three or four times. The word *viewless*, also, is introduced far too often.

Coleridge said of the same poems that "seldom, if ever, was the emergence of an original poetic genius above the literary horizon more evidently announced." Wordsworth made the amendments Dorothy suggested.

There is evidence to suggest that Wordsworth was in Paris during late September 1793, but as Annette was in Orléans, it is unlikely that he went to France in order to see the mother of his daughter. His trip, it seems, was for other reasons, and he returned in October with a sense of himself as a failed revolutionary, a failed father, a failed lover, a family failure with no vocational calling and with no one to believe in him apart from his sister, whose love and faith he must not fail. Dorothy was busy unthreading herself from the Cooksons so as to be free for whatever William had in store for the two of them: she was certain they would be united in Halifax by November 1793, then certain it would be for Christmas and her twenty-second birthday, but Mr. Griffiths never appeared. Eventually, presumably without her escort, she left the rectory in Forncett in February 1794, never to return. After six weeks in Halifax, William and Dorothy set off together, in the manner of an elopement.

She and William began their "pilgrimage," as Dorothy later called it, by coach to Kendal. From there she "walked, with my brother by my side, from Kendal to Grasmere, eighteen miles," arriving in the Lakeland village at sunset and seeing "a rich yellow light on the waters" in which "the islands were reflected." This was Dorothy's first view of Grasmere, where they stayed for the night in an inn overlooking the church. The next day they continued "from Grasmere to Keswick, fifteen miles, through the most delightful country that was ever seen." At Keswick, they stayed at Windy Brow, the farmhouse belonging to Wordsworth's friends Raisley and William Calvert.

It is appropriate that Dorothy uses the term "pilgrimage" to describe the partnership with William that began at this point, and not only because of the conscious simplicity of their journeying. When they set out together from Halifax, "two glad foot travellers through sun and shower," as Wordsworth later remembered, they were pilgrims in search of healing and enlightenment who had turned their backs forever on their former lives. Walking from one life into another, the pilgrim inhabits a liminal realm, and William and Dorothy Wordsworth were what we might call threshold walkers. "Who doth not love to follow with his eye," wrote Wordsworth in *The Prelude*,

> The windings of a public way? The sight
> Hath wrought on my imagination since the morn
> Of childhood, when a disappearing line,
> One daily present to my eyes, that crossed
> The naked summit of a far-off hill
> Beyond the limits that my feet had trod,
> Was like an invitation into space
> Boundless, or guide into eternity.

This walk "beyond the limits" and over the "disappearing line" was to be Dorothy's rite of passage, the first threshold of her life.

At Windy Brow she found, in anticipation of the role that their moonlight arrival at Dove Cottage would play in five years' time, her journey's end. Writing to Jane Pollard, Dorothy described finding in the home and its setting the kind of peace and transformation one might experience at the tomb of a wonder-working saint. Windy Brow is not a house in her description but a state of mind; Dorothy's vocabulary has become one of sublimity and grandeur. What she encounters in this sacred spot overwhelms her senses and challenges her into exploring a new and richer sense of self:

> You cannot conceive anything more delightful than the situation of this house. It stands upon the top of a very steep bank, which rises in a direction nearly perpendicular from a dashing stream below. From the window of the room where I write I have a prospect of the road winding along the opposite banks of this river, of a part of the lake of Keswick, and of the town, and towering above the town a woody steep of a very considerable height whose summit is a long range of silver rocks. This is the view from the house, but a hundred yards above, it is impossible to describe its grandeur. There is a natural terrace along the side of the mountain which shelters Windy Brow, whence we command a view of the whole vale of Keswick . . . This vale is terminated at one end by a huge pile of grand mountains in whose lap the lovely lake of Derwent is placed, at the other end by the lake of Bassenthwaite, on one side Skiddaw towers sublime and on the other a range of mountains not of equal size but of much grandeur, and the middle part of the vale is of beautiful cultivated grounds interspersed with cottages and watered by a winding stream which runs between the lakes of Derwent and Bassenthwaite.

For William and Dorothy alike, their careers as walkers began as acts of disobedience. William's life-changing march across the Alps four years earlier had taken place when he should have been studying, thus earning him the disapproval of his uncles, while this, Dorothy's first substantial walk, earned her the disapproval of her uncle Christopher's wife, known as Aunt Crackanthorpe.

As William's Alpine letter home to Dorothy, wishing she could share with him the beauty of the views, contained an emerging vocabulary his sister had not known him to use before, so Dorothy's defense of her unconventional behavior to her aunt has about it a newfound dignity. No longer the dutiful relation, she is confident, rational, collected: she writes as someone who is freed. There is a magnificence to her reply:

> I am much obliged to you for the frankness with which you have expressed your sentiments upon my conduct and am at the same time extremely sorry that you should think it so severely to be condemned. As you have not sufficiently developed the reasons of your censure I have endeavoured to discover them, and I confess no other possible objections against my continuing here a few weeks longer suggest themselves, except the expense and that you may suppose me to be in an unprotected situation. As to the former of these objections I reply that I drink no tea, that my supper and breakfast are of bread and milk and my dinner chiefly of potatoes from choice. In answer to the second of these suggestions, namely that I may be supposed to be in an exposed situation, I affirm that I consider the character and virtues of my brother as a sufficient protection, and besides I am convinced that there is no place in the world in which a good and virtuous young woman would be more likely to continue good and virtuous than under the roof of these honest, worthy, uncorrupted people . . .
>
> I cannot pass unnoticed that part of your letter in which you speak of my "rambling about the country

> on foot." So far from considering this as a matter of condemnation, I rather thought it would have given my friends pleasure to hear that I had courage to make use of the strength with which nature has endowed me, when it not only procured me infinitely more pleasure than I should have received from sitting in a post-chaise—but was also the means of saving me at least thirty shillings . . .
>
> I am now twenty years of age and such have been the circumstances of my life that I may be said to have enjoyed [W's] company for a *very few* months. An opportunity now presents itself of obtaining this satisfaction, an opportunity which I could not see pass from me without unspeakable pain.

Exchanging the nursery, the parlor, and the cultivated garden path for the liberty of the highways and byways, Dorothy walked out of the life that she and others expected of her, out of a hierarchy in which she, a poor relation, was at the bottom of the pile. Walking was an act of defiance, but it was also an assertion of her sense of homelessness and the pilgrim's liminality; she was placing herself in the unknown, somewhere between the past she was leaving and the future she was ready to embrace. Walking for Dorothy—the sense it offered of greater possibilities, the freedom it unleashed, the desire it inspired to go further and higher and deeper, to look more intensely, more closely around her, into the life of things—was a physical expression of her longing.

For William, walking was symbolic of his restlessness, his sense of uprootedness, his support of the poor and unaccommodated for whom the Revolution in France was being fought. As he put it in 1795: "I have some thoughts of exploring the country westward of us, in the course of next summer, but in an humble evangelical way, to wit *à pied.*" Wordsworth's identity as a poet was bound up with walking: walking was his way of writing—"A hundred times when in these wanderings / I have been busy with the toil of verse," he wrote in *The Prelude*—and in his writing he depicted himself walking. He was, as Seamus Heaney wryly puts it, a pedestrian poet; through walking, Wordsworth defined himself, but walking and writing were also in vogue. John Thelwall, the peripatetic radical whom Wordsworth would shortly come to know, agreed that "I pursue my meditations on foot"; Jean-Jacques Rousseau found that body and mind worked as one, he walked his way inward. "I can meditate only when I am walking," he declared in his *Confessions*. "When I stop, I cease to think; my mind works only with my legs." Coleridge, William Hazlitt recalled, "liked to compose in walking over uneven ground, or breaking through the straggling branches of a copse-wood," while Wordsworth's preferred realm was "walking up and down a straight gravel-walk, or in some spot where the continuity of his verse met with no collateral interruption."

Walking, Dorothy and William could talk without risk of being overheard or interrupted. Their conversations as they tramped through Cumberland would have been unlike those "long, long conversations" as they paced the garden path at Forncett. From the narrow concerns of provincial life Dorothy was suddenly submerged in major issues. William proudly belonged to "that odious class of men called democrats"; he was living intensely in the historical moment; his philosophical, governmental, and ethical concerns were the concerns of the day. Fired up by the political situation he had seen in France, dragged down by his personal situation, William was experiencing a profound crisis, and Dorothy was the person to whom he turned.

Her brother's incipient genius, his sense of immediacy, of urgency, and of modernity, gave Dorothy, as Wilberforce had done four years before, a direction and a purpose. She emerged from this walk with a project: she had committed herself to William. This commitment entailed more than simply devoting herself as a sister to her brother's best interests; it meant constructing herself as a vital part of his aesthetic. As they walked between Kendal, Grasmere, and Keswick, whether consciously or not, they revised their sibling bond, making it spiritual rather than biological, a twinship of souls rather than of blood. There was no turning back now, no possibility of a future for William with Annette. Dorothy and William built a vision of what they would be together: the poet and his sister, the courtly lover and his maiden. From this union would emerge his new poetic identity and the voice of her journals. It was now that they laid the foundations of the utopian poetic life they would, five years later, write into being in just this spot, with William playing the hero and Dorothy the heroine of each other's writings.

Chapter Two

TO HAVE AND TO HOLD: HOME

Thrice hath the winter moon been filled with light
Since that dear day when Grasmere, our dear Vale,
Received us; bright and solemn was the sky
That faced us with a passionate welcoming,
And led us to our threshold, to a home
Within a home . . .

—WILLIAM WORDSWORTH, *Home at Grasmere*

I do not know how a cottage may do me with a wife.
But I am sure it would suit me with a sister.

—THOMAS BABINGTON MACAULAY, *Macaulay's Letters*

It is the summer of 1800, and William has been away from Dove Cottage for more than three weeks. The journal Dorothy is keeping to give him pleasure describes wading through time. *I sate till I could hardly drag myself away I grew so sad,* she writes on the eleventh day that she has been without him. With her brother visiting Mary, Dorothy is living elsewhere, attending more often to what doesn't happen than to what does. Each day of his absence has been organized around walking the three miles to Ambleside to send and pick up the post, even when the disappointment is inevitable. *Oh! That I had a letter from William!* she writes on the very day that he departs. *No letters!* she records two days later, on

May 16. On May 20, *No letters!* On May 27, *I walked to Ambleside with letters . . . I expected a letter from Wm. In the morning went to Ambleside,* she writes on May 30, *forgetting that the post does not come till the evening. How was I grieved when I was so informed.* On June 3, *No letter, no William.* By June 4, she is waiting not for his letters but for the sound of his step on the road: *I brought home lemon thyme & several other plants, & planted them by moonlight. I lingered out of doors in the hope of hearing my Brothers tread. I would not go far from home,* she wrote on June 5, *expecting my Brothers.* On June 6, *No William! I slackened my pace as I came near home fearing to hear that he was not come.*

Then, late on June 7, the clock-ticking tension breaks like a storm; William has come home again. She hears the creak of the gate and the quick familiar pad up the path to the front door. Looking back, as she fills in her account of the day, Dorothy can see that it had an anticipatory quality all along; rain had threatened in the morning while she was picking gooseberries and baking them in a pie, but the skies had cleared by the afternoon, and she gathered sod and plants from the hill and orchids from the lakeside to put in their garden.

Dorothy records her last day alone before William's return in terms of domestic bliss: there are no views described, no gazing has been done, no major walks have been taken, her pleasures are gained from puddings, tea, plants, watering, and weeding: she pictures herself in these pages as a happy housewife. The tone of her journal has changed since her first entry three and a half weeks earlier: having described loneliness and melancholia, Dorothy is now keen to stress the joy of being home at Grasmere:

> *I did not leave home in the expectation of Wm and John, & sitting at work till after 11 o'clock I heard a foot go to the front of*

> *the house, turn round, & open the gate. It was William——after our first joy was over, we got some tea. We did not go to bed till 4 o'clock in the morning so he had an opportunity of seeing our improvements—the birds were singing, & all looked fresh, though not gay. There was a greyness on earth and sky. We did not rise till near 10 in the morning . . . The evening was cold & I was afraid of the tooth-ach for William. We met John on our return home.*

This should be the last time that Dorothy Wordsworth writes in her journal. Had she stuck to her resolution to keep up the entries only until William *comes home again* from his visit to Mary at Gallow Hill, our final image of her would be welcoming him back in the moonlight, with John's return the following evening—of less significance than William's impending toothache—recorded as an afterthought. While we know what she ate, drank, and planted that day and whom from the vale she saw, we have no idea what Dorothy said or what she thought. What do she and William talk about all night after their *first joy was over*, and how does that *joy* express itself? They must have discussed his agreement with Mary and the problem of what to do about Annette; they must also have discussed his agreement with Dorothy, and the role she would play in his future. Is it when they are sitting up until four in the morning that she presents to him the notebook that holds the tale of destitution that she has been writing in his absence? How does William respond to her journal? Does he read what Dorothy has written with the *pleasure* she anticipates, praising her ability to produce prose that is sometimes indistinguishable from "a large portion of every good poem," as he puts it in the Preface to *Lyrical Ballads*? Is this why she continues with the journal after his return?

Had William read Dorothy's journal that night, he would have seen from her second entry, dated May 15, 1800—the day after he and John departed—that she had already lost enthusiasm for the project. She dutifully notes the dreariness, drudgery, and eventual disappointment of the day spent alone, but there is no sign of her either wanting to give William any particular *pleasure by it* or writing so as not to *quarrel* with herself. It is as if she had temporarily forgotten the journal's purpose: *A coldish dull morning—hoed the first row of peas, weeded &c &c—sat hard to mending till evening. The rain which had threatened all day came on just when I was going to walk.* She later told Jane Pollard that without her brothers during this time, "I felt myself very lonely while I was within doors." Their home became empty and desolate, a place of work rather than of comfort and pleasure. This is neither the dream cottage she has conjured up so many times nor the warm embrace described by William in his poetry. The mood of Dorothy's second entry is one of anger and self-pity.

Despite the weight of her melancholia, on May 16, two days after William has left—*I had many of my saddest thoughts & could not keep the tears within me*—Dorothy is ready to put together, albeit in discontinuous and staccato sentences, an impression of continuing life. Her entry for that day, whereby she ticks off a checklist of items, typifies the style of the journal to come. She first records the weather, *Warm & mild*; then the garden, *transplanted radishes*; after which, in the following order, she describes her walk, *walked to Mr. Gells*; the woods, *extremely beautiful with all autumnal variety and softness*; her longing, *Oh! That we had a book of botany*; the flowers, *The primrose still pre-eminent among the later flowers of the spring*; the birds, *I was much amused with the business of a pair of stone-chats*; her letter writing, *wrote to Mary Hutchinson*; her walk to the post, *After tea went to Ambleside*; her disappointment, *No letters!*; her route home, *returned by Clappersgate*; the image of

Grasmere, *very solemn in the last glimpse of twilight*; her mood, *very melancholic*; and what she ate, *hasty pudding*. Business and banality rest unselfconsciously alongside metaphor and beauty: *washed my head . . . Rydale was very beautiful with spear-shaped streaks of polished steel.* Dorothy concludes, as she will often do, by relating an encounter with a vagrant whose voice she tries to catch: *I met a half crazy old man. He shewed me a pincushion, & begged a pin, afterwards a halfpenny. He began in a kind of indistinct voice in this manner: "Matthew Jobson's lost a cow. Tom Nichol has two good horses strained—Jim Jones's cow's broken her horn &c &c."* Two days later, on May 18, she notes a little girl from Coniston who *came to beg. She had lain out all night—her step-mother had turned her out of doors.* Dorothy always writes down the stories that are close to home.

To push through the hours, she has been reading. Dorothy reads ballads while William is away, but she varies her diet with Shakespeare, selecting for herself on May 17 *A Midsummer Night's Dream*, whose pastoral mood is in keeping with the lifestyle she and William are trying to promote. "The lunatic, the lover and the poet" are a threesome perhaps too close to give her pleasure, and she opts next for tragedy and histories, reading *Timon of Athens* on the eighteenth, *Macbeth* on the twenty-fifth, *King John* on the twenty-ninth, and *Richard II* on June 3. Dorothy is an acute and impressionable reader, but she does not say which of these plays she enjoyed the most, or why. She has immersed herself in Shakespeare, but his imagery does not seep into her journal writing in the way that her brother's words will.

Of more significance is her homemaking. She and William are busy constructing their garden, and like Milton's Eve, Dorothy has been transplanting plants and flowers from the valley to their own patch of land, adding orchids, lemon thyme, and rock ranunculus to the radishes and peas. When not hoeing and planting, she has been scrubbing, drying, and ironing—each stage of the household wash taking up a full day—plus nailing up the beds, binding the carpets, mending the clothes, and even making her own shoes. Running their home requires her to work her very fingers to the bone. But while she notes in her journal the domestic tasks performed, her entries are increasingly concerned with transforming the idea of Dove Cottage from an exhausting site of physical labor into the mythical center of their lives. At the same time as recording the regular headaches that take her early to bed, she commemorates a paradise of peace and stillness: *I walked towards Rydale & turned aside at my favourite field,* she wrote on May 26. *The air & the lake were still—one cottage light in the vale, had so much of day left that I could distinguish objects, the wood; trees & houses.* She sits on the shore and listens to the birds singing on the opposite side of the lake. The beauty brings on a sadness so heavy that she cannot move, and she quotes a line by William: "When pleasant thoughts bring sad thoughts to the mind."

Dorothy's journal is a description of home but also a creation of it. Following her second entry, on May 15, in which she was so lackluster, she begins a portrait of Grasmere that is essentially restorative, like a good mother. *It calls home the heart to quietness,* she wrote of the valley on May 16, when she returned from Ambleside without letters. *I had been very melancholy in my walk back . . . But when I came to Grasmere I felt that it did me good.* She is engaged every bit as much as her brother in the project of idealizing their life together, and her journal does in prose what *Home at Grasmere,* which Wordsworth had begun in March that year, does in poetry. Here he recalls how as a schoolboy he had first seen the vale and thought, "What happy fortune were it here to live." "Embrace me, then, ye Hills, and close me in," he now exclaims, when the soft and verdant valley welcomes him back to her breast. Grasmere is

> A termination, and a last retreat,
> A Centre, come from wheresoe'er you will,
> A Whole without dependence or defect,
> Made for itself, and happy in itself,
> Perfect Contentment, Unity entire.

Their centerless lives are now sealed together by the healing capacities of home.

Colonizers, the Wordsworths have been taking over the valley. They name the local landmarks after their family and friends: a wood at the northeast end of Grasmere becomes Brothers Wood, a stand of fir trees opposite becomes John's Grove, a gate by White Moss becomes Sara's Gate, after Sara Hutchinson, Mary's sister; a rock in Bainrigg Wood becomes Mary Point. Another rock is named also after Sara, but becomes known as the Rock of Names when Coleridge, William, Dorothy, John, Mary, and Sara all carve into it their initials. Wordsworth, in his *Poems on the Naming of Places*, dedicates a natural spot to Dorothy and remarks, "Soon did the spot become my other home, / My dwelling, and my out-of-doors abode." Now he is at Gallow Hill, another of his "other homes," and Dorothy herself has been homemaking across the vale. Two years earlier, in her Alfoxden Journal, she had expressed her relief that we cannot "shape the huge hills, or carve out the valleys according to our fancy," but her former affectation is long forgotten. On May 18 she writes, *Walked to Ambleside in the evening round the lake. The prospect exceedingly beautiful from Loughrigg fell. It was so green, that no eye could be weary of reposing upon it. The most beautiful situation for a house in the field next to Mr. Benson's*. The next day she walks up into the *Black Quarter*, the name she and William give to Easedale, where she sees among the rocks *the most delightful situation possible for a cottage commanding two distinct views of the vale & of the lake*. The following Wednesday, sitting on the grass above Jenny Dockeray's farm and admiring the view, she thinks, *If I had three hundred pounds & could afford to have a bad interest for my money I would buy that estate, & we would build a cottage there to end our days in*. She wants everywhere to be her other home and sees homes everywhere. She also seeks out people without homes. In a rare moment of direct social comment, she notes down a remark made to her by their friend John Fisher, when she is walking back from Ambleside disappointed in her hopes for a letter from William. *He talked much about the alteration in the times, & observed that in a short time there would be only two ranks of people, the very rich & the very poor, for those who have small estates says he are forced to sell, & all the land goes into one hand.*

Home for Dorothy is something she either is seeking or has just lost. When she lived with her aunt in Halifax, Cockermouth, to which she could never return, was "home." When she moved to her grandparents' house in Penrith, where she "never consider[ed] myself as at home," Halifax became "that dear place which I shall ever consider as my home." Forncett was her first "happy home," and when she later moved with William to Racedown Lodge in Dorset, Dorothy called it "the first home I had." Her recollections of Racedown were "I think [the] dearest . . . upon the whole surface of the island," and yet it was without a second thought that she left for Alfoxden House, in order to be near Coleridge. She began recording her life in the Alfoxden Journal only when she realized that she and William would soon be leaving the house, after which it was Dove Cottage that Dorothy mythologized as being her first home. And the Grasmere Journals were begun at the moment when William was first gone from her, at which point she wandered about the valley as if she had no home to go to.

Dorothy's journal entries in the weeks that William is away recall her early letters to Jane Pollard when she was conjuring up the cottage life she longed to share with her brother: "I assure you I am a very skilful architect I have so many different plans for building one Castle, so many contrivances! Do you ever Build Castles?" Often what she sees in nature is symbolic of her attitude to these castles. Observing a chaffinch, she wrote on May 17: *The skooby sate quietly on its nest rocked by the winds & beaten by the rain.*

Her journals are filled with stories of stormy lives. Week after week she describes the beggars who pass through their valley. It is only when she reports the tales of the homeless that Dorothy's writing takes on any obvious narrative structure. As with the young widow who comes begging on the day that William first goes to see Mary at Gallow Hill, Dorothy grasps hold of these stories with tenacity. She retells them verbatim, impersonating the original narrator. A woman walking to Whitehaven with her wounded husband tells Dorothy:

> *I was an officer's wife I, as you see me now. My first husband married me at Appleby I had £18 a year for teaching a school & because I had no fortune his father turned him out of doors. I have been in the West Indies—I lost the use of this Finger just before he died he came to me & said he must bid farewell to his dear children & me—I had a muslin gown on like yours—I*

seized hold of his coat as he went from me & slipped the joint of my finger—He was shot directly.

Sometimes Dorothy will rewrite these autobiographies in her own words:

On Tuesday, May 27th, a very tall woman, tall much beyond the measure of tall women, called at the door. She had on a very long brown cloak, & a very white cap without Bonnet—her face was excessively brown, but it had plainly once been fair. She led a little bare footed child about 2 years old by the hand & said her husband who was a tinker was gone before with the other children. I gave her a piece of bread. Afterwards on my road to Ambleside, beside the bridge at Rydale, I saw her husband sitting by the road-side, his two asses feeding beside him & two young children at play upon the grass. The man did not beg—I passed on & about ¼ of a mile further I saw two boys before me, one about 10 the other about 8 years old at play chasing a butterfly. They were wild figures, not very ragged but without shoes & stockings; the hat of the elder was wreathed around with yellow flowers, the younger whose hat was only a rimless crown, had struck it round with laurel leaves. They continued at play till I drew very near & then they addressed me with the Begging cant & the whining voice of sorrow—I said I served your mother this morning (The Boys were so like the woman who called at the door that I could not be mistaken)—O! says the elder you could not serve my mother for she's dead & my father's on at the next town—he's a potter—I persisted in my assertion & that I could give them nothing. Says the elder Come lets "away" & away they flew like lightning.

The beggars in Dorothy's journal belong to a world different from the one she describes herself as belonging to; in this other world material details such as money and clothes feature, and people have firm and clear voices, with accents and attitudes. But at the same time as fleshing these figures out, Dorothy represents them as ideas and not individuals, and she gathers together their tales for William to recycle as poems in the same way as she gathers mosses for the garden.

Back in 1795, when they were also homeless wanderers, William and Dorothy left the home of the Calverts at Windy Brow and journeyed together to Cockermouth, where she saw once again the house of her birth. Empty since their father's death, "all was in ruin, the terrace-walk buried and choked up with the old privot hedge which had formerly been most beautiful, roses and privot intermingled—the same hedge where the sparrows were used to build their nests." William then returned to Windy Brow while Dorothy began a peripatetic existence in the North Country, staying with the Speddings at Armathwaite, the Crackanthorpes at Newbiggin Hall, the Griffithses at Newcastle, Aunt Elizabeth at Halifax, and her old friends from Penrith days, the Hutchinsons, in their farm at Sockburn, near Durham. Mary Hutchinson had also managed to make her escape from Penrith and was now keeping house for her brother. "Very different indeed is their present situation," Dorothy wrote to Jane Pollard,

> from what it was formerly when we compared grievances and lamented the misfortune of losing our parents at an early age and being thrown upon the mercy

> of ill-natured and illiberal relations . . . you cannot think what pleasure it gives me to see them so happy; situated exactly as our imaginations and wishes used to represent, when there was little hope that they would be realized. When shall I have the felicity of welcoming you my earliest friend to such a home?

On August 5, 1794, she attended Jane Pollard's wedding to John Marshall of Leeds. Dorothy's fantasies about welcoming Jane to her home required her friend to stay unmarried and be the companion of herself and William: her castles were tumbling down, and still William had no notion what to do with his life. "What will become of me I know not," he wrote to a friend. "I cannot bow my mind down to take orders, and as for the law I have neither strength of mind, purse, or constitution, to engage in that pursuit." For a while he considered moving to London, taking Dorothy with him, and surviving on writing and translating. It was a "very bad wild scheme," thought Elizabeth Threlkeld, and an incongruous idea for a man made unwell by noise and heat and a woman who returned "quite jaded and pale as ashes" from an afternoon spent in Norwich. When they worked as a team in their literary pursuits, William, who was well educated, clearly considered Dorothy, who was undereducated, his equal.

Fifteen months of further separation were to pass until a home of their own did materialize, during which time Dorothy lived "upon the bounty of my friends" and felt her "existence [to be] of very little use." The opportunity that then arose would not free her from dependence on the bounty of others, but she would at least be "doing something," as she put it. A widower friend of Wordsworth's, Basil Montagu, introduced him to the wealthy Pinney brothers, who offered the poet and his sister their empty house,

Racedown Lodge, positioned between Lyme and Crewkerne on the Dorset and Somerset borders. The Pinneys' father had made his fortune from extensive West Indian sugar plantations and was the largest slave owner in Bristol; now that Dorothy was in the orbit of Wordsworth and not Wilberforce she seemed not to mind at whose cost her comfort was secured, and Wordsworth, despite his sympathies for the underdog, seemed not to mind either. Montagu's motherless son, Basil Caroline, born twelve days before William's own fatherless Caroline, was to join them, and the Wordsworths would be paid £50 a year for raising the unhappy child. William's charisma was beginning to impress people other than his sister: not only did the Pinneys offer him Racedown Lodge rent-free, but Raisley Calvert of Windy Brow, who believed William had great talent, had died of tuberculois that January, leaving him £900 so that he could devote himself to his poetic vocation. "He cleared a passage for me," Wordsworth later wrote of Calvert's legacy, "and the stream flowed / In the bent of Nature." Calvert also cleared a passage for Dorothy: a codicil to the will granted William full power to invest any portion of the money "for the use and benefit of his sister." Dorothy had, for the first time in her life, a degree of financial security, and the Wordsworths were able to set up house together. She confided to the "eyes and ears alone" of Jane Marshall, née Pollard, the recent turn of events:

> Know then that I am going to live in Dorsetshire. Let me, however, methodically state the whole plan, and then my dearest Jane I doubt not you will rejoice in the prospect which at last opens before me of having, at least for a time, a comfortable home, in a house of my own. You know the pleasure I have always attached to the idea of home, a blessing which I so early lost.

But when she and William at last found a home, they lived a simulacrum not of the blessing they so early lost but of the married life he had rejected in France. William chose to live not with Annette and their own three-year-old child but with Dorothy and someone else's three-year-old instead. He had doubled his life, abandoning one woman and child to save another woman and child from feeling abandoned. Rejecting his daughter for reasons she would have found inexplicable, Wordsworth was repeating with young Caroline what Dorothy had experienced from her own father.

Dorothy, William, and Basil arrived at Racedown Lodge at midnight on September 26, 1795. Forncett Rectory had been a handsome pile, but Racedown was in a different league: a gentleman's estate replete with statues, it was a large, light, elegant block of a house surrounded by the undulating Dorset hills, some cultivated, others wild, with a view of the sea less than two hundred yards from the door. Although Racedown was one of the several places Dorothy would call "the first home I had," she seems in many ways never to have left, as well as never to have known, her first home. Throughout her life, whenever she was away from the North, she would compare her surroundings with the Cumberland hills from which she was removed at age six. The furze and broom that she now saw in Dorset delighted her more than anything else only "because they remind me of our native wilds." William and Dorothy read extensively from the Pinneys' library, walked two hours in the morning, and developed their garden. Dorothy studied Italian when she could, the translation project shared by herself and William still considered by them a possible

Racedown, drawing by S. L. May

way of earning a living. As the winter drew in, Dorothy described to Jane how they were surrounded by "books, solitude and the fireside, yet I may safely say we are never dull."

Basil took up much of Dorothy's time, and now that she was not under the supervision of her Cookson aunt in Forncett, she could raise the child according to her own methods. "Do not suppose . . . that we make him our perpetual play-thing," she explained to Jane, herself now nursing the first of her dozen children, "far otherwise, I think that is one of the modes of treatment most likely to ruin a child's temper and character." William and Dorothy agreed that the style of childhood advocated by Rousseau was their model. "We teach him nothing at present but what he learns from the evidence of his senses," Dorothy wrote.

> He has an insatiable curiosity which we are always careful to satisfy to the best of our ability. It is directed to everything he sees, the sky, the fields, trees,

> shrubs, corn, the making of tools, carts, etc. etc. etc. He knows his letters, but we have not attempted any further step in the part of *book learning*. Our grand study has been to make him *happy* in which we have not been altogether disappointed.

Basil's childhood, during which he played outside regardless of the "rain . . . falling down upon him or the wind blowing about him," sounds much like the one Wordsworth idealized in *The Prelude*, where he would "sport / A naked savage, in the thunder shower." Through Basil, "my perpetual pleasure," Dorothy and William relived their prelapsarian years. Six months of exposing him to the elements and he turned "from a shivering half-starved plant to a lusty, blooming, fearless boy."

Dorothy was using the same method to turn William, her other perpetual pleasure, from the shivering half-starved plant he had become back into a lusty, blooming, fearless man. Now that he had finally found support for his poetic vocation, temporary relief from financial anxiety, and the home he desired with his sister, Wordsworth's depression, rather than lifting, reached its lowest point. The first months at Racedown were marked by a collapse in him that only Dorothy's touch had the power to repair:

> . . . the beloved Sister in whose sight
> Those days were passed, now speaking in a voice
> Of sudden admonition—like a brook
> That does but *cross* a lonely road, and now
> Seen, heard, and felt, and caught at every turn,
> Companion never lost through many a league—
> Maintained for me a saving intercourse
> With my true self; for, though bedimmed and changed

Both as a clouded and a waning moon,
She whispered still that brightness would return,
She, in the midst of all, preserved me still
A Poet, made me seek beneath that name,
And that alone, my office upon earth.

He and Dorothy often used the image of the moon to describe the waxing and waning of Wordsworth's brilliance.

Guilt at trading Annette and Caroline for a life with Dorothy underpinned his mental state, but a major factor behind his decision to abandon Annette was that without his sister beside him Wordsworth was unable to reach his strength as a poet. An absorption in poetry, by which he sought to unify himself with a nature who "never did betray / The heart that loved her," as he put it in "Tintern Abbey," was possible only after an initial act of disunity and betrayal toward those who loved him.

When Wordsworth emerged from the darkness, it was not as a stronger or more certain person but as a stronger and more certain poet. Dorothy's acute perception and admiration for "common things" had taught him to hear and see again, and she became the audience, the addressee, and increasingly the subject of his poetry.

In the winter of 1796, Mary Hutchinson came for a seven-month stay, the first prolonged period of time she had spent with William and Dorothy together. The most enigmatic figure in the Wordsworth circle, Mary, as she is written about by Dorothy and William, appears devoid of personality. In her one known likeness—a portrait of Mary together with Wordsworth painted by Margaret Gillies in 1839—she sits to the right of her husband before a desk, pen in hand ready to inscribe his words, gazing at him with patient and fixed anticipation as though the shallow stream of her own mind had never been interrupted by a ripple of thought. William looks not at but past Mary, the trajectory of his vision crossing through hers and resting somewhere in the distance. Thomas De Quincey described Mary in the early days of her marriage to William as tall, plain, and elegant, with a cast in one eye and a powerfully feminine presence. But in the only lines Wordsworth would ever directly write about her, "She was a Phantom of delight," Mary has less presence and more of what might be called "atmosphere":

> A perfect Woman, nobly planned,
> To warn, to comfort, and command;
> And yet a Spirit still, and bright
> With something of angelic light.

The closer Wordsworth became to someone, the less able he was to give the person form. Mary was undemanding, he suggests, barely there except to illuminate others. She was, agreed De Quincey in 1807, "a sunny benignity—a radiant graciousness—such as in this world I never saw surpassed." Mary Hutchinson has come down to posterity as an empty person surrounded by full people, her sole contribution to conversation consisting, so it was reported, in the repetition of "God bless you." Even Mary's sister Sara, who has another nonspeaking role in Wordsworth and Coleridge biographies, has more buoyancy. But the reality seems to have been the opposite: Mary was a full person surrounded by empty people, and the nearer she comes to usurping Dorothy's place at William's side, the emptier Dorothy describes herself as being. That it was Wordsworth rather than Mary who was never fully present and in need of reminding about the presence of others can be seen in a story passed down from Rydal Mount days, that Mary once broke a plate outside his study door in order to alert him to everyday life.

It was Mary who called Wordsworth's great poem *The Prelude*; Mary who contributed the startling metaphor to Wordsworth's daffodil poem—"They flash upon that inward eye / Which is the bliss of solitude"—and she had about her all the deep serenity and certainty of self these lines suggest. Mary must have had limitless reserves of kindness, energy, and patience in order to put up with Dorothy's insecurities and William's self-absorption, but what kept her afloat in the company of the Wordsworths was her sense of humor and her understanding of family loyalty. Dorothy she would never tease, but Mary's gentle mocking of William he found reassuring and relaxing. She was equally bound to her own siblings, and the relationship between William and Dorothy might have exasperated her at times, but it was an intimacy she would never question. Mary Hutchinson was that rare thing, a woman who was contented with herself and at ease in her own sexuality; she possessed, Wordsworth said, "perfect happiness of soul." This made her an immensely attractive figure; Coleridge envied William his catch in Mary, and she was deeply loved by John Wordsworth as well. John "used to walk with her everywhere," Dorothy recalled; "they were exceedingly attached to each other," and it was John rather than William who would show Mary the beauties of Grasmere when they first moved there in 1800. On hearing of Mary's marriage to his brother, John sent her one final note: "I have been reading your letter over and over again My dearest Mary till tears have come into my eyes and I know not how to express myself . . . But whatever fate Befal me I shall love thee to the last and bear thy memory to the grave." In her dependability and indulgence, Mary Hutchinson, the eldest daughter of a large family, was a perfect mother to these orphan boys, a Wendy to a party of Peter Pans.

A letter from Wordsworth to Mary, written eight years after they married, recalls her departure from Racedown in the summer of 1796, when he walked with her part of the way. How different things might have been, he says, had they then thrown caution to the wind:

> You would have walked on Northwards with me at your side, till unable to part from each other we might have come in sight of those hills which skirt the road for so many miles, and thus continuing our journey . . . we should have seen so deeply into each others hearts, and have been so fondly locked in each others arms, that we should have braved the worst and parted no more.

They were as happy in Racedown "as human beings can be" together, wrote Dorothy to Jane during Mary's stay, with the added qualification, "that is when William is at home." In her brother's absence, Dorothy continued, "you cannot imagine how dull we feel." Dorothy and Mary were friends—her early letters are filled with effusions such as: "My dearest dear Mary I look forward with joy to seeing you again"; "I wish from my heart that William and I could be with you"; "I wish that you were here"—but being friends with the woman who will separate you from your only loved one does not make the feelings of jealousy and resentment go away; friendship is as fraught with ambivalence and aggression as enmity or love. Dorothy loved Mary because Mary was lovable, but she was threatened by her as well. "Mary Hutchinson is a most excellent woman,"

Dorothy will tell her brother Richard when William becomes engaged. "I have known her long, and I know her thoroughly; she has been a dear friend of mine, is deeply attached to William, and is disposed to feel kindly to all his family." On one level this was how Dorothy felt—it is certainly how William would have wanted her to feel. But there is little in her correspondence with Mary that is not strained as Dorothy realizes the depth of the growing commitment from which she is excluded, and the letter she writes to Mary after her departure from Racedown that summer—clearly an emotionally loaded occasion between Mary and William—is a case in point. No sooner had their guest set off back to Sockburn than Coleridge leaped over the gate behind the house, jumped the stream, and bounded across the field into the Wordsworths' lives. The manner of his entry they would never forget.

"You had a great loss in not seeing Coleridge," Dorothy wrote to Mary:

> He is a wonderful man. His conversation teems with soul, mind, and spirit. Then he is so benevolent, so good tempered and cheerful, and, like William, interests himself so much about every little trifle. At first I thought him very plain, that is, for about three minutes: he is pale and thin, has a wide mouth, thick lips, and not very good teeth, longish loose-growing half-curling rough black hair. But if you hear him speak for five minutes you think no more of them.

In contrast to Wordsworth, whose great brow and taut features gave him an inward, cerebral look, there was a disarming quality to Coleridge's appearance and his manner of describing it. "As to me," he wrote to John Thelwall,

> my face, unless when animated by immediate eloquence, expresses great Sloth, & great, indeed almost idiotic, good nature. 'Tis a mere carcass of a face: fat, flabby, & expressive chiefly of inexpression . . . As to my shape, 'tis a good shape enough, if measured—but my gait is awkward, & the walk, & the whole man *indicates* indolence capable of energies . . . I cannot breathe thro' my nose—so my mouth, with sensual thick lips, is almost always open.

His mouth was almost always open anyway because Coleridge talked on and on. "I heard his voice as he came towards me—I heard it as he moved away—I heard it all the interval," Keats would say of him. Coleridge's talk, Wordsworth said, was like

> a majestic river, the sound or sight of whose course you caught at intervals, which was sometimes concealed by forests, sometimes lost in sand, then came flashing out broad and distinct, then again took a turn which your eye could not follow, yet you knew and felt it was the same river.

For Coleridge himself, "The stimulus of conversation suspends the terror that haunts my mind."

Left alone with their new friend, Dorothy would never "feel dull." Her letter to the still and steady Mary, aside from informing her that she was missed by neither herself nor William and that their second guest was so much more interesting than their first, reveals a very different person from the buttoned-up young woman who had stiffly described Wilberforce to Jane Pollard as "one of the best of men" before asking not to be teased about him. Coleridge's enthusiasm was infectious, and Dorothy was drawn to him like "bees in swarming-time to the sound of a brass pan," as Hazlitt put it. Ebullient, energetic, and energizing, he was like William had once been, but in his violent mood swings he was more like Dorothy. Coleridge would also quarrel with himself; he, too, would shift between intense vitality and melancholia, from observing, hearing, and articulating with a sharpness that left his companions seeming only half alive, to seeing the world as colorless and himself as without worth.

Wordsworth's relationship with Coleridge began, much as those with Dorothy and Annette Vallon had done, with tremendous velocity. Both he and Coleridge threw themselves headlong into new friendships as though the other figure completed them in some way, and almost instantly they saw one another as different aspects of the same man. Coleridge, whose friendship with the poet Robert Southey had recently ended in bitter disappointment, had a vacancy in his life. Southey had left a "large void in my heart," he said, which he knew no man "big enough" to fill. Wordsworth, he decided, was the right size, and the fact that he then set about making him bigger still is an indication of how large Coleridge discovered his void to be. Wordsworth was to be his poet-god. "Wordsworth is a very great man," he concluded straightaway, "the only man, to whom *at all times* and in *all modes of excellence* I feel myself inferior." Coleridge, who was already well-known as a writer and speaker, was the only man, Wordsworth believed, able to understand his own work. With terms such as these, their friendship was destined to fail.

Unlike for Coleridge, who committed himself to friends as he could never do to his marriage—the word "friend," he said, was "a very sacred appellation"—relationships for Wordsworth became quickly exhausted, and the favorite was soon discarded. Coleridge was not an easy friend. His mind was exhilarating and endlessly stimulating, but he loved too easily and idealized those he loved, needing not equals but mentors. He always longed, so William Godwin noted, "to know some man who he might look up to," and he was unforgiving of failings. When the scheme he had rapidly planned with Southey to set up a pantisocratic community on the banks of the Susquehanna River in Pennsylvania inevitably broke down and Southey opted instead to live with his wife, Coleridge howled in disappointment: "O selfish, money-loving Man! What Principle have you not given up?" This was the mold in which his friendship with Wordsworth was cast. With his gravitas, firm sense of destiny, and adoring sister, Wordsworth provided a new anchor for Coleridge, who spent much of his life adrift. As for Wordsworth, Coleridge was the only person who could make him laugh; in Coleridge's company, Hazlitt noticed, Wordsworth displayed "a convulsive inclination to laughter about the mouth, a good deal at variance with the solemn, stately expression of the rest of his face."

Dorothy was a vital part of William's attraction for Coleridge. She was, Coleridge exclaimed to his publisher Joseph Cottle, "a woman indeed." The youngest of ten children, only one of whom had been a girl and she had recently died, Coleridge romanticized the role of sister. To seal his pact with Southey, Coleridge had married the sister of Southey's fiancée, Edith Fricker, and to Edith he had written:

> I *had* a Sister—an only Sister. Most tenderly did I love her! Yea, I have woken at midnight and wept—because *she* was *not* . . . There is no attachment under heaven so pure, so endearing . . . I know, and *feel*, that I am *your Brother*—I would, that you would say to me—"*I will* be your sister—your *favourite* Sister in the Family of the Soul."

Before the über-sister of his soul appeared in the form of Sara Hutchinson, Coleridge found what he needed in Dorothy. But what was Dorothy's investment in Coleridge, who surely interrupted her time alone with William? Was she in love with him, as many readers have assumed? Robert Gittings and Jo Manton state that "it is surely impossible to use the words 'love' or 'in love' with any meaning about the three. They were all in a state of delighted wonder with one another, a type of which there can be no rational account." Delighted wonder of the type that can provide no rational account is a fairly apt description of love and being in love; add to this the rapidity with which the group's relationship got going, the joyful recklessness of their subsequent behavior, the fact that Coleridge was the first man other than her brother with whom Dorothy had been emotionally intimate, that much of this intimacy took place in the moonlight and was organized around the search for natural beauty, and that, usually so sympathetic to others, she was endlessly hostile to his wife—"who would have made a very good wife to many another man, but for C!!"—and to avoid the conclusion that there was a dynamic between them involving love of some sort is like looking through a telescope with a blind eye. What needs examining is the nature of that love, which had nothing to do with courtship or exclusivity. Dorothy's love for Coleridge was bound up with her love for William, and the love Coleridge and William had for one another. She seemed often unable to distinguish herself from Coleridge at all.

Three's a couple, and from the beginning Dorothy and William preferred to be with one another in a triangle. Dorothy had never imagined a life shared with William as one that would involve just the two of them. Initially she had hoped they would be joined by Annette, and there was a time when she fantasized it would be Jane Pollard. In their first home it turned out to be young Basil

Montagu with whom they lived, and in their second it was Coleridge from whom they were rarely separated; when they later moved into Dove Cottage, they were accompanied by their brother John. During their times alone they would talk of absent friends. *We wished for Mary*, Dorothy writes in her journal when she and William have enjoyed a walk, and there is rarely a point in their Dove Cottage years when Dorothy is not writing to or receiving a letter from Mary or another one of their circle. With this endless exchange of thoughts, news, and comments, the lives of Dorothy and William echo with the sound of other voices, which makes Dorothy's sense of separation when William marries perhaps hard to understand. But for the Wordsworths the experience of loving another person was not only an extension of loving one another; it was also a way of containing their own love, of keeping it balanced and within bounds.

They had known Coleridge a month when they packed their bags and departed Racedown, carried off to Nether Stowey in Somerset by their triumphant friend on a one-horse chaise. The fact that they had no money and gave up a house they were living in rent-free is testament to the urgency of William's and Dorothy's need for Coleridge. His damp and disheveled cottage on the edge of the village was just large enough for himself, his wife, Sarah, and Hartley, their nine-month-old son, but not for the energetic Wordsworths as well, along with their blossoming foster child. While Coleridge talked endlessly to his guests and showed off his woodland kingdom, Sarah Coleridge, uncomfortable with the ways of her husband's new friends, was left holding the baby. The union between Dorothy and William was dependent not only on the presence of a third person but also on the exclusion of a fourth, someone they considered different from themselves, be it Annette, Sarah Coleridge, or eventually Coleridge himself.

Living cheek by jowl in Nether Stowey did not discourage the Wordsworths from continuing to pursue their own "happiness in a little cottage," but they stumbled instead upon a second mansion, one that put Racedown in the shade. For the substantial sum of twenty-three guineas a year, they signed a lease for a furnished house with all the room the Coleridges lacked. Alfoxden, four miles from Nether Stowey, was an isolated nine-bedroom Queen Anne house surrounded by a deer park, woods, and meadows. Unable to look at a landscape without comparing it to the landscape of her birth, Dorothy thought the smooth and sylvan terrains of the Quantocks like the North. "Sea, woods wild as fancy ever painted, brooks clear and pebbly as in Cumberland," she wrote to Mary. "The woods are as fine as those at Lowther [near Penrith] and the country more romantic; it has the character of the less grand parts of the neighbourhood of the Lakes."

Sarah Coleridge was not at first excluded from the group. When the Wordsworths moved to Alfoxden, Coleridge and his wife would walk to see them together, and on a particularly crowded day in their cottage, when Sarah had spilled boiling milk on Coleridge's foot, he had stayed behind in the garden bower while Sarah had gone walking with the guests. John Thelwall once visited Coleridge at Nether Stowey and found Sarah alone, having just returned from Alfoxden in order to do the washing. After sleeping the night in the cottage, Sarah returned to Alfoxden with Thelwall. "Faith," Thelwall told his wife, "we are a most philosophical party . . . the enthusiastic group consisting of C. and his Sara, W. and his sister, and myself, without any servant, male or female." The men spent a good deal of time walking and talking politics and philosophy; a conversation recalled by Coleridge when they were all three seated in the most beautiful part of the glen gives us a sense of their companionship. "'Citizen John,' I said to him, 'this is a fine place to talk treason in!,' 'Nay, Citizen Samuel,' replied he, 'it is rather a place to make a man forget that there is any necessity for treason.'" There was a happy atmosphere at Alfoxden that year, and Dorothy and Sarah must have spent a great deal of time alone together while Wordsworth and Coleridge walked, talked, and wrote. There is no reason to think that relations between them did not start out well.

Sarah Fricker was the eldest of six children, five of them girls, whose mother kept a dress shop in Bristol. Despite having fallen on hard times since the death of their father, the Fricker sisters were middle-class, popular, and fashionable. When he met Sarah at a family party in 1794, Coleridge was consumed with enthusiasm for the pantisocratic scheme he had cooked up with Robert Southey, and the Frickers had already become part of the general fantasy. The idea was that a group of twelve men and twelve women would set up a community by the Susquehanna River, where they would live according to the philosophies of David Hartley and Spinoza. Were a group of pantisocratic friends to marry into this family of sympathetic sisters, how harmonious they would be as they sailed away together into a new world! Mary Fricker, the third sister, had already married the fellow pantisocratist Robert Lovell, while Edith, the second sister, was being courted by Southey. Sarah, at twenty-four, was the only sister left of marriageable age. She was pretty, quick-witted, and well turned out; Coleridge was certainly sexually attracted to her, but, more important, he was as ever drawn in by the appeal of the family such a relationship would allow him to join. And Southey, in his folly, goaded him on: "Our Society will be of the most polished order . . . Our females are beautiful and amiable and accomplished—and I shall call Coleridge my brother in the real sense of the word." What should have been a light fling became the burden of a lifetime, as Coleridge tried to persuade himself that his feelings for Sarah had a durability beyond his enthusiasm for Southey's friendship. "My God!" he wrote after having made some sort of promise to Sarah:

> How tumultuous are the movements of my Heart—Since I quitted this room what and how important Events have been evolved! America! Southey! Miss Fricker!—Yes—Southey—you are right—Even Love is the creature of strong Motive—I certainly love her. I think of her incessantly and with unspeakable tenderness—with all that inward melting away of Soul that symptomizes it. Pantisocracy—O I shall have such a scheme of it! My head, my heart are all alive.

Coleridge wavered in his commitment to Sarah, backed out, and was spurred on to the bitter end by Southey. Once he married, his religious convictions were such that he could never countenance a divorce, however miserable the relationship was to become for them both.

Sarah was older than Dorothy and more worldly, raised as she was in the fashionable southern towns of Bristol and Bath, both of them social hubs. A few years earlier Dorothy had loved bonnets and bows and life at Windsor, and a part of her must have admired Sarah for liking to change for dinner and for wearing nice dresses. While the quarrel that later developed between Sarah and Dorothy was ostensibly between bohemian and bourgeois values, the two women had more in common than Dorothy cared to admit. Each left her family to live with an unconventional and financially unreliable man, each appreciated Coleridge and wanted to keep him in their camp, and each was concerned with class. Sarah thought her husband's friends ill-mannered, which they were: Dorothy helped herself to Sarah's clothes, and even Mary's family considered the surly and taciturn William a "vagabond," but it took only the slightest breeze to blow Dorothy's bohemianism off her like dust. She cut De Quincey when he married "beneath" him, even though Dorothy had known his wife, a local girl, since she was a child and was friends with her parents. She described her Grasmere acquaintances in terms of their social rank:

> We are very comfortably situated with respect to neighbours of the lower classes, they are excellent people, friendly in performing all offices of kindness and humanity and attentive to us without servility—if we were sick they would wait upon us night and day. We are also upon very intimate terms with one family in the middle rank of life, a Clergyman with a very small income.

At times like this, Dorothy belongs more to Jane Austen's Netherfield than to Grasmere Vale.

If Sarah did not throw herself with similar abandon into the schemes that excited Dorothy so much, it was because she had a child to raise, a house to run, and a more certain sense of who she was. And because it was only as "three persons" that Coleridge said he liked his group, "and one soul." Coleridge is largely to blame for Dorothy's dismissal of Sarah; not only did he leave his wife out of his friendship with the Wordsworths, but, because she was not confident about her own opinions, Dorothy's complaints about Sarah increasingly echoed those of Coleridge. "Permit me, my dear Sara," he later wrote,

> without offence to you, as Heaven knows! It is without any feeling of Pride in myself, to say, that in six acquirements, and in the quantity and quality of natural endowments whether of Feeling, or of Intellect, you are the Inferior. Therefore it would be preposterous to expect that I should see with your eyes, & dismiss my Friends from my heart, only because you have not chosen to give them any Share of your Heart.

A miscarriage followed by another pregnancy might have begun the separation of Sarah from her husband's life with the Wordsworths, and she appeared at Alfoxden less and less during 1798. Meanwhile, Coleridge and the Wordsworths "wanton'd in wild Poesy" over the combes of the Quantock Hills, Dorothy finding views that heightened her sensations and allowed her to dissolve into stillness, silence, and emptiness. It was to be a year of trances; the poets wrote about them, and Dorothy practiced them. Like Coleridge's Christabel, who "gathers herself from out her trance," or Wordsworth's Peter Bell, who sits still as a stone until "the trance is passed away," or even the wandering sailor in "Salisbury Plain," who "without sense or motion lay / But, when the trance was gone, feebly pursued his way," Dorothy willed herself into trancelike states and gave herself up to nature. *We lay sidelong on the turf*, she recorded in her journal, *and gazed on the landscape till it melted into more than natural loveliness*. The mind, all three believed, should be a tabula rasa ready to receive impressions, and Dorothy was experimenting in visual excess, seeing so much that she could see no longer.

Her letters back to Halifax from Alfoxden informed her relations that she was "deeper in plays and poetry than ever." As

Dorothy told Mary, William's "faculties seem to expand every day; he composes with much more facility than he did as to the mechanism of poetry, and his ideas grow faster than he can express them." The mood of life in the Quantocks is captured by the young Hazlitt, who recalled sitting on the trunk of an old oak tree with Coleridge hypnotically chanting William's poems, walking for miles on brown heaths overlooking the Channel, and talking metaphysics with Wordsworth while Coleridge explained to Dorothy the different notes of the nightingale. The locals were convinced that these strangers, who were out more often at night than during the day, who did not seem to have any profession, and who hung around the coast, were anarchists spying for the French. A Home Office detective concluded that the group was simply "a mischievous gang of disaffected Englishmen."

During the explorations and night walks, which their neighbors found so suspicious, a poetic collaboration had begun. "The thought suggested itself," Coleridge later recalled,

> (to which of us I do not recollect) that a series of poems might be composed of two sorts. In the one, the incidents and agents were to be, in part at least, supernatural . . . for the second class, subjects were to be chosen from ordinary life, the characters and incidents were to be such as will be found in every village and its vicinity.

It was Wordsworth whose poems would give, as Dorothy's prose would do, "the charm of novelty to things of every day," but the most vital part of Coleridge's explanation of the division of labor is that he did "not recollect" which one of them had the idea of collaborating in the first place. *Lyrical Ballads* might even have been Dorothy's idea; Coleridge doesn't care about distinctions. The three of them were thinking with one another's minds and seeing with one another's eyes.

❧

Dorothy Wordsworth began her Alfoxden Journal on January 20, 1798. She and William had returned from a disappointing trip to London, during which they had failed to get staged his tragedy *The Borderers*, to find that Coleridge had left Nether Stowey for a while to preach in Shrewsbury. They also learned that their unconventional behavior made them no longer suitable as tenants in Alfoxden and they would be leaving in the summer, when the house had been let to someone else. Dorothy was treading Coleridge's native hills without the buzz of his constant chatter. Facing the prospect of losing their magical friend and their "first" real home, she picked up her pen; as she would do in two years' time when she started her Grasmere Journals, Dorothy wrote as a response to loss.

This early journal records their final four months in the Quantocks, and while there is an elegiac note to her writing, it is free from the anxiety that runs through her Grasmere Journals. The credo of their group concern was, as Coleridge put it, "all is contemptible that does not spring out of an affectionate Heart," which might account for the optimism of Dorothy's prose, but another reason for her tone could be that what we have of the Alfoxden Journal is incomplete. The reason for this is that William Knight, the late-Victorian Wordsworthian who first transcribed her notebook journals in 1889 and 1897, omitted those details he felt to be irrelevant or belittling, such as ailments, illnesses, and tears. We know that his edition of the Grasmere Journals was similarly affected by censorious editorial decisions because he told us so: what he called "trivial details," meaning anything relating to their bodies or mutual affection, were erased by Knight, who wanted the Wordsworths preserved as cerebral beings. Because the original manuscript of the Alfoxden Journal disappeared some time after his transcription was "completed," we cannot know how far Knight also simplified this earlier text, thus altering Dorothy's tone. As they stand, the Alfoxden and Grasmere journals are as different from one another as the combes of Somerset from the crags of Cumbria.

The first four sentences of the Alfoxden Journal were copied by Wordsworth into his own notebook; either this, or, as Pamela Woof suggests in her edition of the Alfoxden Journal, Wordsworth composed these lines himself, and Dorothy picked up where he left off, continuing the journal in her own style and in a separate book until April 1798. In contrast to the opening of the Grasmere Journals in May 1800, which has Dorothy sitting on a stone, in the opening entry of the Alfoxden Journal in January 1798, Dorothy is nowhere to be seen:

> The green paths down the hill-sides are channels for streams. The young wheat is streaked by silver lines of water running between the ridges, the sheep are gathered together on the slopes. After the wet dark days, the country seems more populous. It peoples itself in the sunbeams.

This is a mannered performance, an artist's appreciation rather than an intimate journal. It is written in the language of sensibility, drawn up as an exercise in simplicity of form and clarity of speech, subjects with which Wordsworth and Coleridge were currently preoccupied.

If these lines were indeed composed by Wordsworth, then Dorothy's own entry begins with the sentences that immediately followed his:

> The garden, mimic of spring, is gay with flowers. The purple-starred hepatica spreads itself in the sun, and the clustering snow-drops put forth their white heads, at first upright, ribbed with green, and like a rosebud when completely opened, hanging their heads downwards, but slowly lengthening their slender stems.

The differences between the first four sentences and the second two are striking. From a broad, impersonal landscape the passage has now become microscopic. Dorothy brings everything down to earth, her eyes are fixed firmly on the ground. The tender personification of the snowdrops—pure Dorothy—anticipates her later description of the Lakeland daffodils laying down their heads to rest, while the purple-starred hepatica spreading itself out and gazing up to the sky describes Dorothy herself during her Alfoxden days.

Despite her longing for domesticity, Dorothy's journal entries do not mention life in the house. We have no idea what they ate, which rooms they chose to sleep in, or in which they spent rainy days. This is not the purpose of her journal. Instead, having begun by looking at the earth, Dorothy lifts her head and looks upward. The Alfoxden Journal is about the moon, which takes on a richly symbolic value. "The sky spread over with one continuous cloud," she wrote on January 25,

> whitened by the light of the moon, which, though her dim shape was seen, did not throw forth so strong a

> light as to chequer the earth with shadows. At once the clouds seemed to cleave asunder, and left her in the center of a black-blue vault. She sailed along, followed by multitudes of stars, small, and bright, and sharp.

At the same time as Dorothy was writing this, Wordsworth wrote "A Night-Piece":

> ————The sky is overcast
> With a continuous cloud of texture close,
> Heavy and wan, all whitened by the Moon,
> Which through that veil is indistinctly seen,
> A dull, contracted circle, yielding light
> So feebly spread that not a shadow falls,
> . . . the clouds are split
> Asunder,—and above his head he sees
> The clear Moon, and the glory of the heavens.
> There in a black-blue vault she sails along,
> Followed by multitudes of stars, that, small
> And sharp, and bright, along the dark abyss
> Drive as she drives. . . .

Was William borrowing from Dorothy, Dorothy borrowing from William, or was this nightscape scene discussed by them together in such a way that priority of authorship is as impossible to distinguish as when two chefs make a sauce?

During the spring of 1798, Dorothy, Coleridge, and Wordsworth were all discovering voices quite new to them. Dorothy's Alfoxden Journal, her first formal literary exercise, was unlike anything she had written before, and the ballads Coleridge was writing, *The Rime of the Ancient Mariner* and the first part of *Christabel*, introduced an entirely different tone to his writing. Meanwhile, Wordsworth produced nineteen contributions to *Lyrical Ballads*, whose effect would be, as Hazlitt saw immediately, like the turning over of fresh soil.

Wanting to remain a group after the Wordsworths left Alfoxden and became homeless once more, the three hatched a plan to spend a year in Germany. Coleridge, now in receipt of an annuity from the Wedgwood family, would study German philosophy; Wordsworth and Dorothy, poor as church mice, would learn the language with a view to making money from translations. It would be cheaper for them to live in Germany than in England. Basil they would leave behind, along with Sarah, Hartley, and Coleridge's four-month-old son, Berkeley, who were initially to join the party after the first three months. Dorothy believed that Basil should start to mix with other children and it was time his father sent him to school. She would miss her "little companion," as she called him, after he dropped out of her life.

Before setting sail from Yarmouth in September 1798, Wordsworth and Coleridge sold *Lyrical Ballads, with a Few Other Poems* to Joseph Cottle for £50, money they used to fund their trip, and William and Dorothy took a walking tour of the Wye. This was Dorothy's most substantial walk yet, covering over fifty miles in three days. William had last been at Chepstow five years before, "five summers, with the length of five long winters," a very different man from the one he was now. "Lines Written a Few Miles Above Tintern Abbey" was composed as they left Tintern and concluded as they arrived back in Bristol. Here it was written down immediately and with not a word altered, before being placed, at the eleventh hour, at the end of *Lyrical Ballads*. The poem is a meditation on Wordsworth's poetic vocation and a tale of spiritual crisis:

> . . . For I have learned
> To look on nature, not as in the hour
> Of thoughtless youth, but hearing oftentimes
> The still, sad music of humanity,
> Not harsh nor grating, though of ample power
> To chasten and subdue. And I have felt
> A presence that disturbs me with the joy
> Of elevated thoughts; a sense sublime
> Of something far more deeply interfused,
> Whose dwelling is the light of setting suns,
> And the round ocean, and the living air,
> And the blue sky, and in the mind of man,
> A motion and a spirit, that impels
> All thinking things, all objects of all thought,
> And rolls through all things.

Two-thirds of the way through, Wordsworth announces that there is someone on the banks of the Wye with him. The presence of a companion comes as a surprise to the reader, who has reason to believe that he or she alone has accompanied the poet through his thoughts. And even then it is a full eight lines before Wordsworth tells us the identity of the friend sitting with him:

> For thou art with me, here, upon the banks
> Of this fair river; thou, my dearest Friend,
> My dear, dear Friend, and in thy voice I catch

> The language of my former heart, and read
> My former pleasures in the shooting lights
> Of thy wild eyes. Oh! yet a little while
> May I behold in thee what I was once,
> My dear, dear Sister! . . .

How are we to interpret this unexpected tribute to Dorothy in Wordsworth's first great poem, a tribute that would make her famous as his sister? In a curiously ambiguous gesture, Wordsworth both acknowledges her place in his life and reminds her that that place is not by his side, despite her presence as his companion, but *beneath* him; it is the same place he occupied five years earlier, before he matured into the man he is now. Dorothy is an image of his "former" self, his childhood, his lost home. She is his past. Just as he will later wonder in *The Prelude* whether his own "maturer age," "calmer habits, and more steady voice" could ever have "chased away the airy wretchedness" that battened away on Coleridge's youth, Wordsworth here hopes that there will come a time when the "wildness" in Dorothy will be tamed and she will become as cultivated as he has:

> When these wild ecstasies shall be matured
> Into a sober pleasure; when thy mind
> Shall be a mansion for all lovely forms,
> Thy memory be as a dwelling-place
> For all sweet sounds and harmonies . . .

Only, he suggests, when she is reflective rather than simply responsive can Dorothy be placed next to William as his equal. Until then they will be like Narcissus and Echo: he looks at her as into a dark mirror, she repeats back to him what he has already said.

It is in her Grasmere Journals that Dorothy seeks to cultivate her mind as "a mansion for all lovely forms," her "memory . . . as a dwelling-place for all sweet sounds and harmonies," to prove to her brother that she has achieved the inner peacefulness, the trancelike stillness, that he desires for her; that they are, indeed, of one soul.

Their next home inspired Dorothy's most banal writing and William's most sublime. Coleridge was "gay as a lark" on the passage across to Hamburg, Wordsworth "shockingly ill," while Dorothy, who had never before left English shores, spent the journey "vomiting, & groaning, unspeakably." Coleridge drank and debated with the other passengers before sleeping beneath the stars; the Wordsworths cooped themselves up in their cabin. It was a sign of things to come. Coleridge was delighted by the energy of Hamburg, William indifferent, and Dorothy disgusted. She hated cities anyway and found the German streets with their streams of sewage "dirty, ill-paved," and "stinking." Because they arrived at their inn too late to eat downstairs, a *male* rather than a female servant brought the napkins and water to their room. Dorothy noted that the fresh washing of the floor had simply spread the dirt about, and the meal was served without vegetables on their plates or a cloth on the table. In the first of several travel journals she was to keep throughout her life, Dorothy records that she found the locals "cheats," to which William agreed. "It is a sad place," he said. "I have no doubt this city contains a world of good and honest people if one had but the skill to find them."

Dorothy, who had expressed a desire to travel in order to broaden the mind and see what she called "different people and different manners," discovered that travel had the effect instead of limiting her mind. She preferred being around the same people and the same manners; it was *familiarity* by which she was inspired and difference that she feared. The details of common life that she observes in the Grasmere Journals will be artfully suspended on the page like a still life in a frame, but what she sees in Germany makes her appear provincial and narrow-minded, which of course Dorothy was. In her Grasmere Journals she would write about home as no one she had read had done before, imbuing the domestic with a sense of the sublime, but away from home Dorothy's journals were the work of the middle-class evangelical she had been raised to be. The perfect electrometer has become a recorder of small change and foul stenches, the lone nightingale has joined the chorus of Englishwomen everywhere.

Away from home, Dorothy has lost that oceanic feeling. Conversations with William are reduced to a checklist of gripes about local manners. The landlord of their inn she describes as a "greasy face" at the head of the table, "laughing with landlord vulgarity and complaisance at the jokes of his guests"; the baker fiddles them, the soldiers wear belts that make them look like women, and "industry," she concludes, "is the moving spring of the Hamburgher's mind." The meeting with Friedrich Klopstock, described by Coleridge as the "venerable father of German poetry," gives Dorothy a headache that lasts for the next two days. The same encounter moves Coleridge to tears, despite his not having understood a word that has been said.

Dorothy's discomfort, together with the Wordsworths' lack of funds, was taking a toll, and after two weeks the group divided. "So there is an end to our fears about amalgamation," wrote Coleridge's friend Thomas Poole. Poole and his other friends were anxious about the possibility of Coleridge collapsing entirely into

Wordsworth, but it was instead Dorothy and William who were to amalgamate during their time in Germany. While Coleridge bounded across to beautiful Ratzeburg ready to immerse himself in the language, the Wordsworths dragged themselves south in a crowded carriage that Dorothy compared to a dung cart. The shaking of the vehicle, she recorded, "gave me a violent pain in my bowels which was followed by sickness," but at least they were beyond the city's gates and were no longer locked in at six-thirty each evening as they had been in Hamburg. For a moment her old voice returned, when she found a familiar subject: "The same moon that shone when we crossed the channel, now in its wane, lighted the waters of the Elbe; and it was of great use to us during the whole of our journey." But in Lüneburg she again lost inspiration: "All seemed lifeless and dead." After stopping at a number of "wretched" inns, each "more strange and more miserable" than the last—"miserable" and "strange" being adjectives frequently employed in the journal—they arrived in Brunswick, which Dorothy found "an old, silent, dull looking place" populated with "dismal"-looking women. Typical of her attitude to situations she has recently left, Dorothy compares the silence of Brunswick—a silence she has been longing for—to what she now sees as the superior "bustle and gaity" of the once-loathed Hamburg. Neither self-knowledge nor irony was among her characteristics, and in a letter written several months later Dorothy gravely observed that she and William were "struck with the extreme folly of people who draw conclusions respecting national character from the narrow limits of common observation. We have been much with German hosts and hostesses and notwithstanding these persons appeared in every respect as if made in contrast to each other."

Two hundred miles out of Hamburg, they arrived in the remote medieval town of Goslar in Lower Saxony. Beneath the

Harz Mountains, they were back in a landscape that reminded Dorothy of home. The Wordsworths had hoped to mix with literary society of sorts, but found Goslar, so Dorothy put it, full of "petty tradespeople, in general a low and selfish race; intent upon gain." Wordsworth agreed; once the home of emperors, Goslar now housed a "wretched race" of "grocers and linen drapers," the widow of one of whom gave them cheap lodgings. Even Coleridge conceded that it was "an ugly silent old desert of a city," but at least, he reminded them, they had "all in each other." How much did William and Dorothy have "all in each other" in Goslar? What happened to them during these dark, cold, silent months? Here Dorothy's Hamburg Journal abruptly ends, and she and William disappear behind their front door. There is some evidence that they kept a joint journal that has since disappeared, but for the next six weeks Coleridge heard from neither one of them, and during their entire stay their only companions were an émigré priest from France and a deaf neighbor. As Wordsworth said, "With bad German, bad English, bad hearing, and bad utterance you will imagine that we had very pretty dialogues."

What did the locals make of this reclusive so-called brother and sister who could speak no German and had traveled hundreds of miles in order to hide away in spartan rooms during an arctic winter? No wonder Dorothy complained that they were stared at. And what was Wordsworth doing in Germany anyway? He "might as well have been in England as at Goslar," thought Coleridge, who was whirling around on the ice with barons and countesses; how is it that a man who had traveled through revolutionary France was unable to cope with life in a sleepy German mountain town? His insistence on bringing Dorothy along had been a "wrong Step," Coleridge concluded; her presence prevented him from engaging with his surroundings, and yet Wordsworth's writing was, as ever, intensely concerned with his surroundings insofar as he was surrounded by Dorothy. Unlike Coleridge, who wrote nothing in Germany, and Dorothy, who wrote nothing good, Wordsworth infused his writing with an energy almost preternatural.

Time and place were suspended in Goslar, as Dorothy and William sank inward. Wordsworth was in a frenzy of composition; when he wrote at this pitch, he became ill. "As I have had no books I have been obliged to write in self-defence. I should have written five times as much," he told Coleridge by way of explaining his six-week silence, "but that I am prevented by an uneasiness at my stomach and side with a dull pain around my heart." In Grasmere, Dorothy wrote so as not to quarrel with herself, and in Goslar, William wrote in "self-defence." The habitual pain in his side, which disabled him when he had a poem growing within, had not been mentioned for a long time, and never had he before described writing as a means of psychological defense. From what was he defending himself? By what was he being besieged?

That winter was the coldest of the long century, so cold, Dorothy said, that when either of them made the slightest movement, "we were obliged to wrap ourselves up in great coats etc, in order not to suffer much pain from the transition, though we only went into the next room or downstairs for a few minutes." During the five months that Wordsworth and Dorothy were holed up like this, Wordsworth composed most of Book One of *The Prelude*. "Was it for this," the great poem began, as he recalled his Cumbrian childhood from the current position of godforsaken Goslar, "Was it for this / That one, the fairest of all rivers, loved / To blend his murmurs with my nurse's song?" The German boardinghouse also provided the stage for four of his enigmatic Lucy poems: "Strange fits of passion have I known," "She dwelt among th'untrodden ways,"

"Three years she grew in sun and shower," and "A slumber did my spirit seal." Each poem is organized around the figure of an unseen, much-loved girl who is sometimes but not always named Lucy, and whose death the poem's speaker imagines and mourns. Gone were the social and economic concerns of *Lyrical Ballads*; Wordsworth's interest was now inspiration, loss, and himself.

Dorothy turned twenty-seven that Christmas; her marrying days were over, her courtship years she had devoted to William. Her celebrated observations had become ordinary, her journal entries were tired and unimaginative. Living in Racedown, they had been similarly isolated, and William had been similarly depressed, but in her own home she at least had plenty to do. In Goslar their pies were provided, there was no Basil on whom to attend, no garden to look after or library to peruse. Not having German, Dorothy could talk to no one but William, whose writing had become obsessive. Was it for this that she had sacrificed her family and friends?

By February the ice had melted, and the Wordsworths left Goslar. They walked in the Harz Mountains and met with Coleridge before returning in May 1799 to the North of England. "We have now learned," William said, "to know its value," and they went straight to Mary Hutchinson in Sockburn as though this was where the value of their lives lay. With neither home nor money, William and Dorothy settled in Sockburn for the next seven months. Wordsworth quickly fell ill; Coleridge, now back at Nether Stowey with his grieving wife, whose new baby, Berkeley, had died while her husband was in Germany, was summoned to leave home once more and attend to his friend. William had completely recovered by the time Coleridge arrived, and in the company of John Wordsworth rather than Dorothy the two men took what Coleridge called "a pikteresk Toor" of the Lake District. Despite his mockery of the fashion for the lakes, he would fall in love with this land of mist and cloud, with its ever-changing skies and its rocks and stones and trees, in whose air hung, like the tatters of a torn coat, the heavy smell of damp fleece. In Grasmere he and Wordsworth found unchanged the "little unsuspected paradise" that the poet Thomas Gray had described in his journal in 1769. "What happy fortune were it here to live," Wordsworth had exclaimed when he saw the vale as a youth; Grasmere was where they would now settle. "You will think my plan a mad one, but I have thought of building a house there by the Lake side," he wrote to Dorothy, adding, "There is a small house at Grasmere empty which we might take, but of this we will speak."

The Wordsworths left Sockburn for Grasmere that winter, making their way by foot over the Pennines, now hard and gleaming, the snow blowing about them like smoke. "Bleak season was it, turbulent and bleak," Wordsworth recalled of the freezing walk, twenty-one miles on the first day, ten miles on the second, with Dorothy in a striped dress and a straw bonnet. The sight by which she would have been greeted had the sun forced its fingers through the thicket of clouds as they dropped down into the valley is best described by De Quincey, who took over Dove Cottage when the Wordsworths moved out:

> The whole vale of Grasmere suddenly breaks upon the view in a style of almost theatrical surprise, with its lovely valley stretching in the distance, the lake lying immediately below, with its solemn bent-like island of five acres in size, seemingly floating on its

> surface; its exquisite outline on the opposite shore, revealing all its little bays, and wild sylvan margin . . . In one quarter a little wood, stretching for about half a mile towards the outlet of the lake, more directly in opposition to the spectator; a few green fields, and beyond them, just two bowshots from the water, a little white cottage gleaming from the midst of trees, with a vast and seemingly never-ending series of ascents, rising above it to the height of more than three thousand feet.

In the late afternoon of December 20, five days before Dorothy's twenty-eighth birthday, the little white cottage became hers for £5 a year. She furnished it herself, using money that had been left to her in the recent will of their uncle Christopher. Dorothy had never before owned anything.

A former inn called the Dove and Olive Bough, the cottage stood on the outskirts of the village, six hundred yards from the church. It looked onto two other cottages, in one of which lived old Molly Fisher, who would help with the housework, especially with the great washes that would take place every five weeks; to Coleridge, Molly was always the woman who had not heard of the French Revolution. Together with a further two cottages a little up the hill, the group of buildings was called Town End, and it was as Town End rather than as Dove Cottage that Dorothy knew her home. Grasmere then housed 270 people, many of whom worked on the land. It was, said the poet Thomas Gray, "a perfect republic of shepherds and agriculturalists." In the thirty years since Gray's visit, there was still "not a single red tile" to be seen, although the odd "flaring gentleman's house" now broke in upon the world of "peace, rusticity, and happy poverty, in its neatest and most becoming attire." The name of the former inn, which in time became attached to the cottage itself, would have suited the new inhabitants, who associated their home with an enveloping nest, a fresh start, and the cooing mother dove.

A flint wall separates the house from the road, and a short path leads up to a narrow front door, through which can be found an oblong kitchen hall. The ceiling is beamed and low and the walls wainscoted with dark wood, which would have been stained with grease and the smoke of candles and tobacco from the old inn days. One tiny, diamond-paned window looks onto the road, and the floor is cool slate. A door leads off into a smaller room, which Dorothy used as a bedroom until William married, when he and Mary took it over. From here you enter the kitchen, previously the bar of the inn. Upstairs are three more rooms: a sitting room and two bedrooms, one for William and one for guests. A small lumber room later lined with newspapers would serve as a bedroom for William and Mary's children. The "necessary," as Dorothy called it, was outside.

It was on the threshold of the new century that they found their dream cottage, but they were less crossing over into something new than turning back. "We were young and healthy and had attained our object long desired," Dorothy recalled. "We had returned to our native mountains, there to live." Dorothy and William could now regain the childhood they had lost; they had come home again.

Chapter Three

IN SICKNESS AND IN HEALTH: HEADACHES

In the journals that I've kept sporadically, my chirpy entries on the arrival of spring migrants and balmy autumns are repeatedly interrupted by complaints about my internal climate.

—RICHARD MABEY, *Nature Cure*

This heaven gives me migraine.

—GANG OF FOUR, "Natural's Not in It"

For the rest of the summer after William's return to Grasmere from Gallow Hill on June 7, Dorothy fills her journal with images of stillness and what Coleridge calls "sudden charm." No longer pushing back the days in anticipation of his arrival, she is holding on to them fast, searching out moments of pause into which she can slip. Much of her time is spent by the lake with William and John, setting floats for pike, which she will then cook for supper. She likes the water best when it is smooth. *The lake became of glassy calmness & all was still,* she wrote on August 2; *I sate till I could see no longer.* She gazes at stillness as though it were an object and listens to it like a sound. Transparency is as rich for Dorothy as a color. Sometimes she likes moving when everything else is still: *At 11 o'clock Coleridge came when I was walking in the still, clear moonlight in the garden,* or *We rowed home over a lake still as glass.* Rydal Water, she says, *is a dark mirror.* At other times it is she who is a dark mirror while all about her moves. Samuel Beckett describes the feeling in *Krapp's Last Tape,* when his lovers are in the boat: "We lay there without moving. But under us all moved, and moved us, gently, up and down, and from side to side."

Her days, she tells Jane, are

> various yet they are irregular. We walk [every] day and at all times of the day, we row upon the water and . . . sit a great part of our time under the apple trees of the orchard or in a wood close by the lake-side. William writes verses, John goes a fishing, and we read the books we have and such as we can procure.

In her journal she gives a different version of the pattern of her life. Some days they sleep in late, some nights they stay up talking until *the first dawning of the day,* there are days when they go to bed in the afternoon, when it is raining or too cold to sit under the tree, and days when they work hard in the house and garden to maintain their idyll. One day she puts in a new window, some days she makes pies or a shoe and will talk with a peddler or beggar, and most days she gathers flowers and plants for the garden. Once she goes to Ambleside with William to get his tooth drawn; once she simply watches the weather change *from clear to cloudy & to clear again.* Once a lamb wanders up to her as she is lying on a hill; it responds to Dorothy as she responds to nature: *It approached nearer & nearer as if to examine me & stood a long time.* She sews and she mends; she papers William's room and she cooks gooseberries.

But there are also days when she discards the ordinary and

scents out the visionary. On June 16, *Collath was wild & interesting, from the Peat carts & peat gatherers—the valley all perfumed with gale & wild thyme. The woods about the waterfall veined with rich yellow Broom.* On June 23, *the setting sun threw a purple light upon the rocks & stone walls of Rydale which gave them a most interesting & beautiful appearance.* Frugal in all else, Dorothy likes visual excess and finds ecstasy in sudden washes of color. She sees yellow everywhere. On August 25, *Grasmere exceedingly dark & Rydale of a light yellow green*; on August 29, *there was a curious yellow reflection in the water as of corn fields—there was no light in the clouds from which it appeared to come*; on August 31, *A great deal of corn is cut in the vale, & the whole prospect though not tinged with a general autumnal yellow, yet softened down into a mellowness of colouring which seems to impart softness to the forms of hills & mountains*; on September 12, *The Fern of the mountains now spreads yellow veins among the trees*; on September 14, *read Boswell in the house in the morning & after dinner under the bright yellow leaves of the orchard—the pear trees a bright yellow*; and on October 10, *There was a most lovely combination at the head of the vale—of the yellow autumnal hills wrapped in sunshine, & overhung with partial mists, the green & yellow trees & distant snow-topped mountains.* As if she were a mystic, sometimes what Dorothy sees is bathed in radiant luminosity.

They are writing all the time. In the summer and autumn of 1800, Wordsworth put together and sent off to the printer the poems for the new volume of *Lyrical Ballads*, sixteen of which had been written in Germany, twenty of which had been written during the year in Grasmere. He also composed the monumental Preface to *Lyrical Ballads*, which sets out his theory of poetry—"all good poetry is the spontaneous overflow of powerful feelings"—and will become the gospel of Romanticism. Here he defines a poet as a superior being, a man

> endued with more lively sensibility, more enthusiasm and tenderness, who has a greater knowledge of human nature, and a more comprehensive soul, than are supposed to be common among mankind; a man pleased with his own passions and volitions, and who rejoices more than other men in the spirit of life that is in him . . .

and so forth. Dorothy's transcribing of all this was essential; she was fully involved in every line produced by William. On July 26, she records that she *wrote out Ruth in the afternoon*; on August 1, *In the morning I copied The Brothers*; on the morning of October 8, *I copied a part of The Beggar*; on October 12, *copied poems for the LB in the evening*; on October 13, *I copied poems on the naming of places*.

Wordsworth has succeeded in luring Coleridge and his reluctant wife from Somerset to live in his perilous and sheep-filled landscape. Together with their son, Hartley, the Coleridges spend July 1800 in Dove Cottage while Greta Hall, the house they are taking in Keswick, is being prepared. During their stay, Coleridge, Dorothy, and William work on *Lyrical Ballads*. Before the Coleridges leave, the party has an island picnic and a bonfire of fir cones. At the end of September, John leaves Grasmere to take on the captaincy of his own ship, the *Earl of Abergavenny*. He has been at Dove Cottage for ten months. Dorothy's journal entry is brief: *Poor fellow my heart was right sad—I could not help thinking we should see him again because he was only going to Penrith*. As it is, they will never see John in the Lake District again. She sits up late the next night copying out *Lyrical Ballads* for the printer. On October 4—his wedding anniversary—Coleridge reads aloud to the Wordsworths the second part of *Christabel*, the dreamy ballad he had begun in March 1798, when they were living in Somerset, and Dorothy records that they were *exceedingly delighted* by it. The next morning he reads it again, and she and William have *increasing pleasure*. But by the next day Dorothy reports, *Determined not to print Christabel with the LB*. There is no personal pronoun, but we assume that it was William's determination and not Dorothy's to exclude the ballad they have been planning on including for so long. Whatever the reason for its rejection, and Dorothy hints at nothing, from that moment on Coleridge believes that the poet in him is dead.

Dorothy is surface blown this summer. Not for her the ambition expressed by Mary Shelley in her diary: "Let me fearlessly descend into the remotest caverns of my own mind, carry the torch of self-knowledge into its dimmest recesses." Dorothy likes the appearance of things to be calm and reflective and does not want to descend beneath into any mental caverns. On Saturday, June 21,

> *Grasmere looked so beautiful that my heart was almost melted away. It was quite calm only spotted with sparkles of light. The church visible. On our return all distant objects had faded away—all but the hills. The reflection of the light bright sky above Black quarter was very solemn.*

She is happiest when melting away in contemplation of an object, or when watching objects fade out of sight, leaving a reflection or echo behind. Five days later, on June 26,

> *After tea we rowed down to Loughrigg Fell, visited the white foxglove, gathered wild strawberries, & walked up to view Rydale we lay a long time looking at the lake, the shores all embrowned with the scorching sun. The Ferns were turning yellow, that is here & there one was quite turned. We walked round Benson's wood home. The lake was now most still & reflected*

> *the beautiful yellow & blue & purple & grey colours of the sky. We heard a strange sound in the Bainrigg's wood as we were floating on the water it seemed in the wood, but it must have been above it, for presently we saw a raven very high above us— it called out & the Dome of the sky seemed to echoe the sound— it called again & again as it flew onwards, & the mountains gave back the sound, seeming as if from their center a musical bell-like answering to the birds hoarse voice. We heard both the call of the bird & the echoe after we could see him no longer.*

The play of light and sound delights her. She notes of the lake after rain that *those parts of the water which were perfectly unruffled lay like green islands of various shapes.* She is drawn to unruffled surfaces, but the surface of her own life is easily ruffled. On Monday, June 23,

> *W & I went into Langdale to fish. The morning was very cold. I sate at the foot of the lake till my head ached with cold. The view exquisitely beautiful, through a gate & under a sycamore tree beside the first house going into Loughrigg . . . When W went down to the water to fish I lay under the wind my head pillowed upon a mossy rock & slept about 10 minutes which relieved my headache.*

Dorothy spends a great deal of her time turned inward. On June 30, her head aches after dinner and she lies down. When she later recovers and goes outside, the night is *excessively beautiful— a rich reflection of the moon, the moonlight clouds & the hills, & from the Rays gap a huge rainbow pillar. We sailed upon the lake till it was 10 o'clock.* Exquisite and excessive beauty comes accompanied by pain: there is a serpent in the Garden of Eden.

Since the day she began her Grasmere Journals, when Dorothy *arrived home with a bad head-ach*, she has inadvertently kept a record of her cavernous descents. During the first three weeks when William is away visiting Mary, Dorothy describes three further occasions on which a bad headache takes her to bed for the afternoon, and one day when she goes to bed "unwell" after lunch. What emerges from the picture she draws of the long, slow summer and bountiful autumn of 1800 is that she is living between two worlds, an outside world that is silent and still, and an inside world that is tempestuous and turbulent. Her descriptions of the external climate are repeatedly interrupted by reports on her internal climate, and sometimes the other way around. *I was not well in the morning. We baked bread—after dinner I went to bed—William walked into Easedale. Rain, hail & snow. I rose at ½ past 7, got tea, then went to sup at Mr. Oliff's.* When we isolate from the strings of non sequiturs in her journal all reference to the times either Dorothy or William is not well between May 14 and their second Christmas in Grasmere, the bill of health at Dove Cottage is as follows:

May 20 *I was sadly tired, ate a hasty dinner & had a bad head-ach.*

May 24 *I went to bed soon with a bad head-ach.*

May 27 *I had a bad head-ach.*

June 3 *Was not well after dinner & lay down.*

July 25 *In the afternoon from excessive heat I was ill in the head-ach & toothach & went to bed.*

July 29 *I was sick & weary.*

July 30 *I was obliged to lie down after dinner from excessive heat & headach.*

August 2 *I . . . lay down til tea time.*

August 3 *headach after dinner—I lay down.*

August 23 *I was ill in the afternoon & lay down—got up restored by a sound sleep.*

August 25 *Wm not quite well.*

August 28 *I had a headach & went to lie down in the orchard.*

September 7 *I lay down after dinner. Wm poorly.*

October 5 *Wm went to bed very ill after working after dinner . . . still in bed & very ill.*

October 7 *I was very ill in the evening at the Simpsons—went to bed—supped there . . . Found William at home. I was still weak & unwell—went to bed immediately.*

October 8 *I was not quite well in the evening.*

October 18 *My head better—he unable to work.*

October 31 *W very sick & very ill.*

November 7 *Wm still unwell.*

November 12 *I lay down after dinner with a headach.*

November 14 *I had a bad head-ach.*

November 15 *I walked to the top of the hill for a head-ach.*

November 16 *My head aching very much I sent to excuse myself to Lloyds.*

November 22 *Wm not quite well.*

November 23 *Wm not well.*

November 24 *I had the tooth-ach in the night—took Laudanum.*

November 25 *Very ill—in bed all day—better in the Evening.*

November 26 *William very well & highly poetical.*

November 28 *Coleridge was very unwell . . . Great boils upon his neck.*

> December 6 *William was not well had laboured unsuccessfully.*
> December 7 *I was unwell & went to bed till 8 o'clock.*
> December 20 *Coleridge came—very ill rheumatic, feverish.*

What did Dorothy's headaches feel like? In his book *A Treatise on Headaches* (1853), the nineteenth-century doctor J. C. Peters described an entire range of pains experienced by his patients, pains "of a hammering, throbbing, or pushing nature . . . pressing and dull . . . boring with sense of bursting . . . pricking . . . rending . . . stretching . . . piercing . . . and radiating . . . in a few cases it felt as if a wedge was pressed into the head, or like an ulcer, or as if the brain was torn, or pressed outwards." Dorothy says nothing other than that her head "ached"; we do not know if her pain pressed, pricked, stretched, or pierced, or whether it felt different every time. We have no idea how she responded to all these headaches, whether she was resigned to them or exasperated by them. She simply notes their occurrence—usually in the afternoons—and her treatment of them by a few hours of rest.

When she does not record in her journal the state of her own health, or that of William and Coleridge, it will be sure to appear as a subject of concern in Dorothy's letters. In September 1800 she wrote to Jane:

> William's health is by no means strong, he has written a great deal since we first went to Alfoxton, namely during the year preceding our going into Germany, while we were there, and since our arrival in England and writes with so much feeling and agitation that it brings on a sense of pain and internal weakness about his left side and stomach, which now

> often makes it impossible for him to write when he is in mind and feelings in such a state that he could do it without difficulty.

As early as 1787, when they were in Penrith, Dorothy told Jane that William "is troubled with violent head-aches and a pain in his side," adding that she had been suffering from "a pain in my head now and then, but I think crying was the cause of it." Dorothy will rarely mention William's health without then commenting on her own, as if their two bodies were in correspondence, and from her journal it appears that they took turns being well and unwell, with Coleridge joining in when he came to visit. On November 23, 1800, William is *not well*, the next day Dorothy has *the tooth-ach*, the day after that Dorothy is *very ill*, and on the following day William is *very well*. Two days later, Coleridge is *very unwell*.

Composition, particularly revision, made William ill, although he did not at first associate his symptoms with writing. The pain and weakness in his side that Dorothy records coincide with his bursts of creativity; the more powerful the poetry coming out of him, the more profound the pain gnawing away within. In May 1801, Dorothy wrote to Coleridge, "Poor William! His stomach is in bad plight. We have put aside all the manuscript poems and it is agreed between us that I am not to give them up to him even if he asks for them." In October 1803, Wordsworth described his "aversion from writing" as

> little less than madness . . . during the last three [y]ears I have never had a pen in my hand for five minutes, [b]efore my whole frame becomes one bundle of uneasiness, perspiration starts out all over me,

> and my chest is [o]ppressed in a manner which I cannot describe.

Many years into their marriage, Mary described Wordsworth lying in bed "hurting himself with a sonnet." William was, Coleridge believed, a pampered hypochondriac. Coleridge's own symptoms—despair, despondency, self-disgust, "rheumatic fevers, swollen leg joints, boils, agonising nephritic pains, and a swollen testicle"—were the very real effects of addiction to opium, but what was wrong with Dorothy?

Whether she is pulled inward or propelled beyond herself, the rhythm of her life as Dorothy describes it alternates on a regular basis from withdrawal, dejection, and anxiety to intense engagement in the world around her and astonishingly heightened sensory perception. Her predisposition to bouts of depression and euphoria could have been exacerbated by her childhood losses, and further pressure added to her already frail psyche by her brother's and Coleridge's insistence on the superiority of emotion to intellect. What made Dorothy different from other women in their eyes was her capacity for "feeling," part of which was the ability to suffer intensely. Had her "sensibility" not been endlessly encouraged and championed by all who knew her until it became her defining feature, she might have been freed from the rigid confines of her responsiveness. As someone who reacted to, melted into, and mirrored her environment, Dorothy suffered with those around her.

But there is more to Dorothy's condition than shifting emotional states. Back in 1791, she wrote to Jane from Forncett that she had, "during the whole of this summer, without being absolutely ill, been less able to support any fatigue and been more troubled with headache than I ever remember to have been, I have of late had an extreme weariness in my limbs after the most trifling exertions such as going up stairs, etc," and in 1804 she told her friend Catherine Clarkson that "ever since I can remember[,] going into company always gave me violent head-aches," adding that she was made ill by "agitation of mind either of joy or sorrow . . . any strong excitement cures my diseases for a time, but if I am well as surely brings them on." Dorothy's headaches, to which there are sixty-three references in the Grasmere Journals, and which are brought on by agitation and excitement, appear to be migraines. The prime characteristics of migrainous women, according to experts, are to have a small frame, a brisk walk, and an eager mind: Dorothy, who described herself as someone for whom "it is natural . . . to do everything as quickly as I can and at the same time," meets the type. Her attacks were regular, on average two a week and in some weeks one every day. They tended to come on after the midday meal and to disappear with a few hours' rest or sleep. She would sometimes treat the pain with laudanum—a mixture of opium in alcohol—and occasionally with wine, but the cost of both was prohibitive. In general she regarded her headaches as trivial. In a letter to Henry Crabb Robinson written in 1829, Dorothy says that she has just suffered the first serious illness in her life, a good fortune she attributes to having always "been so remarkably strong and healthy."

What distinguishes migraine from a bad headache is that the condition is composite: a migraine always involves more than a headache and sometimes does not involve having a headache at all. Migraine, writes Oliver Sacks in *Migraine: The Evolution of a Common Disorder* (1970), is "a whole realm or region of strange phenomena," as remarkable "as the stars in the sky." It is "a physical event which may also be from the start, or later become, an emotional or symbolic event," and its discussion opens up "an extraordinary landscape . . . a sort of wonderland of nature." Migraine can be divided into either the "common" or the "classical," and within these categories the symptoms can vary from the almost indiscernible stab, felt only with the slightest movement of the head, to Chinese burns of searing, incapacitating violence.

Common migraine, in which an area to either the left or the right side of the head is affected, causing nausea and bowel disorder, can last anywhere between a few hours and several days. Sufferers lie in silence in darkened rooms until the pain wears off. Its "most important emotional colorings," writes Sacks,

> are states of anxious and irritable hyperactivity in the early portions of the attack and states of apathy and depression in the bulk of the attack . . . Feelings of depression will be associated with feelings of anger and resentment, and in the severest migraines there may exist a very ugly mixture of despair, fury and loathing of everything and everyone, not excluding the self.

But preceding the depression can be a period of feeling "dangerously well," as George Eliot, who also suffered from migraine, described it, during which you experience a rush of excitement and intensity. Dorothy's headaches are often preceded by euphoria, as on May 20: *Everything green & overflowing with life, & the streams making a perpetual song with the thrushes & all the little birds, not forgetting the stone chats.* But by the end of the day, *No letters! No papers . . . I was sadly tired, ate a hasty dinner & had a bad head-ach, went to bed & slept at least 2 hours.* Four days later, it is after she gets a letter from William and completes her reply that she goes *to bed soon with a bad head-ach.* A migraine can also be followed by a sense of rebirth. In *On Megrim, Sick-Headache, and Some Allied Disorders* (1873), Edward Liveing observed how

> the abrupt transition from intense suffering to perfect health is very remarkable. A man . . . finds himself, with little or no warning, completely disabled, the victim of intense bodily pain, mental prostration, and perhaps hallucinations of sense or idea . . . and in this state he remains the greater part of the day; and yet towards its close . . . he awakes a different being, in possession of all his faculties, and able to join an evening's entertainment.

Dorothy will describe collapsing with pain after dinner and then rising to enjoy an intensely beautiful evening.

Common migraine can sometimes accompany a regular tension headache and can be cured by a "crisis" of physical or mental activity. "Any strong excitement cures my diseases for a time," Dorothy tells Catherine Clarkson, and she notes in her journal how she *walked to the top of the hill for a head-ach.* Attacks provoked by specific circumstances such as stress, exhaustion, agitation, and passive motion (being still while surrounded by movement) are what Oliver Sacks calls the "Borderlands of Migraine," and it is on these borderlands that Dorothy lived. She was always made ill by emotion. "It does not seem to matter much," Edward Liveing says, "what the character of the emotion is, provided it be strongly felt." Oliver Sacks is more specific: "We find, in practice, that sudden *rage* is the commonest percipient . . . sudden elation . . . may have the same effect." It is little wonder that Dorothy, who reacted to everything but preferred to keep her rage repressed, spent hours of every week in agony. Inclement weather can be another major cause of attack; Dorothy was made ill by thunderstorms all her life, and notes in her journals that she would *lie down after dinner from excessive heat & headach* and how, as she puts it, *in the afternoon from excessive heat I was ill in the head-ach.*

There is also, Liveing says, a form of migraine "trance" in which the sufferer feels a drowsiness so extreme that he falls into a waking sleep or a living death. Dorothy described to Jane back in her Forncett days how she was unable to deal with the tiredness that came on with her headaches, being "less able to support any fatigue and . . . more troubled with headache than I ever remember to have been." Throughout the Grasmere Journals, not least when she is lying on the bed at Gallow Hill on the morning of William and Mary's wedding, unable to hear or see, Dorothy can be found in a trancelike state. Oliver Sacks describes a patient for whom the trance replaced the headache, becoming the sole symptom of his migraine:

> "I go into a trance [the patient tells Sacks] where I am able to hear things around me but can't move. I am soaked with a cold sweat. My pulse gets very slow." The state lasts between one and two hours, rarely less or more than this. He "wakes, if one may use the word," with a feeling of intense refreshment and bounding energy.

"Classical," as opposed to "common," migraines are distinguished by "auras," a term that has been used since antiquity to describe the extraordinary symptoms that precede the headache itself, although as with the migraine trance it is possible to experience migraine auras without then suffering the headache. The manifestations of migraine aura, Sacks writes, "include not only simple and complex sensory hallucinations, but intense affective states, deficits and disturbances of speech and ideation, dislocations of space-and-time perception, and a variety of dreamy, delirious, and trancelike states." Some hallucinations can be no more than rippling, shimmering undulations in the visual field, which Sacks's patients compare to the appearance of windblown water, but there are other patients "who cannot bear to think or talk of their attacks, and always refer to them with horror though this is clearly not on account of the pain they occasion." For Edward Liveing, "good descriptions" of attacks of this kind "are hard to obtain, because many aura phenomena are exceedingly strange—so strange as to transcend the powers of language; and good descriptions are made rarer still by the presence of something uncanny and fearful, the very thought of which causes the mind to shy." These auras are characterized by "scotomata," the commonest feature of migraine apart from the headache. Scotomata, or darkness and shadow, are defined by Sacks as "dramatic disturbances in vision and the visual field, taking the form of strange and often twinkling brilliances (scintillating scotomata), or strange blindnesses and absences of vision."

Dorothy's migraines for the most part appear to have been common, but it is possible to find in the Grasmere Journals accounts of what might be the scintillating scotomata of classical migraine. For example, on April 29, 1802, she describes how *William lay, & I lay* side by side in John's Grove, silent and still as the dead:

> *He thought it would be as sweet thus to lie so in the grave & to hear the peaceful sounds of the earth . . . The Lake was still*

> *there was a Boat out. Silver how reflected with delicate purple & yellowish hues . . . —Lambs on the island & Running races together by the half dozen in the round field near us. The copses greenish, hawthorne green—Came home to dinner then went to Mr. Simpson. We rested a long time under a wall. Sheep & lambs were in the field—cottages smoking. As I lay down on the grass, I observed the glittering silver line on the ridges of the Backs of the sheep, owing to their situation respecting the Sun—which made them look beautiful but with something of a strangeness, like animals of another kind—as if belonging to a more splendid world . . . I was sick & ill & obliged to come home soon. We went to bed immediately.*

The dreamlike day begins with a trancelike state, of which Dorothy and William quite possibly have quite different experiences. This is followed by a vision of glittering sheep, which Dorothy finds *strange* and otherworldly, and ends with her being *sick & ill*, by which it is reasonable to assume that she has a headache. Her account of April 29 conforms to what Sacks describes as the uncanny aspect of the aura as well as "the sense of stillness and timelessness" that auras convey: "Such states may wax in depth or intensity, but this occurs despite the absence of any experiential 'happening.' Also typical is their difficulty or impossibility of adequate description . . . We are inevitably reminded of William James's listing of the qualities of 'mystical' states: ineffability, abstract quality, transiency, passivity." Might it be that Dorothy's mystical descriptions are signs of migraine rather than marks of fine sensibility? When she records on October 1, 1800, *flashing light from the beams of the sun*, perhaps it really is flashing light that she sees before her; when, on April 15, 1802, *a sheep came plunging through the river . . . its fleece dropped a glittering shower under its belly*, she might not be writing metaphorically; when she describes how, lying *upon the steep of Loughrigg my heart dissolved in what I saw*, perhaps that is exactly what happened and she does feel herself dissolving. She may like it best when the lake is unruffled not because it looks nice but because the gentle motion on the surface of water makes her sick.

Sometimes what she sees can seem like visions—Sunday, June 20:

> *We lay upon the sloping Turf. Earth & sky were so lovely that they melted our very hearts. The sky to the north was of a chastened yet rich yellow fading into pale blue & streaked & scattered over with steady islands of purple melting away into shades of pink. It made my heart almost feel like a vision to me.*

Her entries recall the accounts of her own visions written down by the twelfth-century nun and mystic Hildegard of Bingen, which Sacks diagnoses as being without doubt migraine auras. Hildegard describes what she sees as "beheld neither in sleep, nor in dreams, not in madness, nor with my carnal eyes, nor with the ears of the flesh, nor in hidden places; but wakeful, alert, and in the eyes of the spirit and the inward ears." Hildegard's visions always involve light. On one occasion, "the light which I see is not located, but yet is more brilliant than the sun, nor can I examine its height, length or breadth, and I name it 'the cloud of the living light.'" Dorothy sees strange light everywhere. *The night was wild*, she wrote of February 8, 1802:

> *There was a strange mountain lightness when we were at the top of the White Moss. I have often observed it there in the*

> *evenings, being between two valleys. There is more of the sky there than any other place. It has a strange effect sometimes along with the obscurity of evening or night. It seems almost like a peculiar sort of light.*

Hildegard's auras bring with them flashes of ecstatic happiness in which she is disengaged from time and space, as they did also for Dostoevsky, who described how

> there are moments, and it is only a matter of five or six seconds, when you feel the presence of the eternal harmony . . . a terrible thing is the frightful clearness with which it manifests itself and the rapture with which it fills you. If this state were to last more than five seconds, the soul could not endure it and would have to disappear. During these five seconds I live a whole human existence, and for that I would give my whole life and not think that I was paying too dearly.

For Sacks, the subject of migraine aura is "touched with the incomprehensible and the incommunicable." In its presence, he feels he has approached what Kant calls "the terrifying sublime."

Dorothy's headaches sometimes spiral her into her body like water drawing down a drain. At other times they expunge her body altogether and propel her outward into *a more splendid world*. It is the experience of physical erasure that she prefers, leaving her as nothing but a pair of observing eyes. The desire to dissolve into what she sees—what she calls *melting* or *fading* away—together with her capacity for self-denial and the frugality of her diet suggest that Dorothy may have had what we recognize now as anorexic tendencies, which were possibly a reaction to the internal incarceration brought on by her headaches. Alive to all her senses and physically agile and fit, Dorothy would seem to live intensely in her body, and yet she responds with less pleasure to what she puts into herself than to what takes her out of herself. From the self-starvation of medieval mystics to the refusal to eat of Samuel Richardson's Clarissa, watching the body shrink is a way of experiencing consciousness without the encumbrance of corporal presence, and this is what Dorothy attempts to achieve.

Self-imposed hunger is a condition defined by refusal: refusal to listen to the body's demands, refusal to accept what is offered or to participate in the sharing of food, and refusal to consider the consequences of starvation. Susan Levin, in a rich and insightful study of her writing—*Dorothy Wordsworth and Romanticism* (1987)—sees refusal as Dorothy Wordsworth's most striking characteristic: "refusal to generalize, refusal to move out of a limited range of vision, refusal to speculate, refusal to reproduce standard literary forms, refusal to undertake the act of writing . . . Dorothy sets down various progressions in her life, but she refuses to make connections."

The Wordsworths were poor, and their cuisine was modest, added to which the plain-living, high-thinking ethos of their household did little to encourage pleasure in consumption. There were three hot meals a day served up at Dove Cottage, Sir Walter Scott reported after a visit, and two of them were porridge or what Dorothy calls "broth." Scott would escape through the spare-room window to satisfy his hunger in the local pub. But if Dorothy went hungry, it was not because they had no money but because she feared change. Stopping the body is a way of preserving the past. Dorothy's weight plummeted not while she was at Dove Cottage but during her time in Racedown, when she was acting as mother to young Basil Montagu, running a large house and garden without help, and nursing William back to mental strength. Having always lived in homes where someone else put the food on the table, Dorothy for the first time would have been responsible for feeding herself and those around her. In 1791 she had told Jane Pollard that she weighed a healthy eight stones; in the autumn of 1800 she told her:

> I first lost my flesh in Dorsetshire having [caught] a violent cold attended with a swelled face, violent toothach and many symptoms of fever. I was never fat afterwards though less thin than I am at present, and I am afraid I will never regain the stone and a quarter of flesh which I have lost.

It wasn't until 1810, eight years after William married, when he and Dorothy left Grasmere to visit friends and relations, that she showed signs of recovery. Dorothy, as William wrote home to Mary,

> is grown very fat and looks better than she has done, since she had that complaint at Racedown: Her throat and neck are quite filled up . . . I never saw a more rapid and striking improvement in the health and appearance of anyone. She has a most excellent appetite, as good a digestion and is never tired.

During her first year of living with William, instead of spreading herself out in the sun like hepatica as she had expected to do,

Dorothy was wilting. Was the reality of William's company a disappointment to her? Did she feel overwhelmed by his mental state and in need of some nurturing herself? Was her emaciated appearance, to use that tired expression, "a cry for help"? It was since the Racedown days that she had been very thin, although William told Mary in the spring of 1802 that Dorothy "does fat one day and lean the other, but fat and jolly for half a year together." Dorothy told Catherine Clarkson, "When I am well my appetite is often much larger than that of any of my female friends but it is very irregular." She was rarely well. Her weight clearly oscillated along with her headaches and her moods. Denying herself food was a form of martyrdom as well as a means of maintaining control over a life whose terms were increasingly dictated by her brother's requirements.

William recovered his strength in Racedown by feeding off what Dorothy had to offer, adopting her "ears and eyes" as his own, and redefining his sister as a bottomless source of sensibility, endlessly available for his consumption. Before she became responsible for maintaining Wordsworth's phenomenal ego and nurturing his future greatness as a poet, nothing much had been asked of Dorothy, other than to make herself generally agreeable. Giving herself up to William's, and thus the world's, greater good required pushing herself to the limit. Her Grasmere Journals describe one February night when William goes off to bed tired and ill, leaving Dorothy, who has already *written in his letter to Coleridge*, writing four further letters on his behalf. Her account of what she went through while her brother slept contains an anger toward him more easily expressed on the page than in person:

> *Wm left me with a little peat fire—it grew less—I wrote on & was starved. At 2 o clock I went to put my letters under Fletcher's door. I never felt such a cold night. There was a*

> *strong wind & it froze very hard. I collected together all the clothes I could find (for I durst not go into the pantry for fear of waking William). At first when I went to bed I seemed to be warm, I suppose because the cold air which I had just left no longer touched my body, but I soon found that I was mistaken. I could not sleep from sheer cold.*

The next day she records that while William's night had been better, her *head ached my bones were sore with the cold of the day before & I was downright stupid. We went to bed but not till William had tired himself.*

Dorothy's eating was, like her prose, measured and controlled rather than dramatic and extreme; she ate with caution and precision, taking in just enough fuel to keep herself going: *I felt myself weak, & William charged me not to go to Mrs. Lloyds . . . so I ate a Beef-steak thinking it would strengthen me so it did, & I went off.* Food appears throughout her journals, which open with William and John setting off to Gallow Hill with *cold pork in their pockets* and close with Dorothy's supper of tapioca and a trip to buy William some gingerbread. She eats meals of gruel, boiled eggs, apple tarts, "hasty pudding," black cherries, and cold turkey. Only once does she describe indulging herself, when she *feasted on gooseberries at Silver Hill.* She is very aware of food and concerned that everyone has enough to eat. She documents the consumption of other people more often than her own: we do not know what she had to sustain herself while William and John ate the cold pork she had prepared for their walk. She will note throughout the journal that *William is eating his broth* or that *I gave him his dinner a Beef Steak*, and she once boils *Coleridge a mutton chop which he ate in bed.* One morning, after she has breakfasted alone, she watches William as he sits *with his Basin of Broth before him untouched &*

a little plate of Bread & butter he wrote the Poem to a Butterfly!— he ate not a morsel . . . Dorothy consumes every word he writes and knows exactly how much or how little he consumes himself: she is responsible for every mouthful.

The preparation of meals took up a great deal of her day. She baked several times a week, always pies, cakes, and bread, she picked and prepared the fruits and vegetables from the garden, she boiled beef and mutton and stuffed and roasted the pike caught on the lake. Dorothy's meals were served without ceremony. Food takes on significance for her only at times of heightened intimacy, as when she and William are caught momentarily alone in the cottage and she is suddenly alert to every detail in

Scullery maid, drawing by John Harden

their domestic lives: *I went & sat with W & walked backwards & forwards in the Orchard till dinner time—he read me his poem. I broiled Beefsteaks. After dinner we made a pillow of my shoulder, I read to him & my Beloved slept.* Or: *We were in deep silence & love, a blessed hour. We drew to the fire before bed-time & ate some broth for our suppers.* These scenes are organized around William's comfort rather than her own; it is her brother she is feeding rather than herself. Without William's company, she will sometimes eat a little hasty pudding before going to bed, the bland mixture of oats and water being easy on her increasingly toothless gums. Sometimes she will not bother eating at all.

There is a gain to illness, too, which can be reward enough for suffering. Illness is a shared experience, and Dorothy enjoyed the physical proximity that being ill allowed herself and William. Being ill broke down barriers and created intimacy, the sickroom folding nurse and patient in on one another like fields under snow. If writing was the problem, reading was the cure: *William was very unwell . . . he went to bed, I read to him to endeavour to make him sleep*, she writes on January 29. He is *still poorly* on February 11—*we made up a good fire after dinner, & William brought his mattress out, & lay down on the floor I read to him the life of Ben Jonson & some short poems of his which were too interesting for him, & would not let him go to sleep.*

She describes nursing more often than being nursed, but she took her turn at being comforted. "Really it is almost a pleasure to be ill, he is so good and loving to me," Dorothy told Sara Hutchinson. There is much to be gained from recovery as well, and Dorothy told Catherine Clarkson in 1804, "I have been so well that my dear Brother's heart has overflowed with joy in looking at me for some time past." Another perspective on Dorothy's condition emerges from a later passage in the same letter to Mrs. Clarkson. She describes one of her migraine attacks in which "violent headaches" and sickness are followed by "yellow and pale looks . . . pains in the bowels, thirst, and want of appetite," and asks Mrs. Clarkson, a friend of the Bristol physician Thomas Beddoes, to

> tell Dr. Beddoes that at all times when I am not in uncommon strength (as I was before the last attack) after writing for any length of time or doing anything that exercises my thoughts or feelings, I have a very uneasy sense of want and weakness at my stomach, a mixture of emptiness, gnawing, and a sort of preparation for sickness—eating always removes it for a time.

Internal pain and weakness after writing or thinking are more William's problems than Dorothy's, which suggests that the two shared their symptoms in the same way as did Henry James and his own adored sister, Alice, who also spent much of her time being ill while keeping a diary of her brother's achievements. Henry gives her "calm and solace," Alice wrote after one of her own attacks, "by assuring me that my nerves are his nerves and my stomach his stomach." This is what James called "the pain of sympathy," and in his notebooks he planned a story about a brother's relationship with his sister in which each "can only abound in the same sense, see with the same imagination, vibrate with the same nerves, suffer with the same suffering: have, in a word, exactly, identically, the same experience of life. Two lives, two beings, and *one* experience." Coleridge described it as "though we were three persons it was but one God."

The first notebook of the Grasmere Journals ends abruptly in mid-sentence on December 22, 1800, with William and Sara Hutchinson, who has come to stay, walking home after dining with their new neighbors. Dorothy's final entry—*S and Wm went to the Lloyds. Wm dined, it rained very hard when he came home at . . .*—runs into the five verses of Wordsworth's poem "The Complaint of a Forsaken Indian Woman," which Dorothy had copied into the back of the notebook. It is three days before her twenty-ninth birthday and twelve months since she and William first arrived at Dove Cottage. As the first year of the new century draws to a close, Dorothy records writing to Catherine Clarkson that William finished composing "Michael," which was to be included in *Lyrical Ballads* as a replacement for Coleridge's *Christabel*, staying with Coleridge in Keswick, baking, starching, ironing, copying for William, being visited by Sarah Coleridge and baby Derwent, and sweeping the chimneys. When we leave her, Coleridge, suffering from the effects of opium addiction, is falling apart in body and mind. His desperate state, the rejection of his ballad, the failure of his marriage, and his growing love for Sara Hutchinson will occupy Dorothy for the next year.

Coleridge had first met Sara Hutchinson the previous autumn, when he visited her brother's farm at Sockburn near Durham. Recently returned from Germany, he had been summoned north to see a sick Wordsworth, who had recovered sufficiently by the time he arrived to invite him on a considerable walk through the Lake District of his childhood. Coleridge then returned alone to Sockburn for a further week, probably without the knowledge of his wife. Dorothy was there with Mary and Sara; to have Wordsworth's devoted women—he would call them Wordsworth's "three wives"—all to himself was very heaven. Nothing Coleridge experienced as he spun about Germany came close to the devastating effect of those few days of stillness in Sockburn, and it was now, in late November 1799, that he appears to have fallen in love with Sara. An entry in his journal, part of which was written in Latin to disguise it from Sarah Coleridge, describes the fatal evening: "Nov 24th—the Sunday—Conundrums & Puns & Stories & Laughter—with Jack Hutchinson—Stood round the Fire, and I held Sara's hand for a long time behind my back, and then for the first time, Love pierced me with its dart, envenomed, and alas! Incurable." An addict, Coleridge satisfied his senses without concern for the consequences. Emotions for him were immediate and overwhelming. His love expressed itself as grand and tragic, but it was a response not to the power of beauty or sexual allure but to domestic coziness, warm fires, and lighthearted fun. Coleridge seems at first to have been equally drawn to Mary, whose attachment to William he had not then realized, and two years later, in his "Letter to Sara Hutchinson," he recalled an evening during that fatal week when the three of them lay on the sofa, Mary with her head on his lap, Sara with her eyelashes playing on his cheek. Coleridge was tremendously vulnerable to intimacy such as this: "Such joy I had that I may truly say, / My Spirit was awe-stricken with the Excess, / And trance-like Depth of its brief Happiness." Nurturing, sensuous women represented for him the natural state of femininity. Never drawn to bluestockings, he liked female intelligence to be instinctive and immediate, untroubled by the conspiracy of thought or doubt. He dropped the *h* that was originally in Sara's name to distinguish her from his wife, and in his poetry he rearranged the letters so that she became "Asra."

Physically, Sara was closer to Dorothy than she was to slender, serene Mary. A small, plain, strong-jawed countrywoman prone to plumpness, with a cloud of light red hair and a swift stride, she was quick in her movements, responsive in conversation, and reassuring in her responses. She had about her a self-sufficiency deeply attractive to Coleridge, who had landed himself a wife now wholly dependent on him. Sara was also a sharp critic of poetry. "If Sense, Sensibility, Sweetness of Temper, perfect simplicity and unpretending Nature, joined to shrewdness and entertainingness make a valuable woman, Sara Hutchinson is so," he decided. Sara, like Mary, was dependable and undramatic, happy to lead a quiet life, unwavering in her emotions. Coleridge saw in Sara what he saw in all those he loved—a form of salvation. The most revealing aspect of her character is that she never gave Sarah Coleridge cause for jealousy. So unlikely was she as a femme fatale, so solid was she as a friend, and so uncomplicated was her support of others that Coleridge's wife continued to direct her jealousy toward the Wordsworths. The most significant aspect of Sara Hutchinson as far as Coleridge was concerned, however, had nothing to do with her personality; it was that she was the sister of Mary, just as Sarah Fricker had been the sister of Southey's fiancée, Edith. In this respect, descriptions of her are essentially unnecessary. Sara Hutchinson was a fantasy figure, idealized, as Wordsworth was and Southey had been, to an impossible degree. She bore the burden of Coleridge's love with remarkable character. She was responsible, so Coleridge told her, for his greatest happiness and his greatest sorrows, for his emotional awakening as well as his destruction. There is no evidence that their relationship was ever consummated, but it is unlikely, given how few times they were alone together, that sexual relations could have taken place more than once. It was Sara's lot to spend her life devoted to a married man whose love for her was apparently killing him.

Nonetheless, initially Sara seems to have enjoyed her flirtation with their celebrated guest. Coleridge shone his brightest on opening nights, particularly when he was in the company of comfortable groups; his initial encounter with Sarah Fricker had also been when she was surrounded by family, and he had stolen the show then as well. As with everyone who found themselves faced with Coleridge's great gray eyes, his wild dark hair, his childlike enthusiasm for more or less everything, his brilliance, his learning, and his energy, Sara Hutchinson, who had never left the North of England, was dazzled. Apart from which, his praises had long been sung by Dorothy, beginning with the letter she sent Mary from Racedown in which she described Coleridge's first visit to their house. When he arrived at Sockburn, Coleridge met a family predisposed not only to like but to love him, to see him as one of their own.

The next time we meet Dorothy, Sara Hutchinson has left Grasmere after a stay of four months, and Coleridge has been ill all year with gout and rheumatic fever. The pace of life at Dove Cottage has changed, and Dorothy has ceased to benefit from the triangular relationships in which she shares William with Coleridge or Mary. We know nothing, however, about how this change comes about because her journal notebook for December 22, 1800–October 10, 1801, has been either lost or destroyed. The only picture we have of Dorothy between the end of the first notebook and the start of the next surviving one is a letter she wrote to Mary Hutchinson on April 29, 1801, after visiting Coleridge in Keswick. Sarah Coleridge was not a good nurse to her husband, Dorothy concluded, but her chief fault as a wife lay in her "want of sensibility and what can such a woman be to Coleridge? She is an excellent nurse to her sucking children (I mean to the best of her skill, for she employs her time often foolishly enough about them) . . . she is to be sure a sad fiddle faddler."

Apart from her endorsement of Coleridge's love for Sara Hutchinson, which Dorothy always encouraged, there is the usual edge to what she tells Mary. The suggestion here is that she, Dorothy, *is* a good nurse to William while Mary, having less sensibility than Dorothy, might not be as perfect a wife to him in the future as Dorothy currently is herself. Also striking, however, is Dorothy's hostility to the bond between mother and child, and she will say something similar to Catherine Clarkson of Mary's firstborn: "I began to be afraid that she was suckling Johnny too long." There is envy in Dorothy's remarks about Sarah Coleridge, directed toward the pleasure Sarah takes in her children and the pleasure the children take in having such a loving mother, but there is also the discomfort of recognition. In her own nurturing relationship with William, on whom she employs her own time often foolishly enough, Dorothy is herself a sad fiddle-faddler.

Were the lost journal to turn up, it is unlikely that prosaic remarks such as these would ever have found their way in. At the best of times "Mrs. C" is mentioned in Dorothy's journals only occasionally and only in passing; beyond the comments she makes in her letters, she never records any feelings she might have about Sarah Coleridge. To do so would be to concede that Sarah had a role in Dorothy's carefully constructed world, and Dorothy's efforts go toward erasing and not enhancing the significance of Coleridge's wife.

The next surviving installment of the Grasmere Journals, beginning October 10, 1801, was written in the small blue notebook that Dorothy had used for her Hamburg Journal in the autumn of 1798. Already contained in the back are lists of expenses incurred on the journey to Germany and William's drafts for "The Brothers" and "Emma's Dell." Many of the pages have been cut out. Dorothy's first entry begins at the front of the book and records Coleridge's return to Keswick *after we had built Sara's seat.*

From October to December the illnesses at Dove Cottage remain constant. On October 15, Dorothy holds her head under a water spout during a walk and is afterward unwell, taking laudanum when she gets home. On October 19 she is *ill in bed all day.* Mary arrives for a two-month stay at the end of October. On November 10, Coleridge goes to London to work as a journalist on the *Morning Post*, leaving Dorothy feeling as she usually does only when William goes away:

> *Poor C left us . . . every sight & every sound reminded me of him dear dear fellow—of his many walks to us by day & by night—of all dear things. I was melancholy & could not talk, but at last I eased my heart by weeping—nervous blubbering says William. It is not so—O how many, many reasons have I to be anxious for him.*

William's unsympathetic response is born of frustration; Dorothy and Coleridge are in a state on a regular basis. In Wordsworth's thrall, they have both grown weaker as Wordsworth has gained in strength. Dorothy and Coleridge each see themselves as on the outside of self-contained units: Dorothy is excluded by the bond between Wordsworth and Mary, while for Coleridge the group from which he feels increasingly left out consists of Wordsworth, Dorothy, and Mary.

Dorothy's subject continues to be the climate, external and internal. Sometimes it is hard to tell which is which, as in her entry for November 24, when she goes to meet William, who is overcome when out walking by himself. *He had been surprised & terrified by a sudden rushing of winds, which seemed to bring earth and sky & lake together, as if the whole were going to enclose him in; he was glad he was in a high road.* His experience might be literal or metaphorical, the sudden onslaught of weather could be subjective or objective; Dorothy does not make the distinction. Now that autumn is here, the air has turned bitter with a hard frost, and there is a roaring wind on the lake; meanwhile, she and William are passing their illnesses back and forth like batons in a relay. Dorothy is ill, she goes to bed, she soon recovers, with William taking over the pain. When William and Mary return fresh and well from a walk, Dorothy is laid low; when she gets up, he lies down. Occasionally they all three suffer together, as when Coleridge writes to them about his own poor state and no one is then able to sleep, but this calamity is less frequent. On November 13, William is *better than I expected*; on the fourteenth, Dorothy is *in bed all day very unwell*; on the eighteenth, she and Mary walk together and William stays behind *being sickish.* On the twenty-third, William is too ill to walk in the morning, Dorothy is unwell after dinner, and Mary has a headache that night. The next day, *We all were well except that my head ached a little.* William is ill on December 1; Dorothy is ill on December 2, 3, and 4. On December 28, *William, Mary & I set off on foot to Keswick . . . We were tired & had bad head aches . . . we all went to bed. My bowels very bad.*

Dorothy dislikes the demands that illness makes on the self, while for Wordsworth explorations of his physical and mental boundaries are second nature. She seems unaware of the pattern of her headaches, never writing anything along the lines of "I was ill again, the usual headache"; "The best way to cure my head is to lie down for two hours"; or "If it's not me, it's William. When will it end?" She does not document a self in process; like a goldfish going round and round in its bowl, surprised each time by the same piece of coral, she writes as if each illness were the first one.

During this autumn of illnesses, the engagement between Mary and William is made public, although a date for the wedding is not yet fixed. *Molly* [Fisher] *was very witty about Mary all day,* Dorothy writes on November 16. *She says: "ye may say what ye will, but there's naething like a gay auld man for behaving weel to a young wife."* The happy couple were both thirty-two, but William, like Dorothy, could pass for twice that age.

When she emerges from the darkness of her bedroom, Dorothy stretches outward, expanding herself into broader horizons, landscapes that are grander, more sublime, than before. *In speaking of our walk on Sunday Evening the 22nd November,* she writes after a headache,

> *I forgot to notice one most impressive sight—it was the moon & the moonlight seen through hurrying driving clouds immediately behind the Stone man upon the top of the hill on the Forest side. Every tooth & every edge of Rock was visible, & the Man stood like a Giant watching from the roof of a lofty castle. The hill seemed perpendicular from the darkness below it.*

Dorothy feels reborn. It is in these states of euphoria that she describes how things "seem" to her imagination rather than detailing what is real. For example, describing her favorite birch tree *yielding to the gusty wind with all its tender twigs,* she places it on the threshold between reality and fancy:

> *The sun shone upon it and it glanced in the wind like a flying sunshiny shower—it was a tree in shape with stem & branches but it was like a Spirit of water—The sun went in & it re-*

> *sumed its purplish appearance the twigs still yielding to the wind but not so visibly to us. The other Birch trees that were near it looked bright & cheerful—but it was a Creature by its own self among them.*

Her preferred literary device is what Keats called the "pathetic fallacy." If there is a star, a plant, or a birch tree *by its own self,* Dorothy identifies with it. After the birch tree she notes, *I saw a solitary butter flower in the wood.*

A few days after Dorothy's thirtieth birthday on December 25, 1801, Mary left Dove Cottage to visit her aunt in Penrith. Dorothy and William walked with her to Keswick, cold mutton in their pockets. They stopped for roasted apples and all had headaches. When they arrived at the Coleridges', Dorothy's bowels were bad. They then traveled on by packhorse to Eusemere, the Ullswater home of their friends Thomas and Catherine Clarkson, dining on porridge and Christmas pies at a roadside inn. The cold and ice on the roads were such that Dorothy *was often obliged to crawl upon all fours & Mary fell many a time.* They parted from Mary by Stainton Bridge—*Dear Mary! There we parted from her—I daresay, as often as she passes that road she will turn in at the Gate to look at that sweet prospect*—after which the Wordsworths stayed on at the Clarksons'.

The presence of Thomas and Catherine Clarkson in the life of Dorothy during these years is interesting because, as Wilberforce had done back in the days of Forncett, or as William had done when he returned from France in 1794, Thomas Clarkson represented a larger universe than any she had known before. As a

Cambridge undergraduate, Clarkson had published "An Essay on the Slavery and Commerce of the Human Species, Particularly the African," the influence of which reached even Jane Austen in her Hampshire vicarage, who declared herself in love with its author. He then helped form the Society for the Abolition of the Slave Trade, where he served as a fact finder, collecting evidence, such as iron cuffs and thumbscrews, from the crews of ships docking between Liverpool and Portsmouth. Mentally and physically exhausted, he temporarily retired in 1794 and built Eusemere, the house where Dorothy, who would become close friends with his wife, Catherine, had first met them a few months before. As ever, Dorothy records these visits—during which she must have listened to the men discuss the traffic in human beings—as if nothing but a few pleasant anecdotes had been exchanged. It is Catherine Clarkson's stories that Dorothy wants to preserve rather than anything else that might have been said: *Mrs. Clarkson amused us with many stories of her family & of persons whom she had known—I wish I had set them down as I heard them, when they were fresh in my memory*. The long tale Dorothy then narrates, concerning Mrs. Clarkson's old aunts, recalls the record she keeps of the life stories of beggars. The breadth of Thomas Clarkson's experience has the effect of drawing her further into her own narrow realm.

Dorothy gives more space to the extended departure of Mary than she has given to anything in her journal so far. Her record of the journey back to Grasmere from Eusemere repeats the imagery used by William in *Home at Grasmere*, in his depiction of their dramatic arrival in the valley two years earlier:

> Bleak season was it, turbulent and bleak,
> When hitherto we journeyed, and on foot,
> Through bursts of sunshine and through flying snows,

Paced the long Vales . . .
The frosty wind, as if to make amends
For its keen breath, was aiding to our course
And drove us onwards like two Ships at sea.
Stern was the face of nature; we rejoiced
In that stern countenance, for our souls had there
A feeling of their strength.

Dorothy writes:

On Saturday 23rd January we left Eusemere at 10 o'clock in the morning, I behind Wm Mr. C on his Galloway. The morning not very promising the wind cold. The mountains large & dark but only thinly streaked with snow—a strong wind . . . We struggled with the wind & often rested as we went along—a hail-shower met us before we reached the Tarn & the way often was difficult over the snow but at the Tarn the view closed in—we saw nothing but mists and snow & at first the ice on the Tarn below us, cracked & split & yet without water, a dull grey white: we lost our path & could see the tarn no longer. We made our way out with difficulty guided by a heap of stones which we well remembered—we were afraid of being bewildered in the mists till the Darkness should overtake us . . . There was no footmark upon the snow either of man or beast. We saw 4 sheep before we had left the snow region. The Vale of Grasmere when the mists broke away looked soft & grave, of a yellow hue—it was dark before we reached home . . . O how comfortable and happy we felt ourselves sitting by our own fire when we had got off our wet clothes & had dressed ourselves fresh & clean . . . We talked about the Lake of Como, read in the descriptive sketches, looked about us, & felt that we were happy.

We indulged all our dear thoughts about home—poor Mary! We were sad to think of the contrast for her.

There is also an echo in Dorothy's journey of the Ancient Mariner's perilous voyage to "the land of mist and snow," only Dorothy's adventure is represented as epic, triumphant, and joyful; the sympathy spared for "poor Mary" would be better off saved. Once home, Dorothy prepares a *broiled gizzard* and *some mutton & made a nice piece of cookery for Wms supper*. It is the only time she describes producing a celebratory meal.

The next day she is unwell and lies down for the afternoon, after which she rises *fresher and better*. William is *tired with composition* on January 25, and on the twenty-sixth Dorothy has a dull morning filled with reading through the newspapers, writing her journal, and waiting by the kitchen fire for William to be ready for their walk. In the evening she begins a letter to Mary, after which she and William *sate nicely together & talked by the fire till we were both tired, for Wm wrote out part of his poem & endeavoured to alter it, & so made himself ill. I copied out the rest for him. We went late to bed*. In her final sentence of the entry, Dorothy notes that *Wm wrote to Annette.*

This is the first time that the existence of Annette Vallon is referred to in the journal, and the letter that William writes, presumably telling her of his engagement to Mary, is of enormous moment. William's final separation from Annette is a reminder to Dorothy that her brother is happy to discard people when their appeal has waned. Wherever they live once William and Mary are married—and Dove Cottage would be too small to house a growing family—Dorothy will once again be relegated to surplus relation. Her tone does not change as she records the occasion of William's breaking the cataclysmic news to Annette, but her reaction to the changes about to take place can be measured by her entries over the following days.

Now that William wants his life to roll forward, Dorothy, Canute-like, is commanding back the waves. The day after William writes to Annette is described as one of calm after a storm, the shores are reflected in the lake in exactly the way that Dorothy likes, the *bees were humming about the hive*, Dorothy copies out William's sonnets, and William uncharacteristically *wasted his mind in the Magazines*. It is all *delightfully pleasant*. After supper they *sate by the fire & were happy only our tender thoughts became painful—went to bed at ½ past 11*. The next day the slump that began the previous evening sets in. It had been wet during the night, and now there was a *downright rain*. William wrote an epitaph, and *they were both in miserable spirits*. They played cards with a neighbor before splashing home with a flickering lantern. From her bed downstairs, Dorothy listens to William throughout the night as he lies tormented and sleepless in his bed upstairs. He wakes the next morning *unwell* and goes back to bed, where, *to endeavour to make him sleep*, Dorothy reads to him, before reading the first book of *Paradise Lost* to herself. They then receive a *heart-rending letter from Coleridge* that makes them both *as sad as we could be*, and William considers going to London to see his friend. Replying to the letter that evening, Dorothy feels *stupified*, a word she later uses to describe Coleridge when he comes in with his eyes swollen from the wind: *He seemed half Stupified.*

The next day William thinks he looks ill and asks Dorothy to set down the story of Barbara Wilkinson's turtledove. As with many of the stories Dorothy records, this one bears uncanny resemblance to the emotional dynamics of Dove Cottage:

> *She had 2 turtle doves. One of them died the first year I think. The other bird continued to live alone in its cage for 9 years,*

> *but for one whole year it had a companion & daily visitor, a little mouse that used to come & feed with it, & the Dove would caress it, & cower over it with its wings, & make a loving noise to it. The mouse though it did not testify equal delight in the Dove's company yet it was at perfect ease. The poor mouse disappeared & the Dove was left solitary till its death.*

Who are the two cooing doves and who is the indifferent mouse? Why has this story of three figures, two losses, and one solitary death caught William's imagination, and why, having asked Dorothy to preserve it for him, does he never do anything with it? It is a tale of abandonment and inequality, one party feeding off the other. The caressing turtledove longs for a more emotionally nurturing bond with the disappearing mouse. The fate of Dorothy was very much on William's mind.

On January 31, after a night during which *William had slept very ill . . . was tired & had a bad headache,* Dorothy begins the process of memorializing Grasmere as a site for herself, Coleridge, and William. What she writes now is elegiac:

> *We walked round the two lakes—Grasmere was very soft & Rydale was extremely beautiful from the pasture side . . . We sate down a long time in different places. I always love to walk that way because it is the way I first came to Rydale & Grasmere, & because our dear Coleridge did also. When I first came with Wm 6½ years ago it was just at sunset. There was a rich yellow light on the waters & the Islands were reflected there,*

but the surface of the lake is now ruffled: *Today it was grave & soft but not perfectly calm.* They sit by the roadside close to the stone where Mary had carved her *dear name.* William deepens the cut with his own knife. There is a breeze on the water, a disturbance that sometimes looks as if it were coming all the way up from the bed of the lake. Then Dorothy finds a strawberry blossom in a rock, which she *unrooted rashly* but *felt as if I had been committing an outrage, so I planted it again—it will have but a stormy life of it, but let it live if it can.*

The first two weeks of February are wretched, with William unable to sleep and Dorothy's migraines occurring almost daily. She lies in bed until three one day, reading Smollett's *Life*. Dorothy reads a great deal of biography; making sense of lives is much on her mind. The next week she reads to William the life of Ben Jonson, whose poetry they both admire. On the ninth, she watches the funeral procession of a woman who has drowned herself pass by the cottage. A hiatus is reached on February 14, when William, having decided that he must see Mary, sets off for Penrith in a pair of new pantaloons from London. He spends three days traveling for the benefit of a few hours' discussion about Annette. Dorothy notes that the hepatica, instead of spreading itself out in the sun as it did in Alfoxden, is *half-starved*. Left alone, she eats *a little bit of cold mutton without laying cloth & then sat over the fire reading Ben Jonson's Penshurst & other things* before walking out before sunset. She stands at Sara's Gate and then, when she comes in view of Rydal Water, casts *a long look at the mountains beyond. They were very white but I concluded that Wm would have a very safe passage over Kirkstone, & I was quite easy about him.* With this sentence, Dorothy runs out of pages, and the Grasmere Journals meet the Hamburg Journal at the other end of the book.

William being away, Dorothy has time on her hands, so she takes up another notebook and continues the entry. The book she finds is a second one of those they had left unfinished in Germany. She turns over the first pages, which contain the lines by William about hurrying from snare to snare, which will become the woodcock-stealing passage in *The Prelude*, and his record of the conversations in Hamburg with Klopstock that had given her a headache, and her account of the journey from Hamburg to Goslar that had also made her ill, and continues the Grasmere Journals, on a clean page with *Sunday 14 February 1802. See the morning former book. After dinner a little before sunset I walked out*. She notes a family of travelers she meets on her walk, with a wild young daughter whose *business seemed to be all pleasure—pleasure in her own motions*. Dorothy then climbs into William's bed, where she sleeps badly, *for my thoughts were full of William.*

The next day she collects a reply from Annette and writes one to Coleridge. These letters are making her ill. She has another bad night. She has persuaded herself not to expect William's return on February 16, *because I was afraid of being disappointed*, but he comes home just before teatime. When he walks through the door and kisses her, *his mouth and breath* are *very cold*. The temperature of William's kiss, seemingly full and on the lips, is an unexpected inclusion in the journal, but from now until the wedding Dorothy prizes gestures like this. They both sleep better that night. But for the rest of February, William continues to be ill, and Dorothy, for the first time in her journal, begins to score through entries that describe her symptoms. On Wednesday, February 24, she describes *a rainy morning—I slept badly & was unwell in the morning—I went to bed directly after Breakfast & lay till William returned from Rydale with letters—he brought a short one from C and a very long one from Mary* before crossing it out and writing instead: *Wednesday 24th. A rainy day*. The next day she notes, *I was bad in my bowels,* before heavily crossing the sentence through. Two days later, on February 27, she writes and then inks over, *I was again obliged to go to bed in the afternoon—not [well?]—we did not walk today.*

Spring was coming in Grasmere, and Dorothy notes that

> *the Moon hung over the Northern side of the highest point of Silver How, like a gold ring snapped in two & shaven off at the Ends it was so narrow. Within this Ring lay the Circle of the Round moon, as distinctly to be seen as ever the enlightened moon is.*

Sometimes, as Freud said, a cigar is just a cigar, but the symbols that Dorothy sees in the night sky are the stuff of dreams. The gold ring, which William will soon slip onto her finger before later removing in order to slip onto Mary's, is here divided in two rather than shared, and William, always the moon in Dorothy's mythology, becomes more distinct and enlightened than ever before, while Dorothy is shorn away. It is not long before Dorothy realizes that the moon is the only thing in the darkness that can be seen.

TO FORSAKE ALL OTHERS: INCEST

It was a strange love, profound, almost dumb, as if brother and sister had grown together and shared not the speech but the mood, so that they hardly knew which felt, which spoke, which saw the daffodils or the sleeping city.

—VIRGINIA WOOLF, "Dorothy Wordsworth," from *The Common Reader*, Second Series

What remain[s] constant, in all the cases that I have read about sibling incest, is that the siblings are looking for something that is felt to be missing . . . sibling incest and parental abandonment go hand in hand.

—PROPHECY COLES, *The Importance of Sibling Relationships in Psychoanalysis*

Before they had finished breakfast on the morning of March 4, 1802, the horses arrived for William's trip to the Calverts at Windy Brow. There was a flurry in the cottage as pens were made, poems put in order for copying, and clothes flung together. Once William had gone, Dorothy busied herself with tidying the strewn drawers and sorting out the shirts *which we had thrown here & there & everywhere* in the rush. She filed two months' worth of newspapers, boiled eggs for lunch, transplanted snowdrops for the garden, noted that the bees were busy, that William had a *rich bright day* for his journey, and that the robins were singing. *Now for my walk*, she writes before pausing to exclaim: *I* will *be busy, I* will *look well & be well when he comes back to me. O the Darling! Here is one of his bitten apples! I can hardly find it in my heart to throw it into the fire. I must wash myself, then off—.*

It is one of those moments when the reader feels jolted awake, afraid he or she might have missed something that came before. Nothing in the previous day's entry offers an explanation for the level of intimacy Dorothy feels now. On the contrary, March 3 had been dreadful, and it was all her own doing: *I was so unlucky as to propose to rewrite The Pedlar,* Dorothy wrote in a brief entry. *Wm got to work & was worn to death, we did not walk I wrote in the afternoon.* A few days earlier she had added to the margins of her entry for February 28, *disaster Pedlar.* No doubt Dorothy had encouraged William to push on with the poem he had abandoned in despair, which task left him drained and her wretched.

As with her appearance by the poet's side at the end of "Tintern Abbey," the sudden vividness of Dorothy's person this morning is so unexpected, so immediate, you wonder how long she has been in the room without your noticing. Our presence at the door seems voyeuristic; we are not prepared to witness emotion as undiluted as this. The warmth and urgency of her tone are startling, but so, too, is the scene she paints: a woman is bustling about, scolding herself for her tears, and summoning up the strength to pull through yet another of her darling's absences. She then pauses in her tracks at a sign of his recent presence, and invests the now-browned apple with all the tenderness she feels for its consumer. The shift in tense is disconcerting, as when a conventional frame in a film is followed by the jerkiness of a handheld camera, but there is something else as well that feels not right. Where is Dorothy's usual melancholia and sense of abandonment when William leaves her? On his previous trips, time has stopped and her movements become torpid, but today there is fluster and even silliness; she is jittery, tearful, slightly euphoric. She feels for some reason especially close to William: during her walk Dorothy *sate down where I always sit I was full of thoughts about my darling. Blessings on him.* When she returns home, she works at her German, reads *Lyrical Ballads*, and then writes him a letter before going to bed.

Dorothy's journal entry for March 4 has about it a postcoital intensity: the late breakfast, the last-minute haste of William's departure, her determination to disguise from him her feelings, her dreaminess as she sorts through his clothes and clears away his mess. There is also a terrible foreboding: the apple is bitten, paradise is lost.

Torpor soon sets in. The next day Dorothy again *wrote to William. Read the LB, got into sad thoughts, tried at German but could not go on—Read LB—Blessings on that Brother of mine! Beautiful new moon on Silver How.* When she wakes the following morning, she has *a bad head ache* and so stays in bed until one o'clock. That night she cannot sleep, but when William returns on March 7, she sleeps well. A letter from Mary on March 8 is followed by another headache; on March 9, William reads Dorothy *a beautiful poem on Love* by Ben Jonson. Perhaps it is "Epode," in which Jonson compares the tempests of lust to the calm of chaste love:

> The thing they here call love, is blind Desire,
> Arm'd with bow, shafts, and fire;
> Inconstant, like the sea, of whence 't is born,
> Rough, swelling, like a storm;
> With whom who sails, rides on the surge of fear,
> And boils, as if he were
> In a continual tempest. Now, true Love
> No such effects doth prove;
> That is an essence far more gentle, fine,

Pure, perfect, nay, divine;
It is a golden chain let down from heaven,
Whose links are bright and even,
That falls like sleep on lovers, and combines
The soft and sweetest minds
In equal knots: this bears no brands nor darts,
To murther different hearts,
But in a calm and godlike unity
Preserves community.

Chaste love as a "golden chain" recalls the image used by Dorothy in the letter she wrote to Jane Pollard in 1793: "Neither absence nor distance nor Time can ever break the chain that links me to my Brothers." But William is about to loosen the chain that links his mind with Dorothy's, and to embark on the swelling seas of sexual desire. Dorothy is not well that evening.

On March 13, he begins the business of trying to separate from his sister and to write without the influence of her ears and eyes: *After tea I read to William that account of the little Boys belonging to the tall woman & an unlucky thing it was for he could not escape from those very words, & so he could not write the poem, he left it unfinished and went tired to bed.* There is a hint of pleasure in Dorothy's tone: he cannot escape from her that easily. The next day he writes a poem about the golden chain that links the two of them together. Sitting at the breakfast table with *shirt neck unbuttoned, & his waistcoat open while he did it,* he pens some lines about a butterfly using Dorothy's very words. *I told him that I used to chase them a little but that I was afraid of brushing the dust off their wings & did not catch them—He told me how he used to kill all the white ones when he went to school because they were Frenchmen.*

Stay near me—do not take thy flight!
A little longer stay in sight!
Much converse do I find in thee,
Historian of my infancy!
Float near me; do not yet depart!
Dead times revive in thee:
Thou bring'st, gay creature as thou art!
A solemn image to my heart,
My father's family!

Oh! pleasant, pleasant were the days,
The time, when, in our childish plays,
My sister Emmeline and I
Together chased the butterfly!
A very hunter did I rush
Upon the prey:—with leaps and springs
I followed on from brake to bush;
But she, God love her, feared to brush
The dust from off its wings.

As in "Tintern Abbey," Dorothy—here "Emmeline"—is bodiless and motionless while Wordsworth uses her to explore his own development. While she still represents her brother's childhood, Dorothy's position in William's imagination has subtly changed: in "Tintern Abbey" she was an image of "what I was once," now she is a "solemn image" of what can never be retrieved, "my father's family."

Throughout the spring, the intimacy between Dorothy and William increases along with his productivity. She refers to him now not as *Wm* but as her *beloved* and her *darling*. While they discuss their plans for the future, William cannot stop composing. They are living in a vortex of poetry; Coleridge claimed that between March and the end of July, Wordsworth produced thirty-two poems. On March 16, Wordsworth wrote "The Emigrant Mother," after which Dorothy read Spenser to him *while he leaned upon my shoulder.* William's butterfly has now joined her nightscape: *The moon was a good height above the Mountains. She seemed far & distant in the sky there were two stars beside her, that twinkled in & out, & seemed like butterflies in motion and lightness.* The next day after dinner *we made a pillow of my shoulder, I read to him & my beloved slept,* and that night while she was walking alone, Dorothy *saw the shape of my Beloved in the Road at a little distance—we turned back to see the light but it was fading—almost gone.* On Sunday, March 21, *William was unwell . . . We had a sweet & tender conversation,* after which Dorothy wrote to Mary and Sara Hutchinson. They then *resolved to see Annette & that Wm should go to Mary.*

Dorothy will accompany William to France in the summer to meet Annette and his nine-year-old daughter, Caroline, but he will go now to Mary alone. The purpose of the meeting with *Poor Annette* is to break the chain that links them both. Dorothy is holding on to her brother's every last breath. On March 23 she writes, *The fire flutters & the watch ticks I hear nothing save the Breathings of my Beloved & he now and then pushes his book forward & turns over a leaf.* On March 24, another major decision is made, although Dorothy calls it a "vow," using the solemn terms of a marriage ceremony. She announces that when William and Mary marry, the three of them will live together in Dove Cottage rather than with Mary and her family at the Hutchinson farm in Yorkshire: *I made a vow that we would not leave this Country for G[allow] Hill.* She writes to Mary to tell her so. Dorothy will no longer be mistress of her home, but her community is at least preserved. She is unwell for the rest of the month.

There is a mystery at the heart of the Grasmere Journals. What is the nature of the love between William and Dorothy? The character of her attachment to him is central to an understanding of what her journal is actually about as well as to an assessment of the quality of her life. Did William feel more intensely toward his sister than he did toward Mary Hutchinson? As a young woman Dorothy fixed her libido on her brother and never moved on, but was the pain she experienced when he married Mary the agony of sexual jealousy or simply resistance to change—or was it something else altogether? She seems confused herself a good deal of the time. If she is unconscious that her love expresses itself as incestuous, it is because addressing what she knows and does not know about her own responses is a continual problem for Dorothy.

It is not especially unusual for siblings separated as children to explore one another sexually as adults; psychologists call the obsessive emotional response between siblings separated as children genetic sexual attraction. Nor is it necessarily a traumatic experience: Melanie Klein believed that incest between brother and sister, as opposed to between parent and child, was a common occurrence and could be healthy and satisfying, paving the way for other successful relationships. Had we the evidence that a sexual relationship of some kind existed between Dorothy and William, then their bond might at least be easier to understand. As it is, what evidence there may once have been no longer survives, although it is unclear what proof we are looking for. Biographers, not having access to their subjects at all hours, tend to be aware that sex has taken place only when a child appears nine months later. Some critics argue that the pages torn out of the Grasmere Journals, the sentences scored through, and the disappearance altogether of Dorothy's original Alfoxden Journal were a way of destroying the evidence, but it is unlikely, given Dorothy's literary style, particularly in the extant formulaic entries of the Alfoxden Journal, that she would keep a note of her sex life with her brother. We are left knowing nothing of what went on physically between them either during the freezing winter in Goslar or on those occasions in Grasmere when Dorothy *petted* William *on the carpet* and came into his room at night to help him sleep, or sat with his head on her shoulder.

The gossip existed even then. De Quincey writes that he had heard as far away as London suggestions of Wordsworth "having been intimate with his own sister." The reason for this story, he suggested, is that it was Wordsworth's habit, "whenever he meets or parts with any of the female part of his own relations to kiss them—this he has frequently done when he has met his sister on her rambles or parted from her . . . without heeding whether he was observed or not." Wordsworth's open embraces were probably not the only reason for the rumors. Wherever they roamed, from Dorset to Germany, Dorothy and William drew attention to themselves because they were insular, secretive, and peculiar and would lie on the ground together gazing at the sky, sit behind walls poring over letters, tramp to the postmistress in the middle of the night to change a word in a letter they had delivered earlier that day, and walk backward and forward along the same path in all weathers, muttering strange incantations. They seemed to be locked inside each other's minds.

The love between brother and sister weaves its way through our culture, appearing in Bible stories, myths, legends, poetry, drama, novels. Both Zeus and Cronus married their sisters, as did a long line of ancient Egyptian gods and kings; in Greek myth, Antigone was both sister and daughter to Oedipus; Cain and Abel fought over Abel's twin sister; Abraham married his sister, Sarah, while King Arthur's son, Mordred, was the product of a night with his half sister, Morgan le Fay. The children playing in the streets in Goslar had been raised on folktales about sibling incest; the lake near the town of Göttingen was said to stand in the place of a castle in which a count had lived who had unwittingly deflowered his own sister. Incest, along with a belief in the sacred nature of childhood, was a fundamental ingredient of Romantic consciousness, so indispensable, as Camille Paglia puts it in *Sexual Personae*, "that even when a sibling does not exist, as in Shelley, he or she *must be invented*." The idea of incest fuels Shelley's *Epipsychidion*, *Cenci*, and *Laon and Cythna*, Leigh Hunt's *Story of Rimini*, and Byron's *Manfred*. Bernardin de Saint-Pierre's popular *Paul and Virginia*, a sentimental novel liked by both William and Dorothy, tells the story of a boy and girl who are raised as siblings and love one another beyond all else. *Wanley Penson*, an anonymous novel that Dorothy read in February 1802, tells the story of another highly idealized brother-and-sister love. Sibling incest is a theme in many texts that the Wordsworths would have known—such as Daniel Defoe's *Moll Flanders*, Fanny Burney's *Evelina*, and Matthew Gregory Lewis's *Monk*—and in many that had not yet been written. There is an incestuous relationship between Helene—who commits suicide—and Anatole in Tolstoy's *War and Peace*; before they drown wrapped in each other's arms, Maggie Tulliver says of her brother in George Eliot's *Mill on the Floss*, "I love Tom so dearly . . . better than anybody else in the world. When he grows up I shall keep his house, and we shall always live together." Jane Austen liked her male characters to be in the position of brother: the heroines of *Emma* and *Sense and Sensibility* both happily marry their brothers-in-law. In *Mansfield Park,* Fanny Price and her brother William fantasize about sharing a cottage, and shortly before Edmund Bertram proposes marriage to Fanny, he grasps her to his breast and exclaims, "My only sister—my only comfort now."

There have also been relationships outside of literature that are not dissimilar to the Wordsworths', such as the one between Thomas Babington Macaulay—great-uncle of Wordsworth's biographer Mary Moorman—and his sisters Hannah and Margaret, whose marriages he experienced as a "living death." His sisters, Macaulay said, have "been everything to me . . . But the affection of brothers for sisters, blameless and amiable as it is beyond almost any human affection, is yet so liable to be interrupted that no man ought to suffer it to become necessary to him." As for Margaret, "The idea of being separated" from her brother "is what I cannot support . . . he has for years been the object of my whole heart." That it was fashionable for siblings with sensibility to relate to one another as ideal partners does not mean that loving one's brother or sister beyond and above anyone else could not be a complicated and bewildering experience, but even taking into account the compounding of sibling and sexual love in the nineteenth century, the feelings Dorothy expresses for William appear extreme. Her journals strain beneath the complexity of her emotions.

In 1954 F. W. Bateson suggested in a book called *Wordsworth: A Reinterpretation* that while they were in Goslar, William and Dorothy realized they were falling in love. The crisis between them resulted in the composition of the Lucy poems, the "desperate remedy" of William's marriage to Mary, and Dorothy's being sacrificed for a greater good. Admirers of Wordsworth responded to Bateson's thesis as though he had defaced a national monument, but none has been able to wash away the stain. Like the boy in the story of the emperor's new clothes, Bateson was only pointing out what was obvious to all: that the relationship between the Wordsworths was an odd one, and that the poems produced during those isolated months in Goslar were very odd indeed. Since the appearance of Bateson's book, the Lucy poems have been raked over for evidence of Wordsworth's state of mind as though they represented the various scenes of a crime. Did he or did he not fall in love with Dorothy while he was in Germany and imagine her death, thus unconsciously freeing himself from guilt? Most critics who have held that there were sexual feelings between the Wordsworths do not suggest that they were ever consummated. Stephen Gill in *William Wordsworth: A Life* thought their relationship in general "unquestionably, profoundly sexual"; John Mahoney in *William Wordsworth: A Poetic Life* believed them "unquestionably, some might say excessively, close"; Kenneth Johnston in *The Hidden Wordsworth* noted their "strong erotic attraction to each other." Molly Lefebure in her biography of Coleridge, *A Bondage of Opium*, is more explicit, arguing that Dorothy's Grasmere Journals provide

> unmistakable evidence . . . that, at Dove Cottage, brother and sister endured an agonising frustration of full physical expression of their love . . . The picture that emerges from the[ir] pages . . . is one of a woman deeply in love with a man who reciprocates her love to the full but is forced to marry another.

An incestuous relationship is specifically one in which *sexual* relations have taken place between members of the same family; love has nothing to do with it. It is expected that family members love one another, and there is no taboo about an all-consuming sibling passion in which the sexual feelings are repressed, even if the effects of such a relationship are more confusing than if sex had been involved. The relationship between the Wordsworths was organized around a notion of perfect and exclusive brother-sister love that was imaginatively assimilated by them both to the point where it became the source of their creative energy, but its physical expression would have been of no interest to them. Wordsworth said that he was "often unable to think of external things as having external existence," and during the Dove Cottage years Dorothy was less a figure of flesh and blood in his life than a poetic idea, which is more or less how she has remained ever since. Despite the biographies of Dorothy herself, it is as William's brilliant and inspirational invention that she has come down to us. Without William, Dorothy has no substance: even in her journal she is hardest to see when she is most alone. Theirs was one of the greatest of all literary seductions: Wordsworth's bond with Dorothy was born of his poetry, organized around his poetry, expressed through his poetry. As for Dorothy, even when she had lost her mind and no longer knew who she was, she could recite her brother's poems word for word, finding the path back into herself through his language. They were more concerned with the effects of pen on paper than with anything expressed by the body, and together William's poetry and Dorothy's journals transformed incestuous love into a mystical ideal. Camille Paglia calls this type of disembodied desire "Romantic incest," which she sees as "a metaphor for supersaturation of identity." Blending into one another, Dorothy and William return to the blissful world of mother and child, free from boundaries and cultural restrictions. The anthropologist Claude Lévi-Strauss argues that the obsession with sibling incest in the culture of sensibility is "at some level related to a wish, not on the existential level of a desire for mating with actual relations, but on the level of memory and nostalgia for a primal state in which no revulsion from incestuous acts or longings was felt." Nostalgia, inspiration, primal states, and supersaturated identity describe the crepuscular landscapes both of the Lucy poems and of Dorothy's Grasmere Journals.

The poems written in Goslar—"Three years she grew in sun and shower," "Strange fits of passion have I known," "She dwelt among th'untrodden ways," and "A slumber did my spirit seal"—are interesting for three initial reasons. The first is the obsessiveness of their theme: the death or possibility of the death of a girl or a woman called Lucy. The second is the question of identity: Who, or what, and indeed *where*, is Lucy? If Dorothy was indeed the model for Lucy, as it has been assumed, then why is she repeatedly killed off? Finally, there is the ambivalence of their tone: What does Lucy's death mean to the poet? How, for example, are we to interpret this sudden thought at the end of "Strange fits of passion"?

> What fond and wayward thoughts will slide
> Into a Lover's head!
> "O mercy!" to myself I cried,
> "If Lucy should be dead!"

Is there an element of hope in the idea, or is it an unimaginable dread? A similar ambiguity resides in the final line of "She dwelt among th'untrodden ways":

> She *lived* unknown, and few could know
> When Lucy ceased to be;
> But she is in her Grave and, oh!
> The difference to me!

What difference *does* it make to him that Lucy is in her grave? Is the difference good or bad? The word is an important one to Wordsworth; he and Dorothy spend a great deal of time thinking about similarity and difference in their relationship. Do the poems express uncertainty about his sister's influence, or about having her with him in Goslar, holding him back from an adventure such as the one Coleridge was enjoying? Are they, as Bateson argued, a means for Wordsworth to rid himself of incestuous thoughts "by killing her off symbolically"?

In the summer of 1802, Dorothy tells Mary that she and William have now swapped bedrooms in anticipation of his forthcoming marriage and that she is recovering from her recent illness in her brother John's bed. "I feel pretty well now," she says, "except that I have a kind of stupefaction and headache about me, *a feeling of something that has been amiss*." When, a few years after William marries Mary, Dorothy wants Dr. Beddoes to know that she has an "uneasy sense" of "emptiness" inside her, it is as though emptiness, as opposed to being a symptom, were the problem itself. Emptiness of this kind is an experience often described by Dorothy, as it is by Coleridge. When he argued with his great friend and collaborator Robert Southey, Coleridge described now having a "void" inside him that no one was big enough to fill. Wordsworth was always attractive to people who felt empty.

In a case study of sibling incest that she titled "On Being Empty of Oneself," the psychoanalyst Enid Balint suggests that there should be an expression "he is empty of himself" to complement the one "he is full of himself." To be full of oneself is to have accepted oneself, to have "identified" with oneself. To be empty of oneself is to experience a void in the place where confirmation or acceptance of one's identity should be, confirmation of the kind that is asked for by a child when he shows his mother a cut or a graze and is told that it will "be all right." This is what Balint calls "feedback," an exchange by which the child sees that he is recognized: "A proper feedback is when the mother receives the hurt, recognises it, does not make too much fuss over it, but just accepts its reality." It was this that was missing for Balint's patient, whose brother had intercourse with her as a child. Without proper feedback from her mother, a void had developed within the little girl. The void in the child can be repeated as an experience for the adult; those who are empty of themselves "do not like to be left alone" and live in what Sándor Ferenczi calls a world of "thinking without feeling and feeling without thinking." Or, as Coleridge put it in "Dejection: An Ode": "I see, not feel, how beautiful they are!"

It would be too easy to say that Dorothy, who deprived herself, was empty while William, who poured out poetry, was full, or that Dorothy filled William while he emptied her. Dorothy and William both knew what it was to feel empty of themselves, and, as with the sharing of their headaches and the dispersal of their words, they filled one another up and emptied one another out by turns.

Nonetheless, something has long been missing for Dorothy. Her early letters edge toward defining what that loss might be. She realizes belatedly that she "at the same moment lost a father, a mother, a home," and recognizes only years after his death "the loss I sustained when I was deprived of a father." She searches around for an explanation for her sense of something being "amiss," telling Jane Pollard that it is in fact their friendship that she misses and variously wondering if it is Jane and William together whom she lacks, or the company of Coleridge, or the want of a home, or the absence of letters to collect from Ambleside, or the sight of the moon in a starry sky. Her journals will often describe what was missing for her during the day, but Dorothy never says that it is her mother she misses. This is a loss she will always see as having been filled—"the loss of a mother can only be made up by such a friend as my dear Aunt"—and yet it is the seamless continuity between mother and child that she tries for the rest of her life to recover with William. Sometimes it seems that it is Dorothy herself who is missing rather than anyone or anything else: when she describes in her journals melting away or dissolving before a view, it reads as though she were enacting her own disappearance. *We lay upon the sloping turf. Earth & sky were so lovely that they melted our very hearts.*

When I read Dorothy's accounts of her love for William in the Grasmere Journals, I am moved in the same way as I am by Catherine Earnshaw's description of her love for Heathcliff in Emily Brontë's *Wuthering Heights*, and it is through *Wuthering Heights* that the peculiarity of the relationship between Dorothy and William can best be understood. Powerful in both cases is the elusive, visionary nature of what each woman is straining to define: her hunger for twinship with the one she loves, her desire to repeat herself in him and to have him repeated in her, her drive to erase any difference between them, her confusion about where she ends and he begins. When Wordsworth writes in "Tintern Abbey" that he sees in Dorothy the "language of my former heart," it is as though she were his double, another version of himself, and in *The Prelude* he similarly refers to her as "Sister of my soul!" When Dorothy writes about William, it is as though a part of her were missing in him, and it is the finding and losing of themselves in each other that is also described by Catherine Earnshaw and Heathcliff. "Fraternal love," Dorothy said, "has been the building up of my being, the light of my path." "I *am* Heathcliff," Catherine explains. "He's more myself than I am." Neither woman is describing, any more than Wordsworth in the Lucy poems, carnal desire. What Dorothy Wordsworth and Catherine Earnshaw experience is depersonalizing, dematerializing, and unsexing. For both, being empty of themselves is fundamental to their relationship with their brothers. Catherine Earnshaw is contained in Heathcliff's body. "I cannot express it," she says to Nelly Dean,

> but surely you and everybody have a notion that there is or should be an existence of yours beyond you. What were the use of my creation, if I were contained here? My great miseries in this world have been Heathcliff's miseries, and I watched and felt each from the beginning: my great thought in living is himself.

The lines could have been written by Dorothy Wordsworth.

Wuthering Heights was published in 1847, four years before selections from Dorothy's journals first appeared in Christopher Wordsworth's *Memoirs* of his uncle William. Not knowing her journals, Emily Brontë gleaned her picture of Dorothy from the poems by Wordsworth in which his sister is addressed, such as "Tintern Abbey," and from Thomas De Quincey's vivid portraits of the Wordsworths that appeared in *Tait's Edinburgh Magazine* in the early months of 1839. It seems unlikely that Brontë would have missed De Quincey's famous essays, given that her family avidly consumed the periodicals and, like many young readers of

Wordsworth's poetry, they aspired to be Wordsworthian: two years earlier, in January 1837, Branwell Brontë had sent some of his poems to Wordsworth, "entreating" him to read and pass judgment on them, "because from the day of my birth to this the nineteenth year of my life I have lived among wild and secluded hills where I could neither know what I was or what I could do."

De Quincey's essays in *Tait's* gave the first public insight into domestic life at Dove Cottage. The Wordsworths were horrified by his account, which was greedily consumed by the public, and his description of William and Dorothy is echoed by Brontë in her later description of Heathcliff and Catherine. De Quincey's portrait of the young Wordsworth is not yet the "bumming and booing" eccentric who has come down to us through folk memory, or the asexual spokesman of leech gatherers and mad mothers; he is a tooth-gnashing and wild-eyed proto–Byronic hero, someone with "animal appetites" and "intellectual passions" both "fervent and strong." Unschooled in gallantry and impatient with social convention, Wordsworth was no more likely than Heathcliff to "burthen himself with a lady's reticule, parasol," or "shawl." "Freedom," De Quincey stresses, "unlimited, careless, insolent freedom—unoccupied possession of his own arms—absolute control over his legs and motions" were "essential to his comfort." As a child, Wordsworth was "austere and unsocial," "haunt[ing] the hills and vales." He and Dorothy were "irritable and even bad-tempered" children, "constantly together; for Miss Wordsworth was always ready to walk out—wet or dry, storm or sunshine, night or day." The adult Dorothy is described as a pagan goddess, untamed and androgynous, all fire and ardor with a "gipsy tan" and an "impassioned intellect." Like Catherine Earnshaw, whose "spirits were always at high water mark," Dorothy was, for De Quincey, "beyond any person I have known in the world . . . the creature of impulse."

Siblings inspire in one another ambivalent emotions. The thrill of loving someone who is the same as you is accompanied by the horror of being replaced by this Identi-Kit model. The oscillation between feelings of narcissism and those of annihilation is something that Emily Brontë understood, and it is in the language used by Catherine and Heathcliff that she describes the dangerous bond between Dorothy and William. Catherine and Heathcliff, raised as brother and sister in the same family, evolve from childhood inseparability into a hybrid of such inward-looking self-consumption that the disappearance of one means the nonexistence of the other. "He's always, always in my mind," Catherine explains to the baffled Nelly Dean, "not as a pleasure, any more than I am always a pleasure to myself, but as my own being. So don't talk of our separation again." The two of them shift between dread of separation and fear of engulfment. Like Dorothy and William, they have sexual desires but not for each other. Sexual desire feeds on distance and difference, and what Catherine and Dorothy describe is proximity and sameness. Catherine's feelings for Linton would count as romantic love in any other novel; she loves him, she says, because he is good-looking and pleasant to be with. Likewise, what Heathcliff feels for Isabella—and what Wordsworth feels for Mary, or what Dorothy may or may not have felt for Wilberforce or Coleridge—is simply what men and women tend to feel for each other. After they were married, Wordsworth wrote to Mary about the state he was reduced to during his bachelor years. "I never suffered half as much as during this absence from you," he recalled.

Love of this kind, which thrives on separation, does not interest Brontë. "There is love," Virginia Woolf said of *Wuthering Heights*, "but it is not the love of men and women." Love between men and women, Catherine explains, is "like the foliage in the woods: time will change it, I'm well aware, as winter changes the trees." Sibling love is different: "My love for Heathcliff resembles the eternal rocks beneath—a source of little visible delight, but necessary." In distinguishing between the foliage in the woods and the rocks beneath, Brontë describes the difference for Dorothy and William between the surface-blown flutterings of sexual desire and the diurnal course of Romantic incest.

Dorothy and William resolve that he will go to Mary alone and that together they will visit Annette in France. The decision is preceded by ominous encounters. First Dorothy is scared by a cow—*the Cow looked at me & I looked at the cow & whenever I stirred the cow gave over eating*—and she sits for half an hour afraid to pass. Then, later that evening, she has a vision:

> *It was nearly dark when I parted from the Lloyds that is, night was come on & the moon was overcast. But as I climbed Moss the moon came out from behind a Mountain Mass of Black Clouds—O the unutterable darkness of the sky & the Earth below the Moon! & the glorious brightness of the moon itself! There was a vivid sparkling streak of light at this end of Rydale water but the rest was very dark & Loughrigg fell & Silver How were white & bright as if they were covered with hoar frost. The moon retired again & appeared & disappeared several times before I reached home. Once there was no moonlight to be seen but upon the Island house & the promontory of the Island where it stands, "That needs must be a holy place" &c—&c. I had many many exquisite feelings when I saw this lowly Building in the waters among the dark & lofty*

1. A silhouette of Dorothy taken in 1806, when she was thirty-four. Friends described her in abstract terms, leaving us with a sense of her energy rather than her appearance.

2. Henry Edridge's portrait shows William Wordsworth in the same year that Dorothy's silhouette was cut. His great brow and taut features gave him an inward, cerebral appearance.

3. The four surviving notebooks in which Dorothy made the entries that have become known as the Grasmere Journals. She wrote not for posterity or to preserve her memories but to defend the world in which she lived from mutability and change.

4. Alfoxden House, in Somerset, where Dorothy and Wordsworth lived for a year from 1797, was one of the places that she called her first "real" home. It was here that she kept her Alfoxden Journal.

5. Goslar, in Lower Saxony, an "ugly, silent old desert of a city" where Dorothy and Wordsworth lived in seclusion during a freezing winter in 1798 and where Wordsworth wrote his Lucy poems.

6. *The Zenith of French Glory* by James Gillray. While Dorothy was walking on the terraces of Windsor Castle, Wordsworth, living in Revolutionary France, had joined "that odious class of men called Democrats."

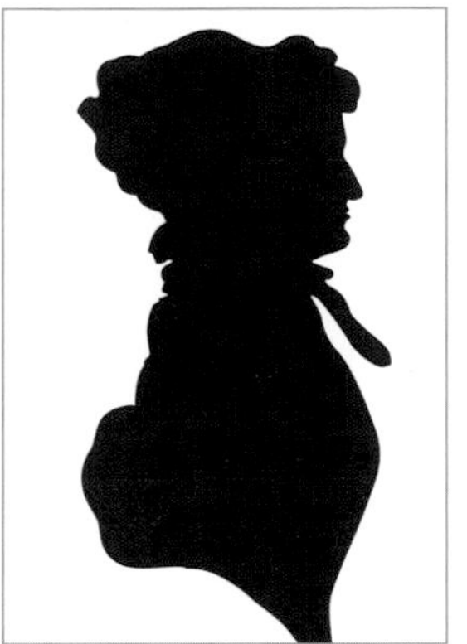

7. Coleridge as a young man. "At first I thought him very plain," Dorothy said of Coleridge; "that is, for about three minutes: he is pale and thin, has a wide mouth, thick lips, and not very good teeth, longish loose-growing half-curling black hair."

8. Sara Hutchinson, Mary's younger sister, whom Coleridge met in 1799. "Love pierced me with its dart," he wrote of her, "envenomed, and alas! Incurable."

9. Thomas De Quincey: writer, opium addict, admirer of Dorothy, and her first biographer.

10. Dove Cottage. "What happy fortune were it here to live," Wordsworth exclaimed when he saw Grasmere as a boy. In the late afternoon of December 20, 1799, he and Dorothy took over the tenancy of Dove Cottage.

11. *Grasmere from the Rydal Road* (1787) by Francis Towne. "The whole vale of Grasmere suddenly breaks upon the view in a style of almost theatrical surprise," wrote De Quincey.

12. The Rock of Names. Dorothy and William named the local landmarks after their family and friends, and together with Coleridge, John, Mary, and Sara, they carved their initials into what became known as the Rock of Names.

13. *Moonlight, a Landscape with Sheep* (ca. 1831–33) by Samuel Palmer. *As I lay down on the grass, I observed the glittering silver line on the ridges of the Backs of the sheep . . . which made them look beautiful but with something of a strangeness, like animals of another kind.* Sometimes Dorothy's mystical descriptions could be signs of migraine aura, defined by Oliver Sacks as "dramatic disturbances in the visual field, taking the form of strange and often twinkling brilliances."

14. Gallow Hill, the Hutchinsons' farm in Yorkshire, from which William and Mary walked to the church in Brompton to be married on October 4, 1802. Dorothy saw from the bedroom window the men running up the avenue to tell her that "it was over."

15. Annette Vallon—Wordsworth's French mistress and the mother of his eldest daughter—became an active counterrevolutionary and Scarlet Pimpernel of sorts.

16. Interior of Rydal Mount. Called by Dora Wordsworth "Idle Mount," the house was Dorothy's final home and the official residence of the Victorian rather than the Romantic poet.

17. In Mary's one known likeness, this portrait taken with Wordsworth in 1839, she sits with pen in hand, ready to inscribe his words, gazing at him with anticipation while he looks past her.

18. Dorothy, aged sixty-two. It is appropriate that she is pictured with pen and paper, as she spent more time writing than she ever did walking or working in her garden. Her lips have folded over her toothless gums, but the "shooting lights" can still be seen in her "wild eyes," although now the brilliant clarity of her vision is aided by spectacles.

hills, with that bright soft light upon it—it made me more than half a poet. I was tired when I reached home I could not sit down to reading & tried to write verses but alas! I gave up expecting William and soon went to bed.

Dorothy often describes herself as a half—she is after all someone who *quarrels with herself*—but this is the only occasion in her Grasmere Journals where she can be heard referring to herself as possessing any poetic talent at all. She has peculiarly little sense of how poetic she is and little certainty over her own judgment: the scene she depicts with such care is less remarkable than many others she describes. Conventionally picturesque, it is the type of scene that was endlessly reproduced in the art and literature of the period; the reflection of the building, the backdrop of the *dark & lofty hills*, the otherness of the appearance of things, were all contemporary clichés. It is a curiously phrased remark, *it made me more than half a poet*: in Dorothy's opinion it is the scene itself that makes the poet, rather than the poet who makes the scene. *More* than half: it is as if her sensibility, which she knows composes half of the poet in William, were tipping the balance.

Over the next month things happen by halves. On April 12, after William has gone to see Mary, and Dorothy, not wanting to be alone, is staying at Eusemere with the Clarksons, she receives a joint letter from the engaged couple, probably about the postponement of their wedding plans until William has been to see Annette. It is late in the evening, and Dorothy tries to read its contents as she walks home:

It was a sharp windy night. Thomas Wilkinson came with me to Barton, & questioned me like a catechizer all the way, every question was like the snapping of a little thread about

> *my heart I was so full of thoughts of my half-read letter & other things. I was glad when he left me. Then I had time to look at the moon while I was thinking over my own thoughts— the moon travelled through the clouds tingeing them yellow as she passed along, with two stars near her, one larger than the other. These stars grew or diminished as they passed from or went into the clouds.*

Dorothy is *full* from a letter only *half-read*, but as it is from William and Mary together, it is only half a letter anyway. When Thomas Wilkinson at last leaves her, it is too dark to finish reading, but the choreography of the night sky dramatizes her fears. This is how things will be in the future: the traveling moon and the two obedient stars, one larger than the other, growing or diminishing as they pass through various clouds. For Dorothy, it is William's brightness that illumines the sky while the smaller of the stars is obscured, but it is in fact her own writing that is starting to shine, and to obscure his.

When William returns on April 13, *the surprise shot through me*. "I believe I screamed," she wrote in a letter, but by the next day she has plummeted from her agitated state and is *ill out of spirits—disheartened*. The Wordsworths begin their journey home from Eusemere, and Dorothy starts to fill herself up with observations and responses. She is writing as she has never done before:

> *The hawthorns are black & green, the birches here and there greenish but there is yet more of purple to be seen on the Twigs. We got over into a field to avoid some cows—people working, a few primroses by the roadside, woodsorrel flowers, the anemone, scentless violets, strawberries & that starry yellow flower which Mrs. C calls pilewort. When we were in the woods beyond Gow-*

barrow park we saw a few daffodils close to the water side, we fancied that the lake had floated the seeds ashore & that the little colony had so sprung up—But as we went along there were more & yet more & at last under the boughs of the trees, we saw that there was a long belt of them along the shore, about the breadth of a country turnpike road. I never saw daffodils so beautiful they grew among the mossy stones about & about them, some rested their heads upon these stones as on a pillow for weariness & the rest tossed & reeled & danced & seemed as if they verily laughed with the wind that blew upon them over the Lake, they looked so gay ever glancing ever changing.

There is something amiss. Dorothy mentions the *black & green* of the hawthorns, the occasional *greenish* hue of the birch trees with the *purple* on the twigs, and the *starry yellow flower*, but says nothing at all about the color emblazoning the vision by the lake. Dorothy is always drawn to the light, she alone sees what sparkles and glitters on the fleece of a sheep or the surface of water, yellow is the color she describes the most in the journals, but the yellow of the daffodils is the one detail she here leaves out. Instead, like a physicist, she records the movement and energy of the flowers as they toss and reel and dance and laugh, *ever glanc-*

Daffodil (Narcissus pseudo-narcissus *L.*), *by Walter Hood Fitch*

ing ever changing, and she notices, too, that those daffodils that are not dancing are weary, and rest their heads. She feels, not sees, how beautiful they are, and this is where the strength of her description lies. But in Wordsworth's tidied-up account of the walk written two years later, something else is going on. In the version published in the 1807 edition of his poems, he does not mention the color, either, referring to "A host of dancing daffodils"; it is only in the revised poem that he replaces "dancing" with "golden." In William's descriptions of the scene he is without Dorothy, wandering lonely as a cloud.

That night they stay at an inn where they have *a glass of warm rum & water*. They enjoyed themselves *& wished for Mary*. The next day,

> *when we came to the foot of Brothers water I left William sitting on the Bridge & went along the path on the right side of the Lake through the wood—I was delighted with what I saw—the water under the boughs of the bare old trees, the simplicity of the mountains & the exquisite beauty of the path. There was one grey cottage. I repeated the Glowworm as I walked along—I hung over the gate, & thought I could have stayed for ever.*

The poem she repeats to herself as she walks along was written by William for Dorothy two days before, just after he left Mary, having made plans for their future. It is a love poem based on an experience he and Dorothy shared back in Racedown days, and he addresses Dorothy as "Lucy":

> Among all lovely things my Love had been;
> Had noted well the stars, all flowers that grew

About her home; but she had never seen
A Glow-worm, never one, and this I knew.

Some readers have seen the glowworm as a symbol inadvertently revealing William's sexual feelings for Dorothy, but I see it as a creature like Dorothy herself, close to the earth and illuminating all it passes. When Dorothy returns to William from the gate, she finds him

writing a poem descriptive of the sights & sounds we saw & heard. There was the gentle flowing of the stream, the glittering lively lake, green fields without a living creature to be seen on them, behind us, a flat pasture with 42 cattle feeding, to our left the road leading to the hamlet, no smoke there, the sun shone on the bare roofs.

The poetry Wordsworth is producing at a daily rate during these weeks is marked by simplicity and optimism, by fancy rather than imagination. There is none of the ambition of *Lyrical Ballads* or the darkness of the Lucy poems, no reaching out for sublimity or interest in the workings, or growth, of the mind. Contentment is the theme of the poem Dorothy found him writing on the bridge at Brother's Water:

The cock is crowing,
The stream is flowing,
The small birds twitter,
The lake doth glitter,
The green field sleeps in the sun;
The oldest and youngest

> Are at work with the strongest;
> The cattle are grazing,
> Their heads never raising;
> There are forty feeding like one!

As William gets happier, his poetry gets emptier of thought, and Dorothy's prose subsequently becomes more full. The jolly ditty above is born of the same sights and sounds that she compiled in her journal, but her description lacks the resistance to ideas and imagination found in William's lines. In his current writing, sublimity is replaced by sentiment, and he is, as he puts it himself in "Tintern Abbey," "more like a man flying from something that he dreads, than one who sought the thing he loved." It is during this spring that William writes of Dorothy, "She gave me eyes, she gave me ears," but he needs more than "the mighty world of eye and ear" to be writing as well as she is now doing. He needs her sense of something "amiss." By remarking on what is missing from the scene—*green fields without a living creature to be seen on them . . . the road leading to the hamlet, no smoke there*—Dorothy adds to the visual field a depth that William takes a detour to avoid. She is much *more than half a poet* these days, and when they return to Dove Cottage, Dorothy is again using the language of halves: *The garden looked pretty by half moonlight half daylight.*

Sitting by the fireside with William that evening, Dorothy fills in her journal and then writes to Mary, enclosing a copy of the poem that William composed during the day. It is a curiously toned letter. Dorothy implores her "dear, dear Mary," who William tells her has become too thin and weak, to

> seek quiet or rather amusing thoughts. Study the flowers, the birds and all the common things that are about

> you. O Mary, my dear Sister! Be quiet and happy. Take care of yourself—keep yourself employed without fatigue, and do not make loving us your business, but let your love of us make up the spirit of all the business you have.

Dorothy tells Mary she is "dear" perhaps once too often, but calls her "Sister" for the first time. Critics have taken the use of this familial term as evidence of Dorothy's acceptance of Mary, but it seems more a recognition of rivalry. It is Dorothy who is the "dear, dear sister" of the circle, and while "sister" was used by them all to denote like-mindedness, Dorothy addresses Mary not as a valued member of their "family," someone who shares their interests already and blends in with their way of life, but as an outsider who needs to be taught their ways and instructed in how to love them. Mary is spoken to as though she were in danger of loving "us" too much, her love for Dorothy assumed to be the same as her love for William. Dorothy has put Mary firmly in her place; it is little wonder that Mary will write to William in years to come of "the blessed bond that binds husband & wife so much closer than the bond of Brotherhood—however dear & affectionate a family of Brothers [&] Sisters may love each other."

Dorothy and William have become a single poetic voice. What interests him these days are "the flowers, the birds and all the common things" that are "studied" by Dorothy with all the energy she can muster in order to distract herself from the business of loving William. He pours out poems in celebration of Dorothy's daisies, linnets, and small celandines; she only has to open her mouth for William to write a poem. They are continually giving one another "feedback": Dorothy sees, hears, or recalls something, William composes some lines about it, William feels ill, Dorothy writes his lines down, William recovers and revises, Dorothy then feels ill on his behalf, she recites the finished poem to William, usually as he lies in bed, tired to death. They recognize and acknowledge one another every step of the way. Dorothy is pleased at the ease with which she inspires him. She writes on April 28, *I happened to say that when I was a child I would not have pulled a strawberry blossom . . . At dinner-time he came in with the poem of "Children gathering flowers."* She notes on April 17 that *I saw a Robin chacing a scarlet Butterfly* and on April 18 that *William wrote the poem on the Robin & the butterfly*. But as he is writing the concluding lines to the poem about the robin and the butterfly, no doubt chanting the words aloud, Dorothy feels overcome. *I was quite out of spirits*, she wrote, *& went out into the orchard—When I came in he had finished the poem.*

William was easily satisfied this spring, but it would be wrong to conclude that the happiness of life in Dove Cottage was at its peak. Every joyful rhyme that Wordsworth writes during these weeks coincides with a sobering entry in Dorothy's journal, suggesting that his optimism is a mood enforced on an atmosphere more opaque than it appears to be and harder to read, not least because, as he later said, his headaches and sleepless nights at this time were due to frustrated sexual longings. On March 26, when William composes "To the Cuckoo" and "The Rainbow," Dorothy is *ill & in bad spirits*. On the twenty-seventh William is interrupted while writing the opening lines of "Ode: Intimations of Immortality" by a delivery of dung, which needs to be spread around the garden. This, Dorothy knows, will be an important poem, bigger and better than anything else he has composed this year, but the next day she *lay down after dinner with a bad head ach*, which continues for the following four days. "Ode: Intimations of Immortality," which took two years to reach the form in which it was eventually published, is a confirmation of William's current mood, but without his fear of reflective thought. The value of common sights associated with Dorothy is questioned in his opening lines:

> There was a time when meadow, grove, and stream,
> The earth, and every common sight,
> To me did seem
> Apparelled in celestial light.

"The things which I have seen I now can see no more," Wordsworth goes on to say of dejection, but by the poem's close his trust in nature is confirmed: "To me the meanest flower that blows can give / Thoughts that do often lie too deep for tears."

On April 21, Dorothy is again upset when Coleridge responds to what Wordsworth has written so far of "Ode: Intimations of Immortality." This comes in the form of his own verses, called by him the "Letter to Sara Hutchinson," which contain an intensely personal, uncensored, and agonized howl of despair at the impossibility of his love and what Coleridge feels to be the loss of his poetical talents. His abjection comes closer to Dorothy's state of mind than the joy Wordsworth is currently gaining from lambs and rainbows:

> A grief without a pang, void, dark, and drear,
> A stifled, drowsy, unimpassioned grief,
> Which finds no natural outlet, no relief,
> In word, or sigh, or tear.

Dorothy listens as Coleridge reads aloud stanza after stanza; she is *affected with them & . . . on the whole, not being well, in miserable spirits.* Now when she looks on William's world, it is with how blank an eye: *The sunshine—the green fields & the fair sky made me sadder; even the little happy sporting lambs seemed but sorrowful to me.* Her lines echo those by Coleridge, which have snagged on her skin like a fishhook: "I see them all so excellently fair, / I see, not feel, how beautiful they are!"

Out the poetry rolls. All spring Wordsworth and Coleridge hurl lines at each other like missiles. When the three of them walk the next day, William repeats a poem he has been composing. "I do not wish to lie / Dead, dead," he chants, "Dead without any company," ending with the incantation "Peace, peace, peace." The sentiment is insistently upbeat to counter Coleridge's gloom, and yet the idea of lying dead was one that seduced Wordsworth, and on April 29 he and Dorothy see what it is like. Dorothy's journal records only how William felt as they lay

> *in the trench under the fence—he with his eyes shut & listening to the waterfalls & the Birds . . . William heard me breathing & rustling now & then but we both lay still, & unseen by one another—he thought that it would be as sweet thus to lie so in the grave, to hear the* peaceful *sounds of the earth & just to know that ones dear friends are near.*

Coleridge had experimented in the same way a year earlier, but he had been alone without any company in a trench he found for himself. On May 1, William and Dorothy lie down together again, this time under a holly tree, *where we saw nothing but the holly tree & a budding elm mossed with* [word deleted] *& the sky above our heads. But that holly tree had about it a beauty more than its own.* Here, in this state of stillness with the beauty above them exceeding itself and the surrounding *landscape fading away,* Dorothy's fourth journal notebook runs out of pages.

By the evening of May 3 there has been a sea change. Wordsworth puts away his suns and celandines and begins to write "The Leech Gatherer," which opens with a "roaring in the wind." He goes to sleep *nervous & jaded in the extreme.* The poem is his reply to Coleridge's "Letter to Sara Hutchinson," his response to the questions that are snapping like little threads around his friend's heart. "I describe myself," William explained to Sara, "as having been exalted to the highest pitch of delight by the joyousness and beauty of Nature and then as depressed, even in the midst of those beautiful objects, to the lowest dejection and despair." He continues to compose as he lies in bed on the morning of May 4, after which he, Dorothy, and Coleridge have a picnic and a walk, reading and repeating the poem in progress as they go. They *almost melted away before we were at the top of the hill.* Dorothy observed that the waterfall beneath the crag *stood upright by itself.* It was, she repeats, *its own self,* unlike the holly tree of the day before, which had about it a beauty *more than its own.*

Neither inspired by nor about Dorothy, "The Leech Gatherer" marks the start of William's move away from his sister's sensibility. He no longer needs the spark of Romantic incest to fire his imagination, and from now until the wedding he will turn to public and cultural matters and write his "Ode to Duty." Other than his tribute to Dorothy in *The Prelude,* William will write nothing further for or about her. He will later say in *The Prelude* that the highest intellectual state to be aspired to by the man of imagination is "singleness":

"No other can divide with thee this work: / No secondary hand can intervene." Not once in his adult life has Wordsworth been in a state of intellectual singleness, but this is not how he wants to be remembered. The Romantic artist, as he is defined in the Preface to *Lyrical Ballads*, is a man who stands apart.

Dorothy, meanwhile, will find solace in her garden. At least nature never did betray the heart that loved her.

TO HONOR AND OBEY: NATURE

Two roads diverged in a yellow wood,
And sorry I could not travel both
And be one traveler, long I stood
And looked down one as far as I could
To where it bent in the undergrowth;
Then took the other, as just as fair.

—ROBERT FROST, "The Road Not Taken"

Not poppy, nor mandragora,
Nor all the drowsy syrups of the world
Shall ever medicine thee to that sweet sleep
Which thou owedst yesterday.

—WILLIAM SHAKESPEARE, *Othello,* act 3, scene 3

In legend, the drowsy syrup that bleeds from the mandragora has a soporific effect. The mandrake is also said to shriek in pain when it is torn from the ground, as will Dorothy when she is uprooted so that William can go for Mary, and between May and the day of their departure in July she is busy preparing the soil.

Her world is inhabited by cries. One night she hears a shout that she thinks might be human: *There was an owl hooting in Bainriggs. Its first halloo was so like a human shout that I was surprised when it made its second call, tremulous & lengthened out, to find that the shout had come from an owl.* Back in November 1800, six weeks after Wordsworth determined not to include *Christabel* in *Lyrical Ballads*, Coleridge, who was spending the night at Dove Cottage, woke screaming, and William in turn cried out three times. Coleridge recorded in his notebooks having had a dream of a woman like Geraldine, the mysterious creature in his rejected ballad,

> whose features were blended with darkness catching hold of my right eye & attempting to pull it out—I caught hold of her arm fast—a horrid feel—Wordsworth cried out aloud to me hearing my scream—heard his cry and thought it cruel he did not come / but did not wake till his cry was repeated a third time.

The previous month, only days after Wordsworth's decision to exclude the poem, Coleridge had recorded another cry, but this time it was not human. "Morning—2 o'clock—Wind amid its [branches] makes every now & then such a deep moan of pain, that I think it my wife asleep in pain—A trembling Oo! Oo! like a wounded man on a field of battle whose wounds smarted with the cold."

There are moans and cries throughout *Christabel* as well. The ballad begins with the "Tu-whit!—Tu-whoo!" of an owl, and when, alone in the woods, Christabel hears Geraldine's bleak moan she carries her, like a bride, over the threshold of her castle gates:

> The lady sank, belike through pain,
> And Christabel with might and main
> Lifted her up, a weary weight,
> Over the threshold of the gate:
> Then the lady rose again,
> And moved, as she were not in pain.

But the pain caused to Coleridge by the rejection of his poem did not go away, and his howls fill the nights, the winds, the lakes, the trees, and the pages of Dorothy's journal. As for Dorothy herself, she had delighted in *Christabel, exceedingly delighted* in it, and she can be found at times crossing "the threshold of the gate" back into Coleridge's dreamlike world.

The optimism of William's mood during the spring is passed. Over the summer nothing but the effect of Dorothy's voice will calm his demons. One night, Dorothy *repeated verses to William while he was in bed—he was soothed & I left him. "This is the Spot" over & over again.* The lines, written for her by Wordsworth two years before, are incantatory:

> This is the spot:—how mildly does the sun
> Shine in between these fading leaves! The air
> In the habitual silence of this wood
> Is more than silent: and this bed of heath,
> Where shall we find so sweet a resting place?
> Come!—let me see thee sink into a dream
> Of quiet thoughts,—protracted till thine eye
> Be calm as water, when the winds are gone
> And no one can tell whither,—My sweet friend!
> We two have had such happy hours together
> That my heart melts in me to think of it.

The next night when William goes to bed, agitated and exhausted, Dorothy reads aloud Shakespeare's "Lover's Complaint" until he sinks into a dream of quiet thoughts. Dorothy has turned into the homesick plant who ministers sleep, and William has become the night owl in Bainriggs.

Night after night he lies wide-eyed and restless; entry after entry of Dorothy's journal will record the effect of his nocturnal existence on their daily lives. His insomnia consumes her: *William was obliged to be in his Bed late, he had slept so miserably; He had slept better than I could have expected but he was far from well; William has got no sleep. It is after 11 & he is still in bed; William had slept very ill; William had slept better—but not well; William has not slept all night; William had not fallen asleep till after 3 o'clock but he slept tolerably; William slept ill, his head terribly bad.* Dorothy does not say what his night thoughts are, but they must include the prospect of meeting Annette and their daughter, and of looking down the road he chose not to travel.

The nights are hellish, but the days are heavenly. The first day of May is *a heavenly morning . . . It was a clear sky & a heavenly morning,* and she and William sow flowers in the orchard and then lie on the ground gazing upward. *Two Ravens flew high high in the sky & the sun shone upon their bellys and their wings long after there was none of his light to be seen.* The second is another *heavenly morning,* and on May 4, *I drank a little brandy & water & was in heaven.*

The final notebook of the Grasmere Journals begins on May 4, 1802. Small and substantial, looking like an artist's sketch pad, it is bound in brown leather with a metal clasp. It already contains Wordsworth's drafts of "Michael," the poem with which he replaced *Christabel,* and "Ruth." Some pages have been cut out from the beginning and end. Dorothy's subject over the late spring and early summer months is nature: what grows and is torn from the earth, and the movements she sees in the air. She is increasingly alert to the birds that migrate and those that stay put.

In her first entry she records seeing a bird *at the top of the crags . . . flying round and round;* it *looked in thinness & transparency, shape & motion like a moth.* She kisses the letters they have engraved on the Rock of Names, and Wordsworth deepens the *T* of Coleridge's initials with a penknife. The moon that night is the one described by Coleridge in his "Letter to Sara Hutchinson," taken from the "Ballad of Sir Patrick Spence": *We had the Crescent moon with the auld moon in her arms.* On May 6, Dorothy writes her journal sitting with William in the garden, where she has brought him his apple. It is one o'clock and

> *the small Birds are singing—Lambs bleating, Cuckow calling—The Thrush sings by Fits, Thomas Ashburner's axe is going quietly (without passion) in the orchard—Hens are cackling, Flies humming, the women talking together at their doors—Plumb & pear trees are in Blossom, apple trees greenish—the opposite woods green, the crows are cawing. We have heard Ravens. The Ash Trees are in blossom, Birds flying all about us. The stitchwort is coming out, there is one budding Lychnis. The primroses are passing their prime. Celandine violets & wood sorrel for ever more—little geranium & pansies on the wall . . .*

Dorothy's garden is an ideal community in which inhabitants come and go harmoniously, each knowing his place. Her detail is simple and exact, drawn with one or two sharp strokes. She puts down what she sees as she works, the image in her mind translating itself with immediate clarity and precision onto the page before her.

Nature is not like this beyond her gate. On May 1, Dorothy had gazed on Grasmere from her old resting place in the Hollins under the rock, and gasped in awe at the excess of it all: *Oh the overwhelming beauty of the Vale below—greener than green.* In the valley the beauty is too great and the green too green; there is a sublimity here, a grandeur in contrast to which the self feels diminished. What she describes now is more like a landscape by Turner. "Turner has no settled process," the artist Joseph Farington noted in his diary, "but drives the colours about till he has expressed the idea in his mind." When the beauty of the valley is overwhelming like this, Dorothy wants to express not a scene but an idea; in the excessiveness of the green she is saying something about the power and terror of what lies within.

Back in the garden her horizons narrow. She does not seek out infinity here, or search for wild and melancholy sights, or for flowers that toss and reel and dance and verily laugh with the wind. In her garden things happen, like Thomas Ashburner's axe, *without passion*, nature does not overwhelm, and colors do not exceed themselves: the apple trees are *greenish* and the woods opposite simply *green*. Everything is ordered.

From the day they arrived at Dove Cottage, Dorothy has been planning her plot of land. "In imagination," Wordsworth wrote to Coleridge on Christmas Eve 1799, "she has already built a seat with a summer shed on the highest platform in this our little domestic slip of mountain." Sloping high behind the cottage, their mountain garden "commands a view over the roof of our house, of the lake, the church, Helm Cragg, and two thirds of the vale. We also mean to enclose the two or three yards of ground between us and the road, this for the sake of a few flowers, and because it will make it more our own." They work together on the orchard and the bower: Dorothy gathers seeds and plants from the woods and the lakeshore; William trains roses, honeysuckle, and scarlet beans up the whitewashed walls, prepares pea sticks, cuts trees, clears paths, spreads dung, cleans the well, and builds steps. John planted a rose tree. Fruits and vegetables grow in abundance: apples, runner beans, broccoli, carrots, gooseberries, onions, potatoes, radishes, rhubarb, spinach, turnips, and mountains of peas, which Dorothy picks every day in the summer.

William builds a seat, but they find seats and bowers all over the valley, too, as though the landscape were made up of sitting rooms. On April 23, Dorothy and Coleridge left him *feasting on silence* and found for themselves a *couch* under the *bower of William's Eglantine*. They lingered looking at the vales:

> *Ambleside vale with the copses the village under the hill & the green fields—Rydale with a lake all alive & glittering yet but little stirred by Breezes, & our own dear Grasmere first making a little round lake of natures own with never a house never a green field—but the copses & the bare hills, enclosing it & the river flowing out of it. Above rose the Coniston Fells in their own shape & colour—not Man's hills but all for themselves the sky & the clouds & a few wild creatures.*

Whether nature is *our own* or *natures own* or *their own*, Dorothy cannot decide, nor can she agree on whether the hills should be *Man's hills*, cultivated and built upon, or *all for themselves*. The problem with Dorothy is that she is uncertain how she feels about the otherness of nature. In June, she sees a house on an island in Windermere where the shrubs that had hidden it from view have been cut away. It was not an improvement, she thought:

> *They have made no natural glades, it is merely a lawn with a few miserable young trees standing as if they were half starved. There are no sheep no cattle upon these lawns. It is neither one thing or another—neither natural nor wholly cultivated & artificial which it was before.*

But for Dorothy, nature in general is *neither one thing or another*; she cannot decide if it should be natural or wholly cultivated and artificial, and at times she cannot even tell which is which.

Sometimes she sees nature according to the picturesque principles laid down by William Gilpin in his popular *A Tour in Several Parts of England, Particularly in the Mountains and Lakes of Cumberland and Westmorland*, and she remakes the scene for herself in the way that he suggests. Trees, Gilpin wrote, can be planted or removed at pleasure by the viewer:

> If a withered stump suit the form of his landscape better than the spreading oak which he finds in Nature, he may make the exchange . . . He may pull up a piece of awkward paling; he may throw down a cottage; he may even turn the course of a road, or a river, a few yards on this side or that.

The beauty of the picturesque lies in regularity, Edmund Burke said in his *Philosophical Enquiry into the Origin of Our Ideas of the Sublime and Beautiful*. The scene should be formed and balanced like a picture in a frame. At other times Dorothy sees in nature a sublimity whose overwhelming beauty is the result of tension, irregularity, excess. The sublime, said Gilpin, is "that which art cannot reach"; it is *greener than green*, and this is what we find throughout the Lake District. "No tame country," Gilpin told his readers, "however beautiful, can distend the mind like this awful and majestic scenery. The wild sallies of untutored genius often strike the imagination more than the most correct effusions of cultivated parts."

When Dorothy looks at her valley these days, she is more likely to see domestic order than awful and majestic scenery. Her trees stand in line like soldiers, she lays down a carpet, creates a parlor, and resolves to continue decorating the next day:

> *The fir tree Island was reflected beautifully—we now first saw that the trees are planted in rows. About this bower there is mountain ash, common ash, yew tree, ivy, holly, hawthorn, mosses & flowers, & a carpet of moss—Above at the top of the Rock there is another spot—it is scarce a Bower, a little parlour, one not enclosed by walls but shaped out for a resting place by the rocks & the ground rising about it. It had a sweet moss carpet—We resolved to go & plant flowers in both these places tomorrow.*

When Dorothy sees the reflection of the fir tree island like this, it is as though she were holding up a Claude glass, the convex hand mirror used by Lakeland tourists to frame and tame the features of the landscape. The viewer, standing with her back to the view, places the glass over the shoulder and looks at the reflection rather than the thing itself. The terror of the landscape is softened, reduced, harmonized; the viewer resembles Perseus avoiding the gaze of the Medusa by looking at the Gorgon's petrifying features only as they are reflected on the sheen of his shield.

In *Lyrical Ballads*, Wordsworth and Coleridge agreed that there would be two depictions of nature: Wordsworth would observe and describe the common things of rural life, and Coleridge would direct his "endeavours" to "persons and characters supernatural, or at least romantic." Dorothy stands on the threshold between these two natures. The Dorothy of "trees planted in rows" is the rural Dorothy of common things who is celebrated by Wordsworth in *The Prelude*, the civilizing influence who during their time at Racedown softened his "over-sternness." Before her gentle touch, William's soul had been a "rock with torrents roaring":

> But thou didst plant its crevices with flowers,
> Hang it with shrubs that twinkle in the breeze,
> And teach the little birds to build their nests
> And warble in its chambers.

Planting flowers and building nests are things that Dorothy does well and will be doing all summer in readiness for Mary. But as she put it herself in a poem she wrote in 1829 about her first walk in Grasmere, "Lured by a little winding path, / Quickly I left the public road." Lured "eastward, toward the lofty hills," she is led away from the ordered world in which she has been placed by Wordsworth, and into Coleridge's nocturnal realm.

In Dorothy's imagination, there are two roads leading to two different natures: the public road preferred by William, where she will meet itinerants and travelers she can talk to on the way, and the little winding path, which will take her deeper into the mysteries of the forest. The diverging roads are best described by the differences between "Michael" and *Christabel*. *Christabel*, with its heady lesbian eroticism, its doves and serpents, woods, spells, and symbols proved too strange even for the Wordsworth of the Lucy poems, and behind his rejection of the ballad for the 1800 edition of *Lyrical Ballads* lay his insistence on nature as a sexless site of benevolence and healing. *Christabel*, which Coleridge was afraid to finish, takes us through the wardrobe door into a Narnia full of wonders; Wordsworth replaced it with his own solid and rural "Michael," which, so the poem begins, is at least "a story . . . not unfit, I deem, for the fireside." Like the two qualities of the mandrake, "Michael" is about attachment to the earth; *Christabel* is set in the locked-up, trancelike world of sleep.

In her relations with nature, as in so much else, Dorothy quarrels with herself. Wordsworth's nature is his teacher and his guide; he describes not what he sees but *how it affects him*, and Coleridge finds in nature an otherness of being from which even he shies away in horror. But Dorothy's nature is divided between the familiarity of her domestic strip of mountain, where nature cooperates with man, and another nature beyond the gate, which, when she stumbles upon it, represents for her a site of awe as opposed to pleasure. The first is a nature with which she identifies, as in her description of the columbine she finds growing on the rocks—*it is a graceful slender creature, a female seeking retirement & growing freest & most graceful where it is most alone*—and the second is a nature that makes her feel like a different person. It is the strange and mysterious realm described in *La nouvelle Héloïse* by Rousseau, who uses the example of mountains as the stage for his sublime transportations:

> Imagine to yourself all these united impressions; the amazing variety, grandeur and beauty, of a thousand astonishing sights; the pleasure of seeing only totally new things, strange birds, odd and unknown plants, to observe what is in some sense another nature, and finding yourself in a new world . . . one isolated in the higher spheres of the earth. In short, there is a kind of supernatural beauty in these mountainous prospects which charms both the senses and the minds into a forgetfulness of oneself and of everything in the world.

Dorothy forgets herself a good deal these days.

On May 7, William finished writing "The Leech Gatherer," and Dorothy sewed frocks for Coleridge's baby son, Derwent. They sat in the orchard in the afternoon, where there was a *thick hazy dull air. The Thrush sang almost continually—the little Birds were more than usually busy with their voices. The sparrows are now fully fledged. The nest is so full that they lie upon one another, they sit quietly in their nest with closed mouths.* Dorothy likes the fact that birds always come home, and there are birds throughout the Grasmere Journals. The thin and transparent mothlike bird that flies round and round on May 4, blackbirds, bullfinches, chaffinches, crows, cuckoos, hens, herons, hawks, owls, ravens, robins, sparrows, stonechats, swallows, and thrushes. There are *little birds busy making love & pecking the blossoms & bits off the trees* as she lies beneath them, there is one bird she cannot identify, *with a salmon coloured breast—a white cross or T upon its wings, & a brownish back with faint stripes,* pecking the dung on the road. Back in April, she had described lying with William in the Hollins, where

> *birds were about us on all sides—Skobbys Robins Bullfinches. Crows now and then flew over our heads as we were warned by the sound of the beating of the air above. We stayed till the light of day was going & the little Birds had begun to settle their singing—But there was a thrush not far off that seemed to sing louder & clearer than the thrushes had sung when it was quite day.*

Sometimes her birds transport her to another world; other times they enter her own world. One day in June, she

> *spoke of the little birds keeping us company—& William told me that that very morning a Bird had perched upon his leg . . . It was a little young creature, that had just left its nest, equally unacquainted with man & unaccustomed to struggle*

> *against Storms and winds. While it was upon the apple tree the wind blew about the still boughs & the bird seemed bemazed & not strong enough to strive with it.*

On May 8 she and William sow scarlet beans. She reads a poem in the *Monthly Review* that makes her think on loss, *Wept, For names, sounds paths delights & duties lost*, and William adds a step to the orchard. On May 12 they bring home

> *heckberry blossom, crab blossom—the anemone nemorosa—Marsh Marygold—Speedwell, that beautiful blue one the colour of the blue-stone or glass used in jewellery, with its beautiful pearl-like chives—anemones are in abundance & still the dear dear primroses violets in beds, pansies in abundance & the little celandine . . .*

She pulls a branch of the taller celandine, and William pulls ivy with beautiful berries, which Dorothy brings into the house and puts over the chimneypiece. Her journal is becoming more and more of a botanical register. On May 14

> *the oak trees are just putting forth yellow knots of leaves. The ashes with their flowers passing away & leaves coming out. The blue Hyacinth is not quite full blown—Gowans are coming out—marsh marigolds in full glory—the little star plant a star without a flower. We took home a great load of Gowans & planted them in the cold about the orchard.*

Dorothy's sentences are turning into lists. What is the purpose of these great inventories? It is as if she wants to hammer home the reality of what she sees so as to give herself some substance: *I name, therefore I am.* Coleridge, for whom nature has never lost its terror, does the same: an entry in his notebook for February 1801 has, in Sara Hutchinson's hand, a transcription of the index to William Withering's *Arrangement of British Plants*, beginning with "Adder's Tongue" and ending, many, many pages later, with "Zannichelly—or Horned Lake Weed." He keeps a list of every known British plant in his notebook precisely because the nature in his poetry is of the kind that he doesn't know and cannot name and might therefore be subsumed. It is the preternatural forest in which Christabel finds Geraldine that Dorothy enters on the evening of May 14. Returning from Rydal with a letter from Sara Hutchinson, she sees that the ordinary day has now become *a strange night*, not least because it is the middle of May but looks like winter:

> *The hills were covered over with a slight covering of hail or snow, just so as to give them a hoary winter look with the black Rocks—The woods looked miserable, the coppices green as grass which looked quite unnatural & they seemed half shrivelled up as if they shrunk from the air. O thought I! what a beautiful thing God has made winter to be by stripping the trees & letting us see their shapes & forms. What a freedom does it seem to give to the storms! There were several new flowers out but I had no pleasure in looking at them—I walked as fast as I could back again.*

When Dorothy describes her *strange night*, she compiles no comforting lists, she does not measure herself against the reality of what she sees, she gives us only the rocks and stones and trees. She knows that she cannot praise nature's beauty without, as Camille Paglia puts it, crossing her fingers first and saying her prayers, because nature, like Geraldine, is really cruel and merciless and could destroy her with a single breath.

In moods such as the one she is in on May 14, Dorothy gets no pleasure from finding new flowers. She will not look them up when she gets home. She loses her desire to give a name to everything she sees, to own the springtime. It has become midwinter in her vale.

On the morning of May 15 she writes, *It is now ¼ past 10 & he is not up. Miss Simpson called when I was in bed—I have been in the garden. It looks fresh & neat in spite of the frost. Molly tells me they had thick ice on a jug at their door last night.* Apart from her peculiar timing, Mother Nature has made a tidy scene. The frost has not destroyed the garden's *fresh & neat* appearance, and the ice is on the jug rather than on the lake. All is in order. But then something strange happens, and Dorothy begins to write up the day again, having forgotten that she has done so already. Nothing, it seems, is in order at all. She puts down the date once more, *Saturday 15th,* only this time she describes it as

> *a very cold & cheerless morning. I sat mending stockings all the morning. I read in Shakespeare. William lay very late because he slept ill last night. It snowed this morning just like Christmas. We had a melancholy letter from Coleridge just at bedtime—it distressed me very much & I resolved upon going to Keswick the next day.*

Her second entry is repetitive and restless, as though she were occupied in the elsewhere of her mind. But it is only here that she notes her own cheerlessness, the madness of the weather, the bad night had by William, the sadness felt by Coleridge, and her own anxiety toward their friend. Dorothy produces two completely different versions of May 15, one describing harmony and the other disharmony.

The next day she fails in her resolution to see Coleridge; May 16 is a typical Sunday, and Dorothy does nothing much at all. *William was at work all the morning I did not go to Keswick. A sunny cold frosty day a snow shower at night. We were a good while in the orchard in the morning.* It is as if there were not a thought in her head. But on a sheet of pink blotting paper fastened into the journal on the opposite page, she produces one of her lists again, only this time she notes the names not of plants or birds or trees but of the people in her world, and she does not *write* so much as *lay* them out, arranging them like an inscription on a tomb. This is a group of friends who have never once been together at the same time, whose relations are maintained vicariously and through a constant exchange of letters. No physical presence is required to keep this particular "family" going, and like the winter gives to the trees, Dorothy gives to the six of them a shape and form:

S. T. Coleridge
Dorothy Wordsworth William Wordsworth
Mary Hutchinson Sara Hutchinson
William Coleridge Mary
Dorothy Sara
. . . .
16th May
1802
John Wordsworth

As with her two entries for May 15, the body of names on the blotting paper provides an alternative entry for the day, an underside to what Dorothy has otherwise recorded. Here are the relation-

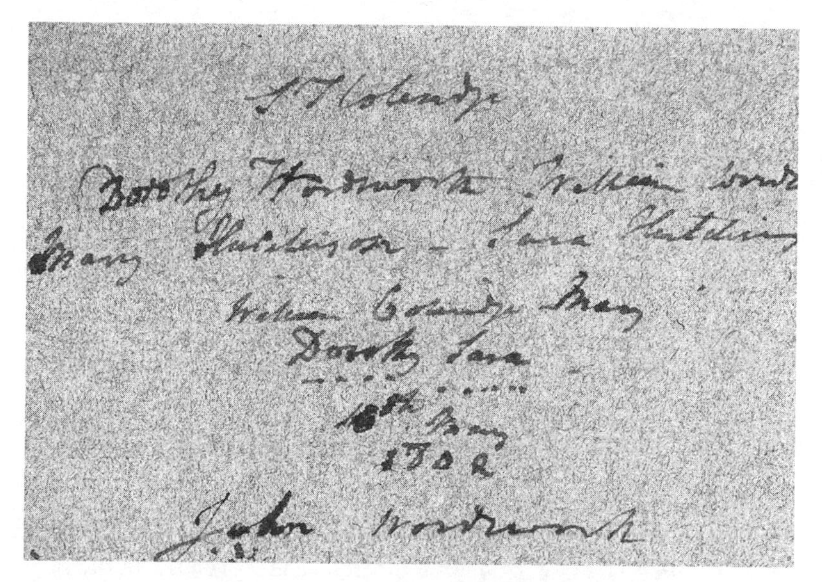

Blotting paper in the Grasmere Journals

ships whose patternings and partnerships she will never discuss in her journal. This summer Dorothy is preparing for change: grouping things together, finding a place for everything. Coleridge is at the forefront of her thoughts, her first concern. But she places him with neither his wife nor the "sister of his soul," Sara Hutchinson. Unpartnered, he is like his Mariner, "Alone, alone, all, all alone." Dorothy and William Wordsworth come next, a comfortable couple sharing the same family name, and Mary and Sara Hutchinson follow, with Mary's name falling directly beneath Dorothy's and Sara's beneath William's as though they occupied the same positions. There is then a new order, one not based around family groups: William, Coleridge, and Mary, with Coleridge now nestling between—coming between?—the future married couple in the same way that he currently stands in the middle of Dorothy and William. William and Mary are never alone in

Dorothy's structure as they will never be alone in married life, but the future grouping, as Dorothy knows, will be not Coleridge, William, and Mary but *herself*, William, and Mary. She sees herself and Coleridge as interchangeable. She also recognizes that she and Mary have swapped places: Mary is with William and Coleridge, and it is now Dorothy and Sara who are partnered together at the bottom of the pile, the two sisterly spinsters, rather than the two Hutchinson sisters, forming a group of their own. This is the order of things on May 16, 1802. John Wordsworth, the other lonely mariner, is remembered only as an afterthought.

As for Coleridge himself, he had never felt part of the group whose relationships Dorothy so neatly defined. One of his notebook entries written back in September 1801 states simply, "W.W. M.H. D.W. S.H." Coleridge saw himself as increasingly on the outside of life looking in: he was in debt, his marriage was failing fast, he was increasingly addicted to opium, and Wordsworth's rejection of *Christabel* from *Lyrical Ballads* had destroyed his belief in himself as a poet. His love for Sara Hutchinson was agonizing, but it was really his love for Wordsworth that was killing him. "By shewing to him what true poetry was," Coleridge told William Godwin, Wordsworth "made him know that he himself was no poet." Unable to write, Coleridge compared himself to an ostrich: "I cannot fly, yet I have wings that give me the feeling of flight." He was "a bird of the earth" looking up to the heavens. He would later describe himself as a great bird of prey in the grip of a snake; opium was a way of "escaping from the pains that coiled round my mental powers as a serpent around the body and wings of an eagle." Coleridge told Godwin how he was once

> a Volume of Gold Leaf, rising and riding on every breath of Fancy—but I have beaten myself back into

> weight and density, and now I sink in quicksilver, yea, remain squat and square on the earth amid the hurricane, that makes Oaks and Straws join in one Dance, fifty yards high in the Element.

Wordsworth is earthbound, too, but in his notebooks in the spring of 1801 Coleridge compares the mind of his mentor not to something squat and square like himself, sitting heavy on the surface through all weathers, but to the soil "on a deep stratum of tenacious Clay, and that on a foundation of Rocks, which often break through both Strata, lifting their back above the surface."

It seems that Coleridge had been lured up to the lakes not to spread his wings and soar the skies, as had been promised by Wordsworth, but to fertilize his friend's own soil. Coleridge now describes with staggering clarity in the "Letter to Sara Hutchinson" his sense of weight and transience:

> To see thee, hear thee, feel thee, then to part—
> O! it weighs down the Heart!
> To *visit* those, I love, as I love *thee*,
> Mary, and William and dear Dorothy,
> It is but a temptation to repine!
> The Transientness is Poison in the Wine,
> Eats out of the Pith of Joy, makes all Joy hollow!
> All Pleasure a dim Dream of Pain to follow!
> My own peculiar Lot, my household Life
> It is, and will remain Indifference or Strife—
> While ye are well and happy, 'twould but wrong you,
> If I should fondly yearn to be among you—
> Wherefore, O! wherefore, should I wish to be
> A wither'd Branch upon a blossoming Tree?

He is living these days "the Night-mare Life-in-Death," as he calls it in *The Rime of the Ancient Mariner*, and Dorothy is thoroughly absorbed by his state. A perfect electrometer, she picks up his moods and suffers them, too. Days after she describes Coleridge and herself in her journal doodle as being essentially exchangeable, Dorothy confirms their identification: *Coleridge not well . . . I not well. C & I walked in the evening wrote to M & S.* On the next day, *Coleridge's Bowels bad, mine also.*

❧

In May, the Coleridges had a frank exchange. "Mrs. Coleridge was made *serious*," Coleridge told Southey,

> and for the first time since our marriage she felt and acted, as beseemed a Wife & a Mother to a Husband, & the Father of her children . . . I on my part promised to be more attentive to all her feelings of Pride, etc etc and to try to correct my habits of impetuous & bitter censure . . . I have the most confident Hopes, that this happy Revolution in our domestic affairs will be permanent.

But like all else in his life, this "happy Revolution" proved transient, and on May 21, Dorothy and William met Coleridge in, of all places, the spot they called "Sara's Rock," where they had *some interesting melancholy talk about his private affairs.* He then came back with them to Dove Cottage, where Dorothy cooked lamb chops. Coleridge wants Dorothy, William, and Mary to live at Greta Hall after the wedding, but Dorothy, whose feelings toward Sarah Coleridge are becoming less and less grounded, does not want this. For Sarah Coleridge's acts of wifely kindness in the wake of the "happy Revolution" in their family affairs Dorothy has nothing but disdain, and it is, as ever, to Sara Hutchinson that she vents her spleen:

> Mrs. Coleridge is a most extraordinary character,—she is the lightest, weakest, silliest woman! She sent some clean clothes on Thursday to meet C (the first time she ever did such a thing in her life) from which I guess that she is determined to be attentive to him—she wrote a note, saying not a word about my letter, and all in her very lightest style . . . is it not a hopeless case?

The snow has now melted, and the weather has become suddenly *very hot . . . a hot wind as if coming from a sand desert.* On Sunday, May 24, Dorothy is ill and takes laudanum. She begins to recover on May 28, when she is *much better than yesterday, though poorly.* She is now in harmony with William rather than with Coleridge: *Wm tired himself with hammering at a passage. I was out of spirits. After dinner he was better & I grew better,* and they sit in the orchard. Dorothy has written nothing about nature all week, but being back in the greenery of her garden again, she checks the seasonal progress:

> *The sky cloud the air sweet & cool. The young Bullfinches in their party coloured Raiment bustle about among the Blossoms & poize themselves like Wire dancers or tumblers, shaking the twigs and dashing off the Blossoms. There is yet one primrose in the orchard—the stitchwort is fading—the wild columbines are coming into beauty—the vetches are in abundance Blossoming & seeding. That pretty little waxy looking Dial-like*

> *yellow flower, the speedwell, & some others whose names I do not yet know. The wild columbines are coming into beauty—some of the gowans fading. In the garden we have lilies & many other flowers. The scarlet Beans are up in crowds. It is now between 8 & nine o'clock. It has rained sweetly for two hours & a half—the air is very mild. The heckberry blossoms are dropping off fast, almost gone—barberries are in beauty—snowballs coming forward—May Roses blossoming.*

Her bustling bullfinches belong in the pages of Thomas Bewick's *Land Birds,* published in 1797. The Wordsworths did not own this book, but many households had a copy, and Dorothy might have seen it on the shelves at the Clarksons'. She would have loved Bewick's tender portraits of the creatures she knew so well, and his descriptions of their characters and habitats. Dorothy catches the humor and charm of her birds with a mixture of scientific objectivity and folk anthropomorphizing. Her flowers, on the other hand, the lone primrose, fading stitchwort, columbines coming into their beauty—which she describes twice—scarlet beans up in crowds and heckberry blossoms dropping off fast, could have been lifted from their soil by Lewis Carroll and transplanted to the Garden of Live Flowers in *Through the Looking-Glass,* where the tiger lily, rose, and daisy like to talk—when there is anybody worth talking to.

The following day Dorothy makes *bread & a wee Rhubarb Tart & batter pudding for William.* In the orchard after dinner, *William finished his poem on Going for Mary,* and Dorothy writes it out. What she calls "on Going for Mary" and Wordsworth called "A Farewell" is the only poem he wrote during the whole of their engagement in which Mary is addressed. The arrival of Mary, he tells the cottage, will change nothing. The point of his new wife, Wordsworth suggests, is that she will have no impact on their lives whatsoever:

A gentle Maid, whose heart is lowly bred,
Whose pleasures are in wild fields gathered,
With joyousness, and with a thoughtful cheer,
Will come to you; to you herself will wed;
And love the blessed life that we lead here.

The poem offers reassurance to Dorothy. They nail up the honeysuckle and sow the scarlet beans, and that evening Dorothy writes out in her journal a new list of names, recording the occasion with solemnity:

Dorothy Wordsworth
William Wordworth
Mary Wordsworth
May 29th 6 o'clock
Evening
Sitting at small table
by window—Grasmere 1802

She has written Mary's new name out in full, as Mary will do for the first time herself on the day of her wedding. This formal list of

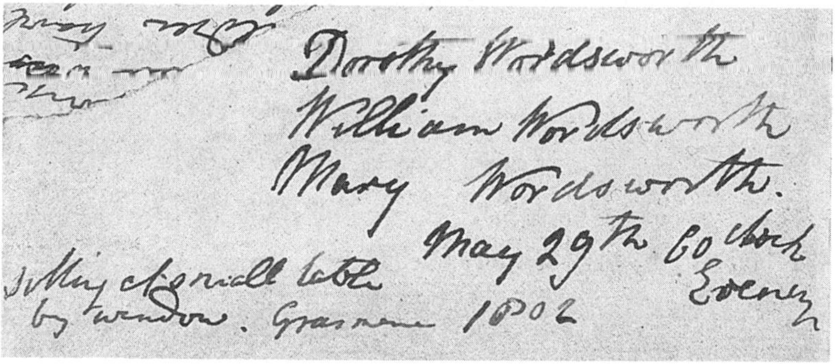
Dorothy Wordsworth
William Wordsworth
Mary Wordsworth.
May 29th 6 o'clock
Evening
sitting at small table
by window. Grasmere 1802

The Grasmere Journals, May 29, 1802

three people, with the time, date, and place, is Dorothy's own version of the marriage certificate.

Strange things are happening. The seasons are out of harmony, and when Dorothy is not ticking off what she sees, she is overcome by forgetfulness. The tangle of double days continues. On June 3 she again writes two entries, the first describing a walk with William into Easedale, where they sheltered from the rain in a cowshed and watched the birds, arriving home together wet and reading from the life and writings of the poet John Logan. *And everlasting Longings for the lost,* Dorothy quotes from Logan's "Ode: Written in a Visit to the Country in Autumn," remarking, *It is an affecting line. There are many affecting lines and passages in his poems*. She finishes her entry and then begins the entry again, *Thursday June 3rd,* this time describing a walk shared with William while dinner is cooking but coming home alone, and walking with him after dinner *upon the Turf path*. She is once more moved by reading, but in this other version of the day it is not lines by Logan that move her but a *very affecting letter* from Mary that arrives while Dorothy is sitting on the window seat reading Milton's *Il Penseroso* to her brother.

On the last day of May she loses one more of her teeth: *My Tooth broke today. They will soon be gone. Let that pass I shall be beloved—I want no more.* Dorothy wants to be *beloved* more than she wants her teeth. Even taking into account her lack of vanity, this is an unusual response to the decay of the body, more appropriate to bearing with a bad haircut than facing life with an empty jaw. Her mood is bizarrely relaxed these days, and on June 2 she records, for the only time in her journal, having *smiled*. Most striking, however, is that what makes her smile is a remark made by the sort of man who would normally make her weep:

> *Yesterday an old man called, a grey-headed man, above 70 years of age; he said he had been a soldier, that his wife & children had died in Jamaica. He had a Beggars wallet over his shoulders, a coat of shreds & patches altogether of a drab colour—he was tall & though his body was bent he had the look of one who used to have been upright. I talked a while to him, & then gave him a piece of cold bacon and a penny—said he "You're a fine woman!" I could not help smiling. I suppose he meant "You're a kind woman."*

There is nothing fine about Dorothy, especially now that she has so few teeth, and she finds the irony of the old man's malapropism entertaining. It is an unusual incident to find in her journal; for once the focus of one of her encounters shifts from the interviewee to the interviewer, and we get a rare sense of how Dorothy seems, not to others but to herself. That night she and William sit *in deep silence at the window—I on a chair & William with his hand on my shoulder. We were deep in Silence & Love, a blessed hour.*

The sudden change in Dorothy's own nature must be unnerving to William, racked as he still is by insomnia and anxiety. Like the climate this summer, brother and sister are out of harmony. Rather than taking on board his emotional concerns as her own, Dorothy finds increasing mirth in her own daily encounters. June 8 is a day of stunning views, and she catches the ferry to Belle Isle on Windermere. On her return journey, an elderly man with a red face looks significantly at the boatman and says,

> *"Thomas mind you take off the directions off that Cask. You know what I mean. It will serve as a blind for them, you know. It was a blind business both for you & the coachman & me & all of us. Mind you take off the directions—A wink's as good as a nod with some folks"—& then he turned round looking at his companion with such an air of self-satisfaction & deep insight into unknown things! I could hardly help laughing outright at him.*

Dorothy is not a humorous person, and what makes her laugh outright—the old man's sense of having deep insight into unknown things—is what she takes profoundly seriously in William's poetry, which is often about such old men.

What is happening to Dorothy? As she sinks deeper into silence with her brother, the voices of those around her appear louder and more clearly defined, and between now and the day of their departure the entries in which she impersonates and records the stories of those she meets will increase. But from where do the mockery and the lightheartedness come? Is she in the grip of a general levity, which allows her to shrug off her need for teeth and to be amused by those people who usually inspire her pity? Does she feel for a moment serenely indifferent to life and whatever it happens to throw at her or any other unfortunate being? Or is it something else altogether? In a letter to her eldest brother, Richard, written on June 10, Dorothy tells him, "I have had the most severe cold I have ever had in all my life, and it has taken hold both of my strength and my looks." She is feeling better, she says, than when she wrote to him last on June 7, but is still "far from well." It was during this severe cold, which goes unmentioned in her journals, that Dorothy enjoyed her boat trip on Windermere. When she is not writing different versions of the same day in her journal, she is taking divergent roads through her journals and letters. In a letter of June 14 she writes, "The Lloyds called in a Chaise, luckily we did not see them; we are determined to cut them entirely as far as Will goes." The entry in her journal reads simply, *Lloyds called*.

Six days after laughing at the sage old man on the Windermere ferry, Dorothy writes a letter to Mary and Sara:

> It is four o'clock and I have scarcely been out of bed two hours today. I cannot well account for it, and as soon as I had got myself dressed I felt so sick that I must go to bed again. I drank three cups of tea and lay in a sort of pleasant half dose till I was roused by your sweet letter, my dear Mary.

After she signs off, William adds two separate postscripts, one to Mary and one to Sara, in which he corrects them for not taking seriously enough the sage old man he described in "The Leech Gatherer," a draft of which they were sent to read. To Sara he writes,

> I will explain to you in prose my feeling in writing that Poem, and then you will be better able to judge whether the fault be mine or yours or partly both . . . You speak of his speech as tedious: everything is tedious when one does not read with the feelings of the Author.

Dorothy then picks up her pen once more, only now her tone is entirely different. "When you happen to be displeased," she writes in her own postscript to Sara,

> with what you suppose to be the tendency or moral of any poem which William writes, ask yourself whether you have hit upon the real tendency and true moral, and above all never think that he writes for no reason but merely because a thing happened—and when you feel any poem of his to be tedious, ask yourself in what spirit it was written.

The letter, which was begun at four, is not finished until eight, by which point Dorothy not only is feeling better, as she notes in her journal, but has become a different person altogether. She signs off by stating that when she arrives at Gallow Hill before going to France this summer, she will "trust to Sara's wardrobe." Dorothy's critical opinion, so much her own five years before, is now, like her dresses, borrowed from others.

When "The Leech Gatherer" was published as "Resolution and Independence," the lines criticized by Sara and Mary had been either altered or removed. The Hutchinson sisters had, William conceded, been right.

By the middle of June they have agreed to leave for Gallow Hill "before the next full moon." William has decided which road they will follow, and Dorothy is insistent on where they will end up. All decisions about their destination have been made by her; they will not live in Gallow Hill or Greta Hall or anywhere other than Grasmere. Now that they have a matter of months before their paths possibly diverge, William and Dorothy find one they travel together again and again. On June 4 *we walked on our favourite path*; on June 5 they walk *late in the Evening upon our path*; on June 8 they walk *first on our own path*; on June 12 she and William walked *first on our own path but it was too wet there*, and on June 13 they walked *first on our own path . . . There was a shower which drove us into John's Grove before we had quitted our favourite path*; on June 14 she refers to *our own path*; on June 15 they walk *a long time in the Evening upon our favourite path*; on June 17 *in the evening walked on our favourite path*, and on June 20 *after tea we walked upon our own path for a long time.*

Richard, their eldest brother, had written to Dorothy in early June about her wishes respecting a settlement upon her after William's marriage. Dorothy replied that she wanted everything to stay the same for the rest of her life, a desire that would be satisfied by an annuity of £60, twice what she was getting from her brothers now. "With sixty pounds a year I should not fear any accidents or changes which might befal me. I cannot look forward to the time when, with my habits of frugality, I could not live comfortably on that sum." The money would enable her to pay her own way in the household, buy a few books, and take a journey now and then, things which, "though they do not come under the article of absolute necessaries, you will easily perceive that it is highly desirable that a person of my age and with my education should occasionally have in her power." Two weeks later a change befalls her that is enough to make anyone smile, but these days Dorothy is in two minds about change. On their father's death in 1783, he was owed £4,500 by his employer, Sir James Lowther, whose refusal to settle his employee's salary and expenses left the Wordsworth children destitute. On May 24, Lowther died, and his heir announced his determination to clear all debts. With this news, which Dorothy heard on June 18, she faced, for the first time in her life, financial independence. But when poverty has brought her all she wants, what could she do with riches? She writes to tell Coleridge, Mary, and Richard the news and by the evening has *a woful headache & was sick in stomach from agitation*. Unable to sleep that night, she joins William in the insomnia that has bedeviled him for the whole month.

The morning of June 19, Dorothy wakes to hear the swallows under her window. Changing bedrooms with William in preparation for his marriage has given her a new focus. The birds have been building their nest on her ledge for the last four days, and she likes to see *their soft white bellies close to the glass*. Watching them through the pane, she sees them as fish in a bowl, with *their forked fish-like tails* swimming *round & round & again they come*. As with the mothlike bird flying round and round on top of the crag that she records in the first entry of the current notebook, and the walking backward and forward on their path with William, Dorothy likes the certainty of a journey's return. One morning while William is at Eusemere she watches the swallows come and go for a full hour, and when their nest is broad enough, they spend both morning and evening sitting on the ledge, twittering to one another. Dorothy's entry for June 19 is also pure chatter, filling in the silence and stifling her shriek. She is nervous and verbose, noting less what she sees around her than what she hears, or can remember having heard before. She recounts an anecdote told by Coleridge about a Quaker woman who set up her own meeting for worship under the mountain Skiddaw; she considers "poor old Willy," whose grave she never passes by without thinking of him; she recalls that Miss Hudson of Workington had called the previous week and said how she loved flowers. When her day ends, she feels that there is shouting as well as singing in the air. *The shutters were closed, but I heard the Birds singing. There was our own Thrush shouting with an impatient shout—so it sounded to me.* The next day, reassured that her anticipated income will not free her from continuing life with William, she *talked sweetly together* with him about how to line their own nest when they disposed of their riches.

These days she can *settle to nothing*. Letters are continuously being sent between Grasmere, Gallow Hill, and Greta Hall; Dorothy never stops reading, writing, or going to the post. Between December 21, 1801, and July 1802, they have also received six letters from Annette, three of which William has answered and two of which have been answered by Dorothy. De Quincey later said that Dorothy wrote Wordsworth's love letters for him during his courtship with Mary, but she wrote his breakup letters to Annette as well. In July she is made *sleepless by letters*. While Molly Fisher helps to prepare the house for their departure, Dorothy reads *A Midsummer Night's Dream* and then begins *As You Like It*, which she takes under the wall near John's Grove, where she can face the sun as she reads. She grinds paint for coloring the walls and whitewashing the ceilings. She paces up and down. When William re-

Swallow, by Thomas Bewick

turns from his visit to Eusemere, where he has discussed with Thomas Clarkson his claim on the Lowther estate, he is *cool & fresh* and smells sweetly. In this sensuous mood, he and Dorothy talk until dawn: *A happy time.*

But on June 25 there is a disaster when the home that has been lovingly prepared for its new inhabitants collapses:

> *When I rose I went just before tea into the Garden, I looked up at my Swallow's nest & it was gone. It had fallen down. Poor little creatures they could not themselves be more distressed than I was I went upstairs to look at the Ruins. They lay in a large heap upon the window ledge; these Swallows had been ten days employed in building this nest, & it seemed to be almost finished—I had watched them early in the morning, in the day many & many a time & in the evenings when it was almost dark I had seen them sitting together side by side in their unfinished nest both morning & night.*

The next page in the journal is torn out, so we do not know the thoughts and events of June 26, 27, and 28. What was it that Dorothy—if it was Dorothy—wanted to forget during these days? The journal picks up again on June 29, and she goes out to *see if my swallows are on their nest. Yes! There they are side by side both looking down into the garden.* But soon a heavy rain beats down on all her hard work, making her roses look *fretted & battered,* spoiling the honeysuckle, and wrecking the peas. Dorothy begins the business of putting the garden back together, and on July 5 the swallows, too, have *completed their beautiful nest.*

The garden repaired, walls repainted, curtains washed and glazed, linen ironed, bedrooms swapped, trees nailed, coal and labor paid for, clothes mended, soil dug, and "The Leech Gatherer" completed and copied out *for Coleridge and for us*, William and Dorothy are ready to leave. On the evening of July 8 they collect letters from Mary, Sara, Coleridge, and Richard, which William suggests they take into the garden. Dorothy is for once *unwilling*, fearing that it will be too dark to see in order to read, or possibly that it will be just light enough to read what she fears to see, *but I saw well enough*. There was a bright moon behind them, and

> *William hurried me out in hopes that I should see her. We walked first to the top of the hill to see Rydale. It was dark & dull but our own vale was very solemn, the shape of helm crag was quite distinct, though black. We walked backwards & forwards on the White Moss path there was a sky-like white brightness on the Lake . . . Glowworms out, but not so numerous as last night—O beautiful place!*

This is Dorothy's final cry as she leaves the cottage on the morning of Friday, July 9; the horse is waiting, the packing done, her words are spreading and sliding over the page as she bids goodbye to her little domestic slip of mountain, journal in hand, ready to note what she sees on the road they will now be traveling:

> *Dear Mary William—the horse is come Friday morning, so I must give over. William is eating his Broth—I must prepare to go—the Swallows I must leave them the well the garden the Roses all—Dear creatures!! They sang last night after I was in bed—seemed to be singing to one another, just before they settled to rest for the night. Well I must go—Farewell.*

Chapter Six

FOR BETTER, FOR WORSE: HONEYMOON

Her bare
Feet seem to be saying,
We have come so far, it is over.

—SYLVIA PLATH, "Edge"

I will be with you on your wedding night.

—MARY SHELLEY, *Frankenstein*

"What, you are stepping westward?"
"Yea."

—WILLIAM WORDSWORTH, "Stepping Westward"

O*n Friday morning, July 9th William & I set forward to Keswick on our Road to Gallow Hill—We had a pleasant ride though the day was showery*. The last part of the Grasmere Journals contains three journeys. First the Wordsworths are stepping eastward to Gallow Hill; next they are traveling south from Gallow Hill to Calais; and finally there is the honeymoon, when Dorothy, William, and Mary will step westward together on the road from Gallow Hill back to Grasmere.

This is the first time that Dorothy has left the central Lake District since the day she arrived two and a half years before, and never has a journey been made with less haste. When she reaches the Hutchinson farm on July 16 and fills in her account of the miles she and William have just completed, her thick brown artist's notebook has become a travel journal. The elegiac tone of the summer months has been replaced by the conversational style of her letter writing. The Grasmere Journals are now a public document; Dorothy is writing a postcard to send to their friends, and her entries have changed from episodic to narrative. Between now and October, the sudden reports that have characterized her style—repetitive, forgetful, and cumulative in their effect—will disappear. Instead, her journal will be formally structured around a beginning, a middle, and an end, as Dorothy comments on the sights they see while she and William work their way down the country, across the Channel, up and down the sands at Calais, and back home again. She documents only their movements; the periods of rest, as at Greta Hall, Eusemere, Gallow Hill, London, and Calais, she passes over. Dorothy will not describe the experience of stillness again until the day of the wedding.

Dorothy's journal has for the first time found a narrative direction, but for William, who is stepping backward into his previous life before he can go forward into a future with Mary, the direction he is facing is not so straightforward.

After leaving Grasmere on the morning of July 9, William and Dorothy ride to Keswick, where they meet Coleridge; this will be the last encounter among the three until the wedding is over. They stay at Greta Hall for two nights; for Coleridge, it is the end of an era. *He was not well & we had a melancholy parting after having sate together in silence by the Road-side.* The end for William and

Dorothy has not come yet, but they continue the walk to Eusemere at a funereal pace, lingering and sauntering so that they can be together for as long as possible before arriving at the Clarksons'. After two nights at Eusemere, they are heading to Leeming Lane on the top of a coach.

> *We had a cheerful ride though cold, till we got on to Stanemore, & then a heavy shower came on, but we buttoned ourselves up, both together in the Guard's coat & we liked the hills & the Rain the better for bringing [us] so close to one another. I never rode more snugly.*

When the sun came out, *every building was bathed in golden light—The trees were more bright than earthly trees, & we saw round us miles beyond miles.* Gone is her detailing of the particular; Dorothy tends now to note the long-range views.

They stop for the night at Thirsk, where their landlady, hearing that her scruffy and weather-beaten guests are planning to walk rather than ride over the Hambledon Hills, *threw out some saucy words in our hearing.* The landlady's attitude, like that of Aunt Crackanthorpe when Dorothy left Halifax to embark on her "pilgrimage" with William seven years before, is a reminder of how offbeat and eccentric their walking appears to the outside world. The German minister Carl Moritz, who walked across England twenty years earlier in 1782, found that "a traveller on foot in this country seems to be considered as a sort of wild man, or an out-of-the-way being, who is stared at, pitied, suspected, and shunned by everybody that meets him." How much worse for the female foot traveler. In *Pride and Prejudice*, written at the same time as Dorothy's journals, even Elizabeth Bennet's relatively short walk to visit her sick sister Jane at Netherfield is a mark of her unconventionality: "That she should have walked three miles so early in the day, in such dirty weather, and by herself, was almost incredible to Mrs. Hurst and Miss Bingley, and Elizabeth was convinced that they held her in contempt for it." For Mr. Bingley's sisters, Elizabeth's walking revealed an "abominable sort of conceited independence, a most country town indifference to decorum."

Sitting footsore on the Hambledon Hills, William *took a Sheep for me, & then me for a Sheep*. They ate and drank at Rievaulx and looked at the ruins of the abbey. All around,

> *thrushes were singing, Cattle feeding among green grown hillocks about the Ruins. These hillocks were scattered over the grovelets of wild roses & other shrubs, & covered with wild flowers—I could have stayed in this solemn quiet spot till Evening without a thought of moving but William was waiting for me, so in a quarter of an hour I went away.*

After a night in a jasmine-covered inn at Helmsley, with a low, double-gavel-ended front, which delighted Dorothy, she and William began the final stage of the journey over Kirkby Moorside, where they were met by Sara and Mary seven miles from Gallow Hill.

"None of our Revolutionary heroes is worth a thing until he has been on a good walk," wrote Bruce Chatwin. Neither William nor Dorothy was revolutionary for long, but walks provided them both with the turning points of their lives, making each, in a small way, heroic. Dorothy's immense walks, her mud-encrusted skirts banging against her sturdy legs, her flimsy shoes, her neck and face often wet and cold, her eyes and ears alert to the beauty of every sight and sound, distinguish her from other women, but closest to her experience of walking is the dramatic description given by the American philosopher Henry Thoreau in 1851. Done properly, Thoreau suggests, walking—like writing—involves vision, risk, abandonment, conviction, total commitment to the journey the self will undergo, and the impact of that journey on the rest of your life:

> If you are ready to leave father and mother, and brother and sister, and wife and child and friends, and never see them again—if you have paid your debts, and made your will, and sealed all your affairs, and are a free man, then you are ready for a walk.

This was the fourth significant walk that Dorothy had undertaken with William, the first being their "pilgrimage" seven years before, the second their walk along the Wye when "Tintern Abbey" was composed, the third their "Long March" nearly three years earlier, when they first came to Dove Cottage from Sockburn. Dorothy had been preparing herself for the significance of this next walk throughout May and June. As she tramped over the Hambledon Hills toward Gallow Hill, she was leaving behind her a great deal more than she had when she had initially walked away from the life of a poor relation. Dorothy's threshold years began and ended with a good walk.

The ten days they spent at Gallow Hill, during which the wedding arrangements would have been finalized, are not mentioned in Dorothy's journals. She picks up her narrative once more to describe the journey she and William take by coach to London. They pass through the town of Beverley, which Dorothy thinks beautiful but whose minster, though *pretty* and *clean*, is *injured*

with Grecian Architecture. The country between Beverley and Hull is *very rich but miserably flat—brick houses, windmills, houses again—dull and endless*, and Hull itself is a *frightful, Dirty, brick housey tradesmanlike, rich, vulgar place*. They leave Hull in the rain on market day and spend the night at Lincoln, arriving in London on July 29. *Wm left me at the Inn—I went to bed &c &c &c—*. After various troubles and disasters they leave on the Dover coach. Dorothy's delight in departing the filthy, noisy capital is apparent in her only description of the city as they cross over Westminster Bridge on their way to the coast:

> *It was a beautiful morning. The City, St. pauls, with the River & a multitude of little Boats, made a most beautiful sight as we crossed Westminster Bridge. The houses were not overhung by their cloud of smoke & they were spread out endlessly, yet the sun shone so brightly with such a pure light that there was even something like the purity of one of nature's own grand Spectacles.*

William's sonnet "Earth has not anything to show more fair" is a product of the same experience, and very probably the same conversation.

On the road out of Canterbury they

> *came to a common, the race ground, an elevated plain, villages among trees in the bed of a valley at our right, & rising above this valley, green hills scattered over with wood—neat gentlemen's houses—one white house almost hid with green trees which we longed for & the parson's house as neat a place which would just have suited Coleridge. No doubt we might have found one for Tom Hutchinson & Sara and a good farm too.*

Within hours of being with the rejected Annette and Caroline, William and Dorothy consolidate their family group in England. They arrive in Dover when it is nearly dark and board the packet immediately, reaching Calais at four o'clock in the morning on the last day of July. There, at 8:00 a.m., *we found out Annette & C chez Madame Avril dans la Rue de la Tete d'or*. This, along with the fact that *we walked by the sea-shore almost every Evening with Annette & Caroline or Wm & I alone*, is all Dorothy writes about Annette and Caroline, who had traveled from Blois to meet them, Calais being a good halfway point for both parties. "Come, my love, my husband," Annette had written to William nine years earlier. "Receive the tender embraces of your wife, of your daughter . . . I love you forever." When he at last arrives, it is because he wants to marry someone else.

Dorothy never wrote about people, other than to record the information she extracted from vagrants, but there are two reasons why the meeting with Annette is not described. First, an account of Annette's character and the type of child William had sired would be inappropriate, given that she wants to share this section of the journal with others. Second, Dorothy wrote up their time in Calais not only after their return to England but after the wedding itself, and Mary was probably seated a stone's throw from the desk where Dorothy now sat, pen in hand. A line had been drawn under Annette.

By way of filling the huge lacunae in her narrative, Dorothy gives two pages to describing the sunsets over the sea. Her writing about France, unlike the journal she kept in Germany, is still aiming at sensibility, but there is nothing peculiar to Calais that catches her interest. Dorothy's vocabulary of melting skies, gem-like colors, reflections in the water, and shapes against the sky is recycled from her Grasmere days, only this time her sentences exist to supplement a silence rather than to describe a state of mind. Because she is working from memory two months later, she uses a pool of stock images. And this time she is writing for an audience; a separate, emended copy of the Calais section of her journal being made for her friends:

> *The Reflections in the water were more beautiful than the sky itself, purple waves brighter than precious stones for ever melting away upon the sands . . . One night, though, I shall never forget. The day had been very hot, and William and I walked alone together upon the pier. The sea was gloomy for there was a blackness over all the sky except when it was overspread with lightning which often revealed to us a distant vessel.*

There is no more frustrating silence in her journal than the one she keeps about their month in Calais. From the evidence of the Hamburg Journal we can surmise that, not liking towns or foreign ways, Dorothy would have been ill at ease in a foreign town, and she instantly notes that the room in which they were lodging was *badly furnished, & with a large store of bad smells & dirt in the yard, & all about*, although in the copy of the description she made for friends, she omitted the complaint about the dirt. The weather was very hot, and Dorothy had a cold (which she also fails to mention in her public version); no doubt her head ached a great deal of the time and her bowels were bad, nor would she be able to eat her customary gruel or drink the tea she so enjoyed. The temporary lull in the ten years of war between their two countries meant that France was now flooded with English tourists rushing across to Paris to see the looted treasures of the Louvre, and Calais was thus overrun with "Lords, lawyers, statesmen, squires of low degree," as Wordsworth put it. Dorothy loathed crowds. From the shore along which she and William walked every day, she could see *far off in the west the Coast of England like a cloud crested with Dover Castle.* They also saw, *as the Evening star sank down & the colours of the west faded away the two lights of England, lighted up by Englishmen in our Country, to warn vessels of rocks or sands.* Did they do anything for the month other than walk up and down the beach gazing longingly toward the horizon? Wordsworth wrote a good deal, but while his Calais sonnets tell us he was disappointed in his revolutionary hopes, they leave us none the wiser about how he felt toward his former lover and their daughter. Apart from a remark in "It is a beauteous evening, calm and free" about Caroline's being less receptive to her environment than either himself or Dorothy—"If thou appear untouched by solemn thought, / Thy nature is not therefore less divine"—we have no idea whether she proved a disappointment to her father or a pleasure.

Dorothy's own position in relation to Annette was a curious one. It was she, rather than Mary, who had usurped her brother's mistress; it was Dorothy who had embraced William when he returned to England, Dorothy with whom he had raised a child at Racedown, Dorothy with whom he shared a home, who read him to sleep, and who *petted him on the carpet* when he felt unwell. It was Dorothy who had mourned him when he went to Gallow Hill, waiting up at night for the sound of his step on the path, and longed for his letters. Dorothy now knew William better than Annette had done, but this had not always been the case. When William fell in love with Annette, he hardly knew Dorothy at all; he hardly knew himself. He was still a chrysalis. Getting to know Dorothy had been a process of self-discovery and self-fulfillment. When William now faced Annette, he saw a stranger in a strange country with a daughter who was also strange to him, but when Dorothy faced her, she must have known that, had Annette and

Caroline been part of William's life for the last ten years, her own life would have amounted to nothing. There would have been no Coleridge, no Germany, no part in William's poetic imagination, none of the intimacy she had relished with her brother, no writing of her own. She would have been an aunt to Caroline and a sister-in-law to Annette instead of having been William's great love.

However, there is no reason to think that the visit was not a success, at least for Dorothy. The length of their stay confirms it, as does Dorothy's comment on their return at the end of the month that they *sat upon the Dover Cliffs & looked upon France with many a melancholy & tender thought*. It was Wordsworth and not she who said on their return that he had never before been so glad to see England again. What happened in Calais seems to be that while William and Annette recognized that their relationship had run its proper course, Dorothy and Annette had formed an intimacy. Dorothy liked and identified with Annette; it was she who kept in touch with her in years to come, she who kept his first love present in William's life. And there was a great deal for her to like in Madame Williams, as Annette—who would never marry—called herself. The sixth and youngest child of the surgeon of the Hôtel Dieu at Blois, Annette, when she met Wordsworth, was twenty-five and generally described as "vivacious," a term that doesn't quite get her combination of heady romanticism with die-hard commitment to the Catholic and Royalist cause. Since William had left France, Annette had become an active counter-revolutionary, a Scarlet Pimpernel of sorts who had successively braved the secret police of the Terror, the Directoire, and Napoleon. She had hidden priests and Royalist refugees in her house, risking her life over and over again to save the lives of others, arranged a prison rescue by rope ladder, and become the subject of a police record while single-handedly raising an illegitimate daughter and posing as a widow. Annette was living through a war that was changing the face of civilization, against which a disappointment in love was like the spilling of a jug of milk.

She was now thirty-six and William thirty-two, but the fact that he looked so much older must have come as a shock to Annette. Their relationship had been explosive and brief, and from her letters—many of which Wordsworth did not receive—it seems that, like most lovers, their principal interest had been the effect they had on each other. She probably knew nothing about his desire to be a poet; she certainly never mentions his ambition. Annette was absorbed in her own emotions; she provided the lover's discourse, and he consumed it. William, while caught up in the political and sexual whirlwind of his time in France, nonetheless left the country without marrying his pregnant lover, nor knowing when or how he would see her again. His excuse for the rapid departure was lack of funds, but of what concern is money to someone who is both in love and involved in a major revolution? It seems an oddly conventional attitude to take in the midst of such turmoil. Wordsworth was passionate, but not passionate enough; a different man might have risked more, a different man would have dealt with the problem of his poverty only after he had secured the hand of the woman he wanted and ensured the legitimacy of his unborn child. As for Wordsworth's disapproving and despairing uncles, they would have found his return to England with a pregnant French Catholic wife less antagonizing than his abandonment of a pregnant French Catholic mistress. In his relationship with Annette, as in all his relationships, Wordsworth provided the caution and she the impulsiveness. He liked in her what he liked in Coleridge and Dorothy: Annette was sensuous, voluble, unstoppable in the flow of her feelings and thoughts.

"My distress would be lessened were we married," she wrote in a typical flow of free association,

> yet I regard it as almost impossible that you should risk yourself, if we should have war. You might be taken prisoner. But where do my wishes lead me? I speak as though the instant of my happiness were at hand. Write and tell me what you think, and do your very utmost to hasten your daughter's happiness and mine, but only if there is not the slightest risk to be run,—but I think the war will not last long. I should wish our two nations to be [reconciled]. That is one of my most earnest wishes. But above all, find out some way by which we can write to each other in case the correspondence between the two kingdoms were stopped.

For quite some time Annette continued to believe that Wordsworth would one day return to her. In another letter she describes to him how she would soon be saying to their daughter how " 'in a month, in a fortnight, in a week, you are going to see the most beloved of men, the most tender of men.' Then my Caroline's heart will be moved, she will feel her first emotion and it will be of love for her father." This emotional pitch was maintained in her correspondence with Dorothy as well:

> His image follows me everywhere; often when I am alone in my room with his letters I think he has entered . . . Ah my dear sister this is my continual state; emerging from my mistake as from a dream I see him

> not, the father of my child; he is very far from me. This scene is often repeated and throws me into extreme melancholy.

Dorothy not only wrote her brother's love letters but also received them.

A month of pacing the Calais sands looking at the sky, and William and Dorothy returned to England. William would meet Annette twice more in his life, and never on his own. As a souvenir of his holiday, he bought a gold wedding ring to give to Mary.

Dorothy was sick all the way back on the packet, and they arrived in Dover at one in the morning on August 30, mounting the coach to London the following afternoon. The journey *was misty & we could see nothing*. Dorothy also says nothing about their stay, which ended up being for the best part of September, extended so that she and William could enjoy the company of John, whose ship had returned from China. "We cannot find it in our hearts to leave him till we have been a few days together," Dorothy told Mary, who was waiting for their arrival. With Christopher down from Cambridge and Richard a London lawyer, the Wordsworth siblings were together again for the first time in years. William and Dorothy lodged in Inner Temple, had dinner with Charles and Mary Lamb, visited Bartholomew Fair, and traveled to Windsor to see their aunt and uncle Cookson, Dorothy's first encounter with them since absconding from Forncett eight years earlier. On the coach back into London she fell ill, delaying their departure to Yorkshire by another week.

In her journal, Dorothy covers their time in London and their journey back to Gallow Hill in one swift sentence: *We stayed in London till Wednesday the 22nd September, & arrived at Gallow*

Hill on Friday 24th September. Having recovered her health sufficiently to travel, she then caught a violent cold on the coach and arrived at Gallow Hill looking thin and ill; Mary on the other hand, who met them in the avenue, was *fat & well. The garden looked gay with astors & sweet peas—I looked at everything with tranquillity & happiness but I was ill both on Saturday & Sunday & continued to be poorly most of the time of our stay.* Jack and George Hutchinson, Mary's brothers, arrived on October 1, and on October 3 Sara helped Mary with her packing.

Then, *on Monday 4th October 1802, my Brother William was married to Mary Hutchinson.* The travel journal has come to a temporary close.

Dorothy begins her account of the morning of the wedding with the crisp forensic objectivity that has by now become the signature of her journal writing, reporting the day, date, and year of this climactic event as if she were informing the Births, Marriages, and Deaths column of the local paper. Only once the scene is securely framed by the solidity of fact does she cautiously introduce herself, measuring, as she does throughout the journal, her own fragility against external reality. *I slept a good deal of the night & rose fresh & well in the morning—at a little after 8 o'clock I saw them go down the avenue towards the Church.* It is surprising that she slept at all, given what the day holds in store, and she seems surprised herself. After she has described the party leaving for the church, which she must have seen from the upstairs bedroom window, she describes the dawn ceremony that took place between brother and sister before they "parted": *I gave him the wedding ring—with how deep a blessing! I took it from my forefinger*

and rose fresh & well in the morning.
at a little after 8 o'clock I saw them
go down the avenue towards the
Church. William had parted from
me up stairs.

= When they were absent
my dear little Sara prepared the
breakfast. I kept myself as quiet
as I could, but when I saw
the two men running up the
walk, coming to tell us it
was over, I could stand it no longer
& threw myself on the bed where I
lay in stillness, neither hearing or
seeing any thing till Sara came
up stairs to me & said "they are
coming." This forced me from the
bed where I lay & I moved I knew
not how straight forward

Entry for October 4, 1802, in the Grasmere Journals

where I had worn it the whole of the night before—he slipped it again onto my finger & blessed me fervently.

These lines should have been read by no one. The two sentences were later heavily scored out in black ink and not deciphered until the Wordsworth scholar Helen Darbishire, using infrared light, transcribed the Grasmere Journals for the first complete edition, published by World's Classics in 1958. It is a curious position for us to be in, snooping around in someone else's room, pulling off the panels to see what more is hidden. Our voyeurism has about it an almost Jamesian quality. Henry James's novels often climax at moments when a sexual intimacy, previously unrecognized by the observer, is revealed, such as when Isabel Archer, in *The Portrait of a Lady,* catches her husband, Osmond, with Madame Merle, "musing, face to face with the freedom of old friends who sometimes exchange ideas without uttering them," or when Maggie Verver, in *The Golden Bowl,* sees her husband standing together with her friend Charlotte on the balcony, or when Strether, in *The Ambassadors,* spies Chad and Madame de Vionnet alone in the boat. In a flash, the Jamesian protagonist recognizes everything that he or she has spent months trying hard not to see. They have been fooled, duped; believing they knew everything, they now realize they have understood nothing. Dorothy's reader is like James's innocent and excluded American: however much we thought we understood of the unusual relationship between the Wordsworths, however much we had imbibed of their intimacy from the previous two and a half years of the Grasmere Journals, we were not prepared to witness a scene like this.

Dorothy has been wearing the wedding ring all night. Perhaps William ceremonially placed it on her finger before she went to bed; it seems possible, given the significance of their ceremony now, and the reassurance of the gesture may account for her having slept during the night. Perhaps he gave it to her in Calais to ensure he did not lose it, and she has been wearing it ever since. Either way, alone together in her room, she removes the ring and gives it to him; he returns it to her finger and *blessed me fervently*. It is this vital phrase, with its surprising juxtaposition of sanctification with heat and passion, and the question it raises of what exactly a "blessing" is in this context and what it would be like if it were done with fervor, that has most alarmed and excited Dorothy Wordsworth's various readers, and yet it seems that Helen Darbishire misread these vital words, a misreading maintained by Wordsworth's biographer Mary Moorman, who edited the revised 1971 edition of the journals. These words, as Pamela Woof writes, "have been taken as confirmation of incestuous feelings between Wordsworth and his sister." Woof, in the latest edition of the Grasmere Journals (2002), suggests that Dorothy in fact wrote, *as I blessed the ring softly*, which makes the exchange rather less charged, reading instead: *he slipped it again onto my finger as I blessed the ring softly*. Examining the manuscript in the Wordsworth Museum, I feel that Pamela Woof is clearly right; Darbishire's error seems born not only from the difficulty of reading the script beneath the heavy attempts to blot it out but also from the fervency of the proceedings. She instinctively associated Dorothy with fervor; it is less an error in transcription than a Freudian slip, what is going on in the bedroom being more *fervent* than *soft*. Quite possibly, Darbishire had De Quincey's essay from *Tait's* in the back of her mind; in his own descriptions of Dorothy, De Quincey refers to her fervency on three separate occasions, speaking twice of her "fervid heart" and once of the way in which her "fervent" feelings robbed her of the dignity that could be found in Mary, who had no fervor about her. However, Woof's rereading of the manuscript does not completely detract from what is fervent in the passage or alter the oddness of the private ritual as Dorothy describes it. Whether William blessed her "fervently" or she blessed the ring "softly," Dorothy at no point records his then *removing* the ring once more. According to her journal, the ring remains on Dorothy's finger forever; we have to assume that Wordsworth then took it off in order to slip it onto Mary's own finger later that morning.

Who scored out the sentence, and why? It could have been Dorothy herself, not wanting Mary to know about the earlier exchange of the ring that she was now wearing; it could have been Wordsworth, unhappy at the thought of Mary knowing that the ring meant for her had been shared with Dorothy; it could have been either Gordon Wordsworth, the poet's grandson who had the family papers in his keeping, or Christopher Wordsworth, the poet's literary executor and first biographer, who felt sufficiently disturbed by the intimacy described by Dorothy to edit it out for future readers. But even now that the lines have been deciphered—albeit until recently incorrectly—and included in modern editions of the journals, scholars continue to find them hard to read, and the scene they describe has taken on the qualities of a fairground mirror among biographers, who see in it either more than is there or less. Kenneth Johnston, in *The Hidden Wordsworth*, has Dorothy dressed for some reason in "bridal white," as though she were Bertha Mason in *Jane Eyre*, trying on the veil of the woman her bigamous husband is about to marry. Juliet Barker, in *Wordsworth: A Life,* describes the ceremony in a single sentence as "an oddly repellent gesture" and says no more about it, as though what was exchanged between brother and sister were of no great significance. John Worthen, in *The Gang: Coleridge, the Hutchinsons, and the Wordsworths in 1802*, calls it "an act of the sheerest love and intimacy" and says that he can find "no evidence" to support the assertion that Dorothy "was too distraught to attend" the wedding, echoing Marianne Kirlew, who wrote of Dorothy in her 1905 book, *Famous Sisters of Great Men*, that on the morning of the wedding "there is no trace of bitterness or undue depression on being thus supplanted." In *Dorothy Wordsworth*, Robert Gittings and Jo Manton say of her journal entry, "No other words could match the transparent truthfulness of this account," and yet for many readers Dorothy's account of the wedding morning is nothing if not elliptical and opaque.

Some biographers pass by the bedroom door without comment, thinking it rude to peep, while others respond to what they see through the keyhole as though it were usual for a sister to wear and bless her brother's wedding ring before falling into a trance. Neither Elizabeth Gunn in *A Passion for the Particular* nor Kathleen Jones in *A Passionate Sisterhood: The Sisters, Wives, and Daughters of the Lake Poets*, both of which give full and sympathetic portraits of Dorothy, has anything to say about her particular passion on the wedding morning, other than to briefly note her unhappiness. What the passage in the journal suggests about the relationship between Dorothy and William is simply too demanding, or too embarrassing, to deal with. These biographers are positioned in relation to their story like Nelly Dean, the toneless narrator of the events that compose *Wuthering Heights*. Kittens are being hung on the backs of chairs, wrists of frozen ghosts are being rubbed against broken glass, and domestic life is generally performed at operatic levels, but Nelly Dean describes the goings-on at the Heights as though it were a suburban bridge party. The conventionality of her narrative voice elides the antisocial feelings that exist between Cathy and Heathcliff in much the same way that many of those who write about Dorothy blithely overlook the inconvenient nature of her love for William.

While Sara Hutchinson prepares the wedding breakfast, Dorothy tries to contain herself upstairs, or, as she puts it, to keep *[her]self as quiet* as she can. She has been up in the bedroom since the wedding party left at a little after eight o'clock. The church in Brompton is a mile from the farm, so, allowing for the walk there and back and a perfunctory marriage ceremony in the middle, she has been as quiet as she can for more than an hour. It is only when she looks out the window and sees *the two men running up the walk, coming to tell us it was over,* that she can *stand it no longer,* and throws herself onto the bed, where she lies *in stillness, neither hearing or seeing anything.* Of all her experiences this morning, Dorothy's glance down the walk is the most shattering. She always measures her own frailty of self against the solid reality of what she sees, she always describes what she sees rather than what she feels, but this look from the bedroom window is the only instance in her journal where seeing becomes a violent rather than a reassuring activity. Dorothy trusts the evidence of her eyes, and what she sees on the avenue—the bride and groom returning as a couple—confirms how vitally self-deceived she has been to believe that William's marriage would include her.

So what is it specifically that for Dorothy is *over*? The spareness of her prose we recognize, as we do her refusal to examine her own responses. But Dorothy's celebrated sensibility now becomes a symptom, and she is overcome by what William calls the "spontaneous overflow of powerful feelings." Throwing herself on the bed, she disengages from the natural world, from outward forms, from her minute observations, from the materiality of domestic life, and, most of all, from William himself. Without these forms to fasten onto, she finds herself sinking down, down. Dorothy Wordsworth, who is generally represented as lacking an unconscious life, can be seen here passing out under its weight.

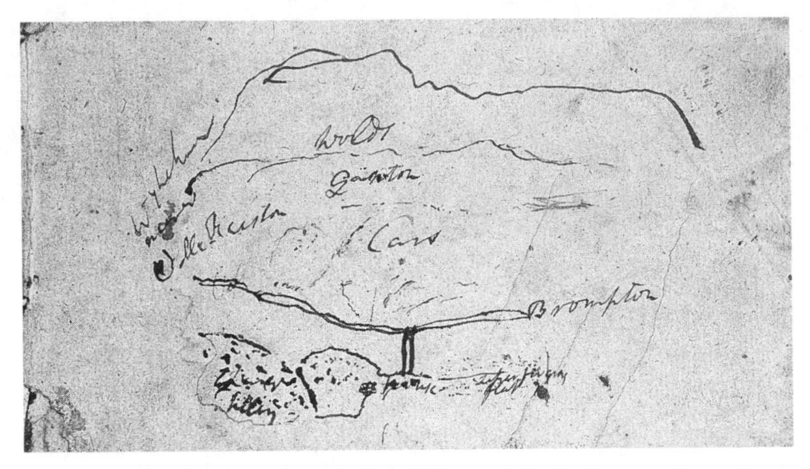

The road to Brompton from Gallow Hill, sketch in the Grasmere Journals

Suddenly—for she is always swift to respond—her world is as still as the seas in which the Ancient Mariner is mired, and she slips into a state of stillness, blindness, and deafness. Her "strange fits of passion" are an example of one of those symbolic moments that punctuate Dorothy's journals and impress them with new dimensions, like her night skies, her lone flowers, William's apple core, and the destruction of the swallows' nest. Her eyes may be open as she lies in stillness on the bed, but they are blank. It is a moment of terror; separation from William, she says, has the power to extinguish her being. Without her eyes and ears she has been reduced to nothingness. Is this the quintessential expression of her Romanticism, aligning her with other visionaries who expire from excessive emotion? "I listen, I call, I cannot even hear my voice," says the French Romantic Senancour's Oberman, "and I am left in an intolerable emptiness, alone, lost, uncertain, borne down by inquietude and astonishment, amidst errant shadows, in intangible and silent space." Alternatively, her trance could be the sign of a migraine, a hysterical seizure, even an orgasm, or what Oliver Sacks calls "vegetative retreat," whereby we protect ourselves from outside threat by passing into a deathlike state; in the animal world possums "play possum" and hedgehogs curl up. It is "an entirely sensible response by any creature to a threat which stumps it," writes the naturalist Richard Mabey, "a kind of ur-depression."

She can have remained like this on the bed only for a minute or two—the wedding party is nearly at the house—but in her account, which begins by noting the hour that the bride and groom left for the church, time now stops, all sounds and actions stop, Dorothy Wordsworth ceases to be. Time is also rushing backward: there is a sense of déjà vu to what she describes. Dorothy has played dead before, in trenches on the Grasmere hills, where she could neither hear nor see; she has lain in stillness on her bed many, many times, neither hearing nor seeing, immobilized by a headache. She has experimented with trances on the Quantocks, she has gazed at the sky until she can no longer hear or see, and night after night, like mandragora, she has soothed William into a stillness where he can neither hear nor see. But it is none of these scenes we recognize when Dorothy lies on the bed at Gallow Hill on the morning of the wedding. The uncanny sense of having been here before can be traced back not to actions but to words. It is to the second verse of the strangest of Wordsworth's Lucy poems that Dorothy returns, the lyric described by Coleridge as an "epitaph," possibly written when the poet "fancied the moment when his sister might die."

> A slumber did my spirit seal;
> I had no human fears:
> She seemed a thing that could not feel
> The touch of earthly years.

> No motion has she now, no force;
> She neither hears nor sees;
> Rolled round in earth's diurnal course,
> With rocks, and stones, and trees.

It is over. No motion has she now, no force; she neither hears nor sees.

The language Dorothy uses in her journals is always precise. Increasingly, her sentences are exercises in verbal exactitude, and so it is surely no accident that the moment she feels the exclusivity and intensity of her relationship with William to be over, she repeats lines of his written when the exclusivity and intensity of their relationship were just beginning, when they were living entirely alone in Germany, shut off from the rest of the world. Dorothy's description of herself on the bed at Gallow Hill echoes Wordsworth's description of the dead girl even down to the peculiar syntax; it would be more idiomatic for him to say not "neither hears nor sees" but "neither sees nor hears," and likewise for Dorothy to say "neither seeing or hearing" rather than "neither hearing or seeing." What she implies by returning at this point in her journal to the language and imagery of "A slumber" is not simply that she now resembles the beloved Lucy but that there can be no separation between her brother and herself. She has folded herself up as the petals of a rose close when dusk settles, and placed herself back in William's imagination: he is writing her lines.

Then, just as suddenly, the volume comes back on, shapes reform, and action begins again. Sara Hutchinson can be heard to say *they are coming*, which forces Dorothy from the bed. But when she rises, she is no longer a part of her body: *I moved I knew not how straight forward, faster than my strength could carry me*, across the room, down the stairs, through the hall, out the door, and onto William's breast. *He & John Hutchinson led me to the house & there I stayed to welcome my dear Mary.*

While Dorothy was lying on the bed and William was walking back from the church, those around the country who were eating their breakfast with the *Morning Post* spread out on the table were reading Coleridge's new poem: "My genial spirits fail," he wrote for the day of his friends' wedding, "And what can these avail / To lift the smothering weight from off my breast?" Coleridge's "Letter to Sara Hutchinson," which, when he had repeated it at Dove Cottage on April 21, had put Dorothy in *miserable spirits*, now appeared, with a few changes, in the newspaper on October 4. Renamed "Dejection: An Ode," the private letter to Sara had become a public letter addressed to "Edmund," Coleridge's intimate name for Wordsworth. William, rather than Sara, is currently the cause of his dejection. It was an unconventional wedding present, but apart from a dress given to Mary by John Wordsworth and a set of forks sent to Dorothy on behalf of William from an American relation, it is the only gift the couple received. "Dejection: An Ode" was a less conventional gift still for Coleridge to present to Sarah, his wife— October 4 being the seventh anniversary of their own marriage. Whom did Coleridge imagine to be the ode's ideal reader on this special day? Was it Sarah, Sara, Dorothy, or Wordsworth to whom he addressed the lines that compound weddings with funerals, "And in *our* life alone does Nature live— / Our's is her Wedding-garment, our's her Shroud!"?

Did Wordsworth and Mary hope, in choosing to marry on the anniversary of Coleridge's wedding, that their friend might feel included in their union? And was it a coincidence that "Dejection: An Ode," written in reply to Wordsworth's joyful "Ode: Intimations of Immortality," should appear today, to remind the groom of how excluded Coleridge actually felt from the celebratory mood? It is hard not to see the poem's appearance on the morning of Wordsworth's wedding as ironic on Coleridge's part; the feelings he expressed were so far away from anything experienced by Wordsworth, particularly on the day of his marriage, that the ode takes on an air of self-parody. Perhaps Wordsworth smiled thinly at his friend's message. For Dorothy, who knew exactly how Coleridge felt and was entirely in tune with the mood of his verse, the irony would be missed.

None of Wordsworth's friends or family attended the wedding. But through the publication of his ode, Coleridge became like his Ancient Mariner, standing outside the door while the wedding feast goes on within, suspending whomever he can with his harrowing tale. Weddings were much on his mind this month, and following the appearance of "Dejection: An Ode," Coleridge wrote the first of five articles for the *Morning Post* about what he called "The Romantic Marriage" that had taken place in the Lake District two days before the markedly unromantic marriage between Wordsworth and Mary. To her parents' delight, Mary Robinson, the daughter of an innkeeper in Buttermere, married a certain Colonel Alexander Hope, who described himself as MP for Linlithgow and brother to the Earl of Hopetoun. It soon became apparent that the "colonel" was a bankrupt, a fraud, and a confidence trickster who had a wife already. The "Maid of Buttermere," as Mary Robinson became known, was catapulted to fame: romantic love had been her undoing, and her seducer was sentenced to hang. It was on her marriage that Coleridge focused during the autumn, with its passion, impulsiveness, failed expectations, and tragic end, rather than the slow-burning, steady, and monogamous love between Wordsworth and Mary.

On October 6 the *Morning Post* carried another of Coleridge's odes, "An Ode to the Rain." Subtitled "Composed before daylight, on the morning appointed for the departure of a very worthy, but not very pleasant visitor, whom it was feared the rain might detain," the ode had been written the previous year and celebrated the privileged time Coleridge spent alone with Dorothy and William at Dove Cottage. "We three dear friends! In truth, we groan / Impatiently to be alone. / We three, you mark! And not one more!" Was it a coincidence that the poem appeared on the very day that Mary was due to arrive at the cottage, making it impossible for the three dear friends ever to be alone together again?

The *Morning Post* carried an entire range of Coleridge's responses to Wordsworth's marriage, from dejection, displacement, and irony, to aggression and black comedy. On October 9, a wedding announcement appeared in the paper:

> Monday last, W WORDSWORTH, Esq. was married to Miss HUTCHINSON, of Wykeham, near Scarborough, and proceeded immediately, with his wife and his sister, for his charming cottage in the little Paradise-vale of Grasmere. His neighbour, Mr. COLERIDGE, resides in the Vale of Keswick, 13 miles from Grasmere. His house (situated on a low hill at the foot of Skiddaw, with the Derwent Lake in front, and the romantic River Greta winding round the hill) commands, perhaps, the most various and interesting prospects of any house in the island. It is a perfect *panorama* of

> that wonderful vale, with its two lakes, and its complete circle, or rather ellipse, of mountains.

The announcement is written in the language of a tourist guide, and the subject becomes the excellent view from Coleridge's house rather than a congratulations to the bride and groom. The Wordsworths believed the spoof was the idea of Daniel Stuart, the *Post*'s editor, but it must have been the work of Coleridge as well, although he never owned up to it. He alone would have known about the honeymoon journey back to Grasmere and the paradisical cottage that awaited them there; the whole piece has about it the kind of parodic humor that Wordsworth usually enjoyed in his friend. Dorothy, always nervous around jokes, was still fuming at Stuart years later—"Upon my Brother's marriage he inserted in the Morning Post the most ridiculous paragraph that ever was penned"—but it would be nice to think that Mary, like John, smiled behind her hand. "It is not quite so bad as I thought it would have been from what you said," was John's cautious reply to Dorothy's outrage.

As soon as we had breakfasted we departed. It is without breaking into a new paragraph that Dorothy picks up her travel journal once more, having completed in the previous sentence her description of the morning of the wedding. They will cover nearly sixty miles by post chaise today, and they leave Gallow Hill in the rain; Mary bids goodbye to her brothers and sisters and also, Dorothy notes, to her home, the house in which Dorothy had refused to live.

This is a journey Dorothy has been thinking about. "My dear

Jane," she wrote to her friend five days earlier, "if this letter reaches you before next Monday you will think of me, travelling towards our own dear Grasmere with my most beloved Brother and his Wife." She then explains to Jane how complex her feelings will be:

> I have long loved Mary Hutchinson as a Sister, and she is equally attached to me this being so, you will guess that I look forward with perfect happiness to this Connection between us, but, happy as I am, I half dread that concentration of all tender feelings, past, present, and future which will come upon me on the wedding morning. There never lived on earth a better woman than Mary H and I have no doubt but that she is in every respect formed to make an excellent wife to my Brother, and I seem to myself to have scarcely any thing left to wish for but that the wedding was over, and we had reached our home once again.

Nothing particular occurred till we reached Kirby, Dorothy notes. They *had sunshine & showers, pleasant talk, love & chearfulness.* This is the mood she determines on for the next two days. Mary is now *dear Mary,* and Dorothy describes nothing but pleasure. It is as if her earlier response had never happened, and yet the fact that she writes down what she went through at all that morning suggests that she wants William to know what she suffered while he was binding himself to Mary for life. But, so far as the journal is concerned, not only is the wedding at last over, *it* more generally is *over.* Dorothy's responses will not be revealed in such a way again.

Mary and William went out of their way to include her in their conversations and observations and to suppress their feelings for one another; Dorothy was treated as a guest of honor, sitting between the newlyweds in the coach. When they reached Kirkby, they sauntered about the graveyard reading the gravestones, and as ever Dorothy recorded the stories that were closest to home. There was one gravestone in memory of five children, the same number as in her own family,

> *who had all died within 5 years, & the longest lived had only lived 4 years. There was another Stone erected to the memory of an unfortunate woman (as we supposed, by a stranger). The verses engraved upon it expressed that she had been neglected by her Relations & counselled the Readers of those words to look within & recollect their own frailties.*

Dorothy's taking note of the moral in her journal would serve as a timely reminder to William.

The honeymoon takes them back through Helmsley, where they stop to rest at the same neat little jasmine-covered inn where Dorothy and William had slept the night before reaching Gallow Hill in July; seeing it once more, Dorothy says her *heart danced*. It is an unconvincing expression, the kind of platitude her writing more usually avoids. The women warm themselves by the kitchen fire and walk in the garden, looking up at Helmsley Castle, and Dorothy then *prevail[s]* upon William to walk around the ruins with her while Mary stays behind. This is probably the first time that she and William have been alone together since he *blessed* her that morning. What do they talk about? Does she tell him how much she suffered while he was at the church? Does he reassure her that nothing will change? *The sun shone, it was very warm & pleasant.*

They continue their journey over the Hambledon Hills, past

Rievaulx Abbey, and on to Thirsk, where they stop for a break at the same inn where the landlady had been so rude to them before, but today she doesn't recognize *the despised foot travellers.* They travel on into the night, breaking the journey at Leeming Lane at eleven in order to sleep. *I am always sorry to get out of a chaise when it is night,* Dorothy commented, her reluctance to deal with the issue of the wedding night perhaps not shared by her travel companions, who have been in her company all day.

William's first night with Mary was inauspicious. *The people of the house were going to bed & we were not very well treated though we got a hot supper.* What were the sleeping arrangements? How many rooms did they have in the inn? Did Dorothy and Mary share a bed? Did all three share a room? Did Dorothy insist on William and Mary being alone together, and they refuse out of regard for her sensitivity? Nothing is mentioned in the journal. The party then sets off again at eight-thirty on *a cheerful sunny morning.* William has been married for twenty-four hours. They cross the Yorkshire Dales; William writes a sonnet about Mary, Queen of Scots, when they pass the castle in which she had been imprisoned. It is not a good poem, and he discards it. As the coach rattles along, he falls *asleep, lying upon my breast & I upon Mary. I lay motionless for a long time, but I was at last obliged to move.* The scene recalls not only Dorothy's state the previous morning but also Coleridge's heartbreaking picture of himself, Sara, and Mary lying on the sofa at Gallow Hill, Sara's eyelashes playing against his cheek.

They pass through Wensley, with Dorothy feeling increasingly unwell, and stop for the night in Hawes. The second night of the honeymoon was more hospitable than the first. *Mary & I got tea, & William had a partridge & mutton chops & tarts for his supper. Mary sate down with him. We had also a shilling's worth of negus &*

Mary made me some Broth for all which supper we were only charged 2/–. But Dorothy vomited and fell into a deep sleep. We can assume she had a migraine. They set off once again at six o'clock the next morning, this time in the rain. They will be home by evening.

The significance of the honeymoon for Dorothy as she travels into *the western sky* is not that she is returning home but that she is retracing her steps. *Every foot of the Road was itself interesting to us, for we had travelled along it on foot Wm & I when we went to fetch our dear Mary.* Her journal had taken a forward thrust during their outward journey, and it was William who was going backward into his past. It is now William who is stepping into the sunset and Dorothy who has lost direction, looking behind her as she goes. She writes up the honeymoon as though she were feeling her way back into herself. Sometimes, after an enormous change has taken place, it is comforting to know that the world is still the same; matching her experience of life after the wedding with life before the wedding gives her solace, and Dorothy describes again and again the experience of returning to places she has shared with William. Nostalgia is the only emotion she allows herself during this highly emotional journey:

> *I was pleased to see again that little path which we had walked upon the gate I had climbed over, & the Road down which we had seen the two little Boys drag a log of wood . . . We recognised the Cottages, houses, & the little valleys as we went along . . . When we went to GH I had walked down this valley alone. Wm followed me.*

But she also describes new sights with enthusiasm, hearing and seeing with greater clarity than when they were traveling east:

> *As we descended the hill there was no distinct view, but of a great space, only near us, we saw the wild & (as people say) bottomless Tarn in the hollow at the side of the hill. It seemed to be made visible to us only by its own light, for all the hill about us was dark. Before we reached Thirsk we saw a light before us which we at first thought was the moon, then Lime kilns, but when we drove into the market place it proved a large Bonfire with Lads dancing round it, which is a sight I dearly love.*

At Wensley, the journey takes on added value when William and Dorothy start to follow the route they took three years before, when they first came to Grasmere, leaving Mary behind at Sockburn:

> *My heart was melted away with dear recollections, the Bridge, the little water spout the steep hill the Church—They are among the most vivid of my own inner visions, for they were the first objects that I saw after we were left to ourselves, & had turned our whole hearts to Grasmere as a home in which we were to rest.*

Garsdale, through which they also pass, is *a dear place to William & me. We noted well the publick-house (Garsdale Hall) where we had baited & drunk our pint of ale, & afterwards the mountain which had been adorned by Jupiter in his glory when we were here before.* When they get to Sedbergh, they stay in the same room where they had spent an evening together on that wonderful first journey. They reach Staveley: *I am always glad to see Stavely it is a place I dearly love to think of—the first mountain village that I came to with Wm when we first began our pilgrimage together.* At Windermere they wait in the rain to change horses. From here it is just a few more miles, and the wedding party arrives back at Dove Cottage, after two days of continuous travel, *at about 6 o'clock on Wednesday Evening, the 6th of October 1802. Molly was overjoyed to see us,—for my part I cannot describe what I felt, & our dear Mary's feelings would I dare say not be easy to speak of.* They inspect the garden by candlelight, and Dorothy gasps at the growth of everything she had left behind.

William and Mary prepare to spend their first night together in Dove Cottage and probably their first moments alone as a married couple, and Dorothy takes herself upstairs to her new bedroom. Her swallows, which she never mentions again, will have now left the nest they so painstakingly prepared and begun their journey south, to winter in Africa.

Mary becomes pregnant immediately.

The next day Dorothy and Mary unpack, and on October 8 they bake bread and walk, *first upon the Hill side, & then in John's Grove, then in view of Rydale*. It is, Dorothy says, *the first walk that I had taken with my sister.* She is alert to first times and last times and always sure to record them. These early days with Mary will be filled with first times as Dorothy tests the waters, seeing how far the newness of everything erases the significance of the old.

On October 9 her journal resumes its daily entries. Having spent a good while setting down the story of the summer journey in a form in which it can—mostly—be read by others, Dorothy is now living back in the present tense. Her entries for the next two days are uninformative: *Saturday 9th. William & I walked to Mr. Simpsons. Sunday 10th Rain all day.* On the eleventh the three of them hunt for waterfalls in the Easedale hills, William and Mary going on ahead, leaving Dorothy sitting on a stone, as she was in her journal's first entry after William left her at Low-wood turning, under the trees. She soon grows cold and catches up with the others, and Coleridge appears at the cottage that night. It is the first time he has seen William since the early summer—*he was well but did not look so.*

In the first week back, Dorothy writes to Annette, goes to Greta Hall (when she is sure that Mrs. Coleridge will not be there), bakes, and has thirteen of the neighbors over to tea. She keeps up her entries for the whole of October, writing up every day except for the week between the twenty-third and the thirtieth, when she is confined to her bed with a toothache that came on during her first walk with William since their return. The walk itself had been *heavenly*. On the thirtieth William goes to Keswick to see Coleridge:

> *Mary went with him to the top of the Rays. She is returned & is now sitting near me by the fire. It is a breathless grey day that leaves the golden woods of Autumn quiet in their own tranquillity, stately and beautiful in their decaying, the lake is a perfect mirror.*

Mary is there by her side all the time; the two women are endlessly together in this tiny space. On the last day of the month, Dorothy and Mary walk to Sara's Gate and look down at Rydal. Dorothy is deeply affected by what she sees:

> *The lake was perfectly still, the Sun shone on Hill & vale, the distant Birch trees looked like large golden Flowers—nothing else in colour was distinct & separate but all the beautiful*

> *colours seemed to be melted into one another, & joined together in one mass so that there were no differences though an endless variety when one tried to find it out.*

Down on the lake, nothing is *distinct & separate*, differences dissolve, and everything melts together. Back in the cottage, Dorothy's distinction and difference from the pregnant Mary will become more and more apparent. When they return, the two both lie on the floor. *Mary slept. I* could *not for I was thinking of so many things.* After tea, they read through old letters. Dorothy is happiest remembering.

Families harbor secrets; we know both most and least about those with whom we share our home. The secret William and Mary kept from Dorothy was the depth and exclusivity of their love, which increased after their marriage. Only when Dorothy's back was turned would they steal a kiss or share a private thought. Noise traveled through the house like a breeze through a broken window; over the summer Dorothy had been able to hear William turning and sighing in his sleep, so the sound of lovemaking from the downstairs bedroom must have been stressful for them all. Letters, when one was away, were shared between the remaining members of the household, and William warned Mary against adding to her letters affectionate remarks that Dorothy might find "obnoxious." In 1810, when William and Dorothy were visiting friends in Coleorton, he burst into song for his wife back at home: "O Mary, I love you with a passion of love which grows till I tremble to think of its strength." His letter, eight years into their marriage, rejoices in their unobserved intimacy:

> Every day every hour every moment makes me feel more deeply how blessed we are in each other, how

> purely how faithfully how ardently, and how tenderly we love each other; I put this last word last because, though I am persuaded that a deep affection is not uncommon in married life, yet I am confident that a lively, gushing, thought-employing, spirit-stirring, passion of love, is very rare even among good people.

"O my William!" Mary herself wrote,

> It is not in my power to tell thee how I have been affected by this dearest of all letters—it was so unexpected—so new a thing to see the breathing of thy inmost heart upon paper that I was quite overpowered, & now that I sit down to answer thee in the loneliness & depth of that love which unites us & which cannot be felt but by ourselves, I am so agitated & my eyes are so bedimmed that I scarcely know how to proceed . . . Indeed my love [your letter] has made me supremely blessed—it has given me a new feeling, for it is the first letter of love that has been exclusively my own—Wonder not then that I have been so affected by it.

Able to write freely without fear of Dorothy's looking over her shoulder, and to talk to her husband without Dorothy being able to hear the murmur of their speech, Mary poured out her love. The presence of Dorothy standing between them can have served only to intensify their mutual desire, snatched moments of intimacy giving married life the flavor of an illicit affair.

Dorothy keeps up her entries for the first eight days of November, but now that William no longer needs her to be his eyes and ears—now that she and he have become *distinct & separate*—it is hard to remember the journal's point. While she records the usual illnesses and changes to the climate, the sense of longing that gave her prose its tension has gone. Dorothy is looking backward now, and her memories take on unusual forms, appearing not only as thoughts but also as repetitions of past scenes and reenactments of earlier poems. William returns from Keswick unwell, and Dorothy, who has been in bed all afternoon, scalds her foot with coffee—*I was near fainting & then bad in my bowels.* She is nursed by Mary, and *with applications of vinegar I was lulled to sleep about 4.* The scene recalls the day, over five years earlier, at Nether Stowey, when she and Wordsworth and Coleridge were first enamored of one another. Coleridge's own small cottage was filled with voracious guests, and Sarah, in all the bustle, spilled boiling milk on her husband's foot. Unable to walk with the party, Coleridge stayed behind in the garden and composed "This Lime-Tree Bower My Prison." "I have lost / Beauties and feelings, such as would have been / Most sweet to my remembrance even when age / Had dimm'd mine eyes to blindness!" Dorothy's scalded foot similarly marks her off as separate from the others, but it is the symbol rather than the cause of her difference from the household.

She is up the next day writing letters. She leaves November 6 blank in her journal, and on the seventh she hears from Coleridge that he is in London, and from Sara that she is in Penrith. William's burst of poetic inspiration over, he begins to translate Ariosto from the Italian. The translations are exquisite. The vale on the eighth is *beautiful*. William continues to work at his translations, but

> *the day was so delightful that it made my very heart linger to be out of doors, & see & feel the beauty of the Autumn in*

freedom. The trees on the opposite side of the Lake are of a yellow brown, but there are one or two trees opposite our windows, (an ash tree for instance) quite green, as in spring.

"Put on with speed your woodland dress," William had written for Dorothy on the first fine day of spring in 1798, "And bring no book, for this one day / We'll give to idleness." In his poem Wordsworth had scorned scholarship and insisted on their walk, but today he stays with his books and his wife, and Dorothy goes out alone. When she writes up her journal later, Mary is sitting in the parlor, and William is working, having had the inevitable upset stomach. *We have a nice fire, the evening is quiet—Poor Coleridge!* Dorothy writes nothing more for six weeks.

The next time she opens her journal it is Christmas Eve, and Dorothy is once more sitting by the fire with William. They have been like this since teatime, she running the heel of a stocking while repeating to him some of his poems, he *turning over the leaves of Charlotte Smith's sonnets but he keeps his hand to his poor chest pushing aside his breastplate.* He listens to Dorothy and reads aloud some sonnets by Milton and some lines from *L'Allegro* and *Il Penseroso*. Mary is baking cakes and pies, and there is a *quiet keen frost* outside. Both women *are well*, and when Coleridge visited them this morning, *we all turned out of Wm's bedroom one by one to meet him—he looked well.* His wife had given birth to a baby daughter, they informed him, the previous day. He calls her Sara. *It was not an unpleasant morning to the feelings—far from it—the sun shone now & then, & there was no wind, but all things looked cheerless & distinct, no meltings of sky into mountains—the mountains like stonework wrought up with huge hammers.* Dorothy's imagery is rarely as austere as this, and what she is defining is again separation and difference. There are no meltings of the sky into the mountains today; the mountains are *distinct*. She writes briefly on *Saturday 25 December 1802. I am 31 years of age.* She is the same age as her mother when she died. Dorothy prepares to take the return chaise to Keswick to share the Christmas festivities with the Coleridges and to see the new infant, but then changes her mind and stays at the cottage, going to Greta Hall on December 30 instead, with William riding ahead for part of the way. They ate

> *some potted beef on Horseback, & sweet cake. We stopped our horse close to the ledge opposite a tuft of primroses three flowers in full blossom & a bud, and they reared themselves up among the green moss. We debated long whether we should pluck & at last left them to live out their day.*

These, the last flowers of the year, are the last flowers Dorothy will describe in the Grasmere Journals. She spends the New Year at Keswick, returning to Grasmere on January 2.

On the morning of January 10 Dorothy stays in bed to have *a Drench of sleep*. Mary has been unwell and in bed a good deal herself, possibly as a result of her pregnancy. By the eleventh it has started to freeze; Dorothy takes William his breakfast in bed, but he doesn't get up until the afternoon. The *blackness of the Cold* puts them off walking, and Mary reads to Dorothy the Prologue of *The Canterbury Tales* while William works *on his poem to C[oleridge]*, as they then called *The Prelude*. It is a day full of Chaucer; Dorothy has already read part of "The Knight's Tale," *with exquisite delight*. Now Mary is copying out some poems, and William is seated beside Dorothy,

> *& here ends this imperfect summary. I will take a nice Calais Book & will for the future write regularly &, if I can legibly,*

> *so much for this my resolution on Tuesday night, January 11 1803. Now I am going to take Tapioca for my supper, & Mary an Egg, William some cold mutton, his poor chest is tired.*

They sit around the fire, the Wordsworth family, the same but different. Their faces flame colored, each about to eat a separate supper while thinking on the year ahead. Mary will have her baby, William will finish his poem for Coleridge on the growth of his own mind, and Dorothy will continue to keep up her journal in the notebook she bought in Calais.

There is one last entry, on Sunday, January 16. It continues to be *intensely cold,* and William has a fancy for some gingerbread. Dorothy braves the weather and walks to the house of Matthew Newton, the village bread maker who has been blind for twenty years. She arrives to find that *the blind Man & his Wife & Sister were sitting by the fire, all dressed very clean in their Sunday's clothes, the sister reading.* It is a mirror image of the tableau of family life she had drawn in her previous entry. The impression Dorothy leaves us with is of another husband, wife, and sister sitting quietly around the fire, the sister reading, the brother no longer able to see. The same, but different.

She writes the word *Monda[y]* in preparation for the next day's entry, but it is left blank. There are no more usable pages now in the leather-bound notebook; Dorothy's ballad has come to a natural close. The last page on which she writes is not even clean, containing already two doodled sketches of chairs, one in pencil, a shadow hovering behind the writing, the other in ink, a solid object floating as if above. They sit among the words with the prescience of the seat reserved for the murdered Banquo, whose ghost will torment Macbeth. The Grasmere Journals, with their passion and their sorrow and their strife, conclude therefore not with prose but with pictures.

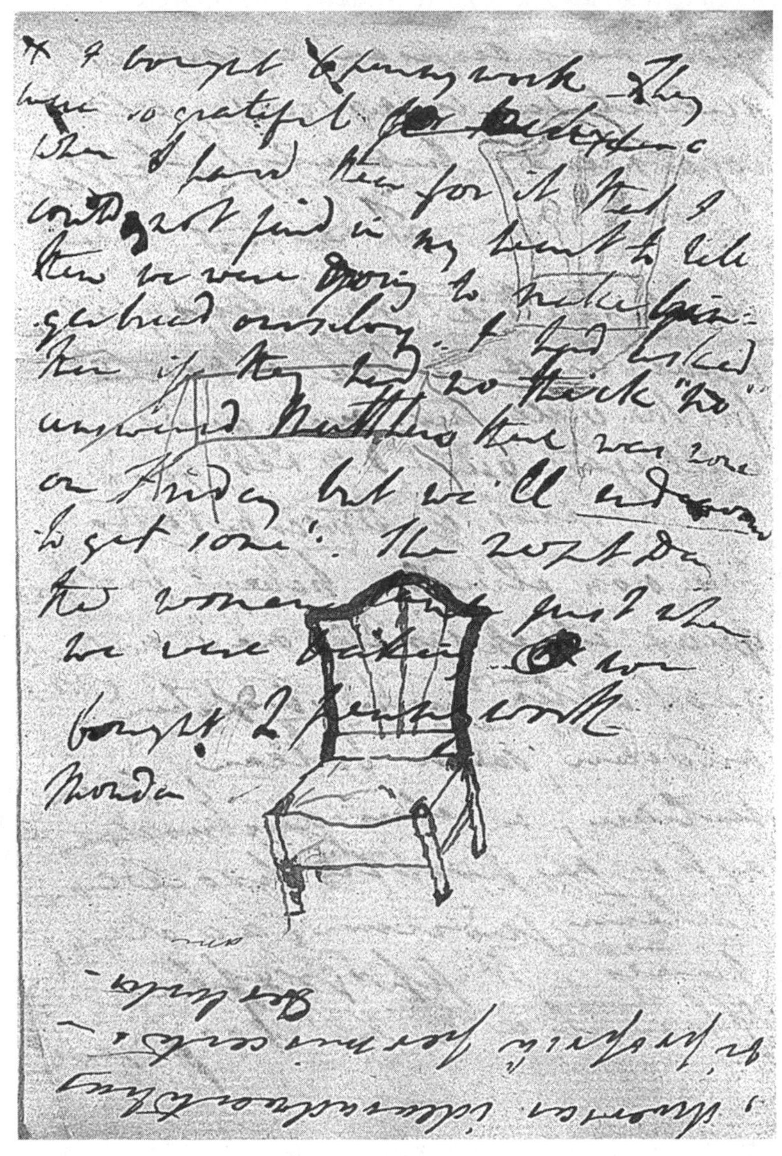
x I bought 2 pennyworth. They
were so grateful when
I paid them for it that I
could not find in my heart to tell
them we were going to make gingerbread ourselves. I had asked
them if they had no thick "No"
answered Matthew there was none
on Friday but we'll endeavour
to get some". The next Day
the woman came just when
we were baking & we
bought 2 pennyworth
Monday

Final page of the Grasmere Journals

Of what was Dorothy thinking as she sketched her empty seats? Her mind was elsewhere, but William's writing is rarely far away. The bed on which she threw herself at Gallow Hill; the fireplace around which they sit; the sightlessness, separation, and silence of family life in the village that winter; the empty chairs—Dorothy's final entries return her to the oddest and most surreal of her brother's poems, written in April of this year:

> These chairs they have no words to utter,
> No fire is in the grate to stir or flutter,
> The ceiling and floor are mute as a stone,
> My chamber is hushed and still,
> And I am alone,
> Happy and alone.
>
> Oh! Who would be afraid of life?
> The passion the sorrow and the strife,
> When he may lie
> Sheltered so easily?
> May lie in peace on his bed,
> Happy as those who are dead.

The image is of peace, but also of death.

Chapter Seven

UNTIL DEATH DO US PART

But Verse was what he had been wedded to.

—WILLIAM WORDSWORTH, "Within our happy castle there dwelt one"

Peace has come to all three, and they live together
in perfect harmony until they die.

—*The Letters of Mary Wordsworth, 1800–1855,*
selected and edited by Mary E. Burton

Who are these coming to the sacrifice?

—JOHN KEATS, "Ode on a Grecian Urn"

Dorothy Wordsworth is fossilized for us in her Grasmere Journals, like the unravished bride of quietness on Keats's Grecian urn. With her wild eyes, woodland dress, and few remaining teeth, she is enshrined in these pages as the eternal threshold figure, caught between the worlds of art and nature, youth and age, joy and dejection; fixed in the silence and slow time of the months between the summer of 1800 and the deep midwinter of 1803, as though nothing happened to her either before or since. So powerful is the effect of stillness and stopped clocks in her writing that it always seems a surprise that she did not emerge fully formed at Dove Cottage aged twenty-eight, like the goddess Athena from the head of Zeus, or to discover that her life did not close altogether with that last supper of tapioca, that she in fact lived on and on, writing other, more dutiful journals, as well as copious letters and even some poems of her own; never leaving her brother, whose family home she shared until her death, a spinster, at the age of eighty-three. But by then she had long lost her reason and was haunting the top of their house like the discarded first wife in Charlotte Brontë's *Jane Eyre*. No longer Wordsworth's "exquisite sister," she was now known as "poor Miss Wordsworth." From being "nature's inmate," as Wordsworth called her, or an "*Inmate* of this vale," as she put it in a poem of her own, for her last twenty-five years Dorothy became a prisoner of the self she had tried so hard to escape.

William and Mary's first child, John, was born eight months after the wedding, with Dorothy no doubt present at the birth. Coleridge and Dorothy stood as godparents, and Dorothy, whose name, De Quincey said, predestined her "to figure rather in the character of aunt than mother," was indeed a devoted aunt, doting on John as only she knew how. Mary had four more children—Dora, Thomas, Catharine, and Willy—who Dorothy always spoke of as "ours," but "Johnny" remained her favorite. "He has blue eyes, a fair complexion, (which is already very much sunburnt,) a body as fat as a little pig, arms that are thickening and dimpling and bracelets at his wrists, a very prominent nose, which *will be* like his Father's, and a head shaped upon the very same model." Baby John accompanied the Wordsworths everywhere, floating in his basket over Grasmere when they picnicked on the island, sleeping by them in the orchard while they worked.

William's children saw Dorothy as their second mother, which made these early years a happy time for her. She was also necessary to Mary, whose dependence on her help was reassuring to someone who needed to be of use in order to feel valued. Mrs. Gaskell leaves us a picture of this period in a letter of 1852, when she describes how Mary, "who is charming," had told her

> some homely tender details of her early married days, how Miss Wordsworth made the bread, and got dinner ready, and Mrs. W nursed all morning, and, leaving the servant to wash-up after dinner, the three set out on their long walks, carrying all the babes amongst them; and certain spots are memorial places to Mrs. W in her old age, because there she sat, and nursed this or that darling. The walks they took are something surprising to our degenerate minds.

It was as William's son that Dorothy loved John, who would always come first for her. Her grief at parting with the baby, six weeks after his birth, when she accompanied her brother and Coleridge on a walking tour of Scotland, recalled her separations from Wordsworth himself: "I have no doubt I shall be as happy as they when I am fairly off, but I do not love to think of leaving home, and parting with the dear Babe who will be no more the same Babe when we return." Dorothy found in loving her nephew a new experience of loss; every change in him, like every parting from him, bringing with it something to be mourned. In 1804, when Mary was taking John on a trip, Dorothy wrote to a friend:

> I do not know how the house will sound without his voice. I shall find a loss even of the very worst he can do—his passionate cries and screams—he is a turbulent fellow, and often when he is in my arms I wish

> for a little quietness, but when he is away the heartsomeness of the house will be gone too.

William and Mary's second child, also called Dorothy but known as Dora, became to her family a version of the aunt after whom she was named. Dora, who was her father's favorite, had, like the young Dorothy, "wild eyes and impetuous movements"; she was "wayward," spirited, and "given to ecstasy." She also denied herself food, and the oscillations in her weight were closely observed by Aunt Dorothy. Wordsworth's love for his daughter and Dorothy's identification with her would dictate the direction of Dora's life. Never able to acknowledge the intellectual ordinariness of John, Dorothy would promote the brother at the expense of the sister, with whom she was quick to find fault. Dorothy was adamant that Dora, brighter than John, was of less value. "Most people think Dora far cleverer, but that is a mistake," she insisted. "Oh! My dear friend!" she exclaimed to Catherine Clarkson of the two young children,

> Johnny *is* such a sweet Creature; so noble, bold, gentle and beautiful—yes! He is a beautiful Boy. D[ora] is very pretty, very kittenish, very quick, very clever, but not given to *thought* . . . They are both sweet in their way; but it must be allowed that John is the finer creature.

It was Dorothy who insisted that Dora be sent away to boarding school so she could break her "abominable habits" and "learn to be a useful girl in the family." One habit to be got rid of was "sucking her tongue," another was pride; Dora, thought Dorothy, was "not unwilling to show off what she can do." William's motivation in allowing his four-year-old daughter to be dragged from the house to travel in a coach by herself to a boarding school in Appleby, where she would stay until she was eighteen, is unclear. He, who had long believed that the best education was to run wild, now allowed Dorothy to reenact with Dora the same trauma that she had experienced at age six. Dorothy described the institution to which Dora was sent as being "more like a large family than a school," recalling the large family in Halifax to which she had been sent as a child. "Much good we are sure she will get—and be saved from a great deal of pain," Dorothy argued as she watched Dora, who clung weeping to her father's legs on his visits, grow up separated from her siblings.

The Wordsworth children were raised among the Coleridge children, Hartley, Derwent, and Sara, much as the second generation of Earnshaws at Wuthering Heights were raised among the second generation of Lintons in Thrushcross Grange. As in Emily Brontë's novel, the lives of the children of Dove Cottage and the children of Greta Hall were to be determined by the unresolved passions and rivalries of their parents. Sara, Coleridge's intellectually brilliant daughter ("Often do we wish that Dorothy was like her in this respect," wrote Aunt Dorothy), grew up hardly knowing her father, but as an adult she suffered, as he had done, from opium addiction. Sara married a Coleridge cousin, flourishing only when she was widowed and able to live alone as a bluestocking in London. Dora, who contracted tuberculosis at school, lived in thrall to her father, who was, as Coleridge put it, "more and more benetted in hypochondriachal Fancies, living wholly among *Devotees*—having even the minutest Thing, almost his very eating and drinking, done for him by his Sister, or Wife." A friend remarked that Wordsworth "was spoiled by having three wives," but once she left school, Dora joined Mary, Dorothy, and

Sara Hutchinson as a member of her father's harem. A natural bigamist, Wordsworth had four wives, but really, as he put it in a poem, "Verse was what he had been wedded to."

In 1805, John Wordsworth went down with his ship, the *Earl of Abergavenny*, leaving the family mired in grief. By 1808, Dove Cottage had grown too small for them all, and Thomas De Quincey, who had recently introduced himself to Wordsworth as an admirer of his work, took over the tenancy. The Wordsworths moved to Allan Bank, on the other side of Grasmere. "We already feel the comfort of having each a room of our own, and begin to love them," Dorothy wrote to Mrs. Clarkson "—but the dear cottage! I will not talk of it." Preparing Dove Cottage for De Quincey's occupation, Dorothy wrote to him of how

> yesterday I sat half an hour musing by myself in the moss-hut . . . Pleasant indeed it is to think of that little orchard which for one seven years at least will be a secure covert for the Birds, and undisturbed by the woodman's ax. There is no other spot which we may have prized year after year that we can ever look upon without apprehension that next year, next month, or even tomorrow it may be deformed and ravaged.

No sooner had he moved in than De Quincey demolished the beloved moss hut and the orchard hedge that she had hoped he would protect, deforming and ravaging both. The essay De Quincey then published in *Tait's* about the characters of Wordsworth and his sister added insult to injury.

By 1811 the Wordsworths had become regular churchgoers and were worried for the health of the king. This was also the year in which the friendship between Wordsworth and Coleridge finally broke down, over a remark William had made to his old friend Basil Montagu, who had offered to have Coleridge stay in his London house. Having just housed Coleridge himself in Allan Bank, during a particularly exhausting period in his friend's life, Wordsworth put it to the teetotaler Montagu that a drink-dependent and drug-addicted guest might not be to his taste, which report, when fed back to Coleridge, he found devastating. "No one on earth has ever loved me," Coleridge howled. The fact that Wordsworth could speak of him in such terms hit him, he said, like a "thunderbolt," and Coleridge disappeared from the Wordsworths' lives. Sarah Coleridge was at last vindicated. "There will never more be *that* between them which was in days of yore," she smugly concluded:

> It has taught C one useful lesson: that even his dearest and most indulgent friends, even those very persons who have been the great means of his self-indulgence, when he comes to live wholly with them are as clear-sighted to his failings, & much less delicate in speaking of them than his Wife, who, being the Mother of his children, even if she had not the slightest regard for himself, would naturally feel a reluctance to the exposing of his faults.

For Dorothy, the absence of Coleridge's stimulation would be tremendous. For years he had shared with her his feelings, thoughts, and experiences; now that he no longer leaped the gate and burst into the house with his startling poems and endless projects,

Dorothy had no further contact with the wider world. It is tempting to think that one reason she changed so quickly from the prototype of Catherine Earnshaw to a provincial Tory is that Coleridge was no longer there to prevent her from doing so.

In 1812, in the space of six months, William and Mary lost two of their children. Catharine, aged four, had long been frail and died after a night of convulsions, and Thomas, aged six, caught pneumonia following measles. In 1813, the poet settled his family at Rydal Mount, a large, handsome house overlooking Rydal Water on the road to Ambleside. This was also the year that Wordsworth became distributor of stamps for Westmoreland, which allowed him to enjoy a steady annual income. In trading the lifestyle of Dove Cottage for the one they would now adopt, Dorothy gave up Cleopatra's Egypt, with all its lawlessness, sublimity, and verbal exuberance, for the austerity of Mark Antony's Rome. Dove Cottage was the home of the aspiring Romantic

Rydal Mount, drawing by Dora Wordsworth

poet, and Rydal Mount the seat of the revered Victorian sage, and it is as such that they are preserved today.

The growth of Wordsworth's wealth and reputation took place alongside the demise of his poetic powers. After the publication of *Poems in Two Volumes* in 1807, he grew steadily famous, and on the death of Robert Southey in 1843 he was appointed poet laureate. The myth of Wordsworth and his wild sister began in their lifetimes; Rydal Mount became part of the tourist route through the Lake District, and strangers would ask to be shown around the house, which for Mary, who was shy, was not always easy. The boys had left home; the housework, once the preserve of Dorothy, was done by servants; and Dora now acted as her father's amanuensis and constant companion. The boredom of life for the Wordsworth women was such that their house was renamed, by Dora, Idle Mount.

Dorothy continued to write, but she never wrote anything again like her Grasmere Journals. In *Recollections of a Tour Made in Scotland*, she preserved her memories of the 1803 trip she took with her brother and Coleridge; she produced a moving account of the death on the Lakeland fells of two locals, George and Sarah Green, who left behind them a bevy of orphans. She recorded excursions on the banks of Ullswater in 1805 and up Scafell Pike in 1818. She kept, during a trip with William and Mary through France, Belgium, Germany, and Switzerland, a "Journal of a Tour on the Continent," and she wrote journals recording a second tour of Scotland in 1822 and a tour around the Isle of Man in 1828, both taken with Mary's sister Joanna. She kept occasional journals of home life and composed occasional verses, three of which were published in Wordsworth's 1815 edition of his poems. She wrote letters until she could no longer hold a pen.

In April 1829, after a winter spent with John, recently ordained deacon for Whitwick, a colliery village in Leicestershire ("Poor Fellow! He wanted me sadly to go with him"), Dorothy collapsed with torturous pains in her intestines: "sickness . . . hot and cold—with pains in the Bowels." It has been remarked by biographers that the months Dorothy kept house for John were a reenactment of the days before her brother's marriage, when she had lived alone with William at Dove Cottage, as well as being a fulfillment of the fantasy of "happiness . . . in my little parsonage" she had described to Jane Pollard when she was still at Forncett. But John's was a "lonely parsonage," Dorothy said, and not a happy one, and the period spent in Whitwick recalls more the winter she spent in Goslar with William. Socially alienated in what she thought a charmless industrial town, whose inhabitants they disliked—"There were not many places with fewer attractions or recommendations than Whitwick," thought Sara Hutchinson—aunt and nephew folded in on one another much as brother and sister had done in Germany thirty years before. The following October, John married. Dorothy was still not well enough to attend the wedding, a grand affair whose "bustle and ceremony" would be, she wrote, "but a melancholic pleasure."

It seemed unlikely that Dorothy, now aged fifty-seven, would survive the Whitwick attack, and from now on the state of her health—more specifically, the state of her bowels—controlled the household at Rydal Mount. "Were she to depart," wrote William, "the Phasis of my Moon would be robbed of light to a degree that I have not courage to think of." Dorothy once again had dominance over William. She became, Mary said, "the Master of her Brother, who humours all her waywardness as quite to enervate him." When Dorothy and William were not living as two halves of the same person, they were taking turns, as orphans often do, at mutual parenting. Dorothy had looked after William during the first act of their adult lives, and he now looked after her. Surely, wrote Dora, "such love as he bears to her is of no common nature." William's fear of losing Dorothy suggests that her presence had not, for him at least, been a burden on his relationship with Mary; on the contrary, healthy or unhealthy, Dorothy was a necessary part of his marriage.

Coleridge died in 1834. Wordsworth, who had been estranged from his friend for years, described him now as "the only *wonderful* man I ever knew." Coleridge and Dorothy, Wordsworth conceded, were the "two beings to whom my intellect is most indebted." For the past five years Dorothy's physical health had deteriorated rapidly, and now her mind had started to become, as she put it in her last journal, "misty dark & blind." In the early months of 1835 William and Mary left Rydal Mount to go to London to secure a job for Willy. "Both in good spirits till the last parting came—," Dorothy wrote, "when I was overcome. My spirits much depressed." Dorothy had always fallen to pieces at partings, and in many ways her response to being left by William when she was sixty-four is no different from her response to his leaving her at *the turning of the Low-wood bay under the trees* thirty-five years before. But this time her depression sank in. That April she received a painful letter from Annette in response to William's rescinding the annuity he agreed to pay their daughter when she married. "And you, kind Dorothy," Annette pleaded, "whom she loves and trusts so much . . . take your niece's part and let her mother die in peace." It is unlikely that Dorothy could do much to influence her brother—"Poor Miss W," wrote Henry Crabb Robinson, "is sinking into imbecility"—but the letter affected her, and she tucked it into the back of her journal, where it remained until it was found in 1970. By the beginning of June, Dora was writing, "Aunt Dorothy grows weaker and weaker." At times it seemed she "had not ten minutes to live," and at other times she "is so bright and strong that you are almost cheated into a belief that she may be spared to you even for years." Her father's heart, Dora said, "is well-nigh breaking." Then, at the end of June, Sara Hutchinson suddenly died, and Dorothy's mind "received a shock," Wordsworth wrote, "from which it has never recovered."

Dorothy had long developed dependencies on opium, which she took twice a day, and laudanum, of which she took between fifteen and twenty-five drops daily; without stimulants, Sara Hutchinson had said, "you would scarcely believe her alive." When the drugs were withdrawn, in the disappointed hope that it might improve her mental health, Dorothy was only happy eating, stealing whole chickens from the kitchen. The once nimble, wiry body became encased in flesh. Her friends all dying and her constitution weakened by drugs, no longer able to walk and with nothing much to do—reading was now impossible because she was, she said, "too busy with her own feelings"—Dorothy became physically violent, verbally abusive, resentful, vulgar, self-pitying, and childlike: "a *clever tyrannical* spoilt child," one friend said; simply "a spoilt child," the more charitable Mary reported. Her pleasures as the years dragged by were no longer watching the birds or the surface of the lake, but waiting for the cuckoo clock to strike the hour, which made her whoop with delight, and splashing water about in a kitchen bowl. Guests to Rydal Mount were kept away from the unkempt figure who prowled the back bedroom on the top floor, squawking like something inhuman, flaying the caps of her nurses with her nails, and bruising their arms with her fists. "We can give her no neighbours but ourselves," Mary said, "or she would terrify strangers to death." William now tended to his sister's every need. "Poor Miss W I thought sunk still deeper into insensibility," Crabb Robinson wrote. "By the bye, Mrs. W says that almost the only enjoyment Mr. W seems to feel is in his attendance on her—and that her death would be to him a sad calamity!!! I cannot help reproaching myself for my inability to conceive this state of mind distinctly."

The Dorothy of fine sensibility and magnetic responsiveness was still recognizable to those who had known her in youth or from the tributes paid to her by Wordsworth in his now famous poems. One female visitor to Rydal Mount, whose great-uncle Tom Wedgwood had been Coleridge's patron, described how

> I was waiting at the door when her chaise drew up, bearing the little shrunken figure from her daily excursion, and I looked into those "wild eyes" which kept all their life and light though the mind had grown dim. There was no dimness in her interest when she heard my name. "From where are you sprung?" she enquired eagerly.

Sometimes it seemed that Dorothy had "quite recovered." Henry Crabb Robinson described a visit to Rydal Mount, where he found

> Poor Miss W in an unexpectedly improved state—Her mind feeble but she talks nothing absolutely insane or irrational, but she has so little command of herself that she cannot restrain the most unseemly noises, blowing loudly & making a nondescript sound more shrill than the cry of a partridge or a turkey. From this she is to be drawn only by a request to repeat Verses which she does with affecting sweetness.

Dorothy in a wheelchair, drawing by John Harden, 1842

"She is, as you know at times," Mary wrote,

> & for a *short space* her own acute self, retains the power over her fine judgement & discrimination—then, & at once, relapses into childlike feebleness—& gives vent to some discomfort by merry sallies or with the impatience of a *petted child* contrives one want after another, as if merely to provoke contradiction. But she *has no delusions*, & we can only consider her state poor thing, as that of premature Dotage.

What is striking about the pattern of Dorothy's madness is how it repeats the pattern of her headaches: it comes and goes. The Grasmere Journals describe her as being very ill and very well on the same day, as being able to shift between motionless trances and energetic walks in the same way that she now oscillated between childlike states and adulthood.

As for Dorothy's namesake, having sent her away as a child, Wordsworth refused to let Dora leave home as an adult. When she wanted, in her mid-thirties, to marry Edward Quillinan, a widower with two young children who was also a close family friend, Wordsworth put his foot down. His argument against letting Dora be with the man she loved was that her health did not permit such privileges; Dora had a weak chest, but what added to her weakness was her refusal to eat. Quillinan referred to Dora's "determination to be unable to eat," which determination increased with her imprisonment. Her self-starvation was, Quillinan told her, "as sure though not as speedy a suicidal process as any other," and visitors in 1834 noted that Dora "eats nothing, says nothing, goes nowhere." Dora ate, Mary said, "about as much as a sparrow might pick . . . Really the food she takes is insufficient to support a life." The doctor assured Mary that her daughter's lack of appetite was "no doubt . . . brought on by anxiety." So while Dorothy, increasingly noisy and growing larger, filled the upstairs of the house, Dora, silent and emptier by the day, shrank before her parents' eyes in the downstairs of Idle Mount.

Only when he was talked round by an influential third party, Isabella Fenwick, did Wordsworth grudgingly give his consent to Dora's marriage, which took place from Mrs. Fenwick's house in Bath in 1841. On the morning of the wedding, however, he was overcome by "a sudden outburst of feeling" and unable to attend the ceremony itself, staying behind to wait for the return of the bride and groom.

Dora then traveled with her husband to Portugal, where in a warm climate she flourished, looking, she said, "like a rose" and eating "like a ploughboy." After six years of marriage, she died of tuberculosis and was buried in Grasmere churchyard by the side of her brother Thomas and sister, Catharine.

George Venables, an acquaintance of the Wordsworths', told Francis Kilvert, who wrote it in his diary, that he had met Dorothy once in her Rydal Mount days. The family was taking tea. "She was depressed and took no part in the conversation and no notice of what was passing. Her brother said he attributed the failure of her health and intellect to the long walks she used to take with him." Wordsworth clearly felt responsible for Dorothy's state, but by fixing the blame on the walks they enjoyed, which are unlikely to have incurred madness, he missed where his responsibility might lie.

William's possessiveness over Dora suggests that marriage for the young Dorothy was never an option, and the experience of Wordsworth's daughter tells us something of what it would have been like had Dorothy defied her brother at any point. But would she have been saved her later suffering had she stayed living with the Cooksons, visiting the Forncett poor, running her Sunday school, and becoming a wife and mother instead of embarking on an odyssey of poetry with her charismatic sibling? Was the exchange of a lifetime of predictable days for a brief spell of intensity in the end worth it? Living with a writer is known to be difficult, but with Wordsworth's egomania, insomnia, and hypochondria; his creative blocks, his endless revisions, his loathing of putting pen to paper, his insistence on adulation, his years of obscurity, his troubled friendship with Coleridge, his dependence on his sister's presence and the accessibility of her every thought, Dorothy surely had it harder than many literary companions.

Virginia Woolf, in an essay on Coleridge's daughter, Sara, who edited her father's work after his death, observed how Sara Coleridge's mighty project involved not "self-sacrifice but self-realisation. She found her father, in those blurred pages, as she had not found him in the flesh; and she found he was herself. She did not copy him, she insisted; *she was him.*" Did Dorothy find or lose herself in her absorption in William? Was her life one of self-sacrifice or self-realization?

The madness of Dorothy Wordsworth was her final threshold. Not fully on one side or the other of the divide between sanity and insanity, when her clouded mind cleared, she would step back into the light to write poems or letters, or enjoy from her bed the two caged doves at the window. At times like this she tried to describe what it was like to be alone in the darkness. "A madman," she wrote to her cousin Edward, "might as well attempt to relate the history of his doings and those of his fellows in confinement as I to tell you one hundredth part of what I have felt, suffered, and done." She ends the letter with a reference to the death of Charles Lamb, who had lived his whole life with his own sister, Mary. "His sister still survives—a solitary twig, patiently enduring the storm of life. In losing her brother she lost her all." After the death of the aunt who had raised her as a girl in Halifax, Dorothy again crossed the line and wrote to Dora about resting places:

> They say I must write a letter—and what shall it be? News—news I must seek for news. My own thoughts are a wilderness—"not pierceable by power of any star"—News then is my resting-place—news! News!
>
> Poor Peggy Benson lies in Grasmere Churchyard beside her once beautiful mother. Fanny Haigh is gone to a better world. My friend Mrs. Rawson has ended her ninety and two years pilgrimage—and I have fought and fretted and striven—and am here beside the fire. The Doves behind me at the small window—the laburnum with its naked seed-pods

> shivers before my window and the pine-trees rock from their base.—More I cannot write, so farewell!

What was wrong with Dorothy Wordsworth? There have been various diagnoses of her condition. Helen Darbishire, in 1958, believed that she suffered from arteriosclerosis, which eventually affected the brain, resulting from the attack of gallstones that first came on while she was at Whitwick. Most recently, Robert Gittings and Jo Manton suggest that Dorothy was the victim of presenile dementia and that her symptoms were similar to those of Alzheimer's. The problem with these diagnoses is that she stayed in this state for over two decades, during which she had occasional bursts of concentration and lucidity, which are against the diagnosis of an organic dementia. As Mary said of Dorothy's illness, "It is a strange case."

In *Dorothy and William Wordsworth* (1927), Catherine MacDonald Maclean argued that Dorothy suffered "a complete breakdown" in her middle age due to emotional and physical exhaustion:

> The austerities of her youth, the passionate ardour of her life with her brother between 1795 and 1802 (there is no doubt that she lived too hard during these years)—the brave voiceless surrender of her joy in 1802, at the time of Wordsworth's marriage—the wear and tear of the bringing up of the Wordsworth family—the constant drain imposed on her strength by the fervour of her spirit—the sapping of her vitality by that extraordinary capacity for sympathy . . . all these no doubt contributed.

But it is the comments made by De Quincey, who knew Dorothy in sickness and in health, that seem as ever the most acute. For De

Quincey, Dorothy was suffering not from exhaustion but from all that she had lost. "I fear that Miss Wordsworth has suffered not much less than Coleridge," he wrote in the last of his *Tait's* essays on Wordsworth, "and, in any general expression of it, from the same cause—viz., an excess of pleasurable excitement and luxurious sensibility, sustained in youth by a constitutional glow from animal causes, but drooping as soon as that was withdrawn." Her collapse, De Quincey implies, was due to the intellectual and imaginative boredom of her life after Wordsworth married and to the long-term effects of suppressed literary talent. She would have been spared her suffering had she been able to read more widely, to write more and to write publicly, to live the life of the bluestocking he believed her—perhaps wrongly—to be, but this was never encouraged. "It is too much to expect of any woman (or man either)," De Quincey believed,

> that her mind should support itself in a pleasureable activity, under the dropping energies of life, by resting on the past or on the present: some interest in reversion, some subject of hope from day to day, must be called in to reinforce the animal fountains of good spirits. Had that opened for Miss Wordsworth, I am satisfied that she would have passed a more cheerful middle-age, and would not, at any period, have yielded to that nervous depression which, I grieve to hear, had clouded her latter days.

These are striking remarks, not least because Freud's insights into the effects of repression were more than half a century away, and De Quincey had not, so far as we know, seen the Grasmere Journals in which Dorothy had recorded her "subjects of hope, from day to day."

My suggestion is that Dorothy suffered from depressive pseudo-dementia, a condition in which severe depression mimics the symptoms of dementia such as cognitive impairment, confusion, forgetfulness, and lack of self-care, and today she would be treated with antidepressants. It is interesting that her collapse did not take place immediately after Wordsworth's marriage, to which she quickly adapted and whose fruits gave her a new sense of purpose. It occurred after the deaths of Coleridge and her close companion Sara Hutchinson, and the departure from Rydal Mount of her beloved John, at which point Dorothy suffered from an extreme form of being empty of herself. In 1833, William told Henry Crabb Robinson that his sister complained of "faintness & hollowness & has an incessant craving for something to support her." There was something missing for Dorothy, as Mary noted: her "restless feelings . . . we attribute to something amiss going on in the head which she rubs perpetually." In an earlier letter to Catherine Clarkson, Dorothy described herself as a container made of entrances and exits in danger of being emptied out:

> Much of the knowledge, which I formerly gained from books has slipped from me, and it is grievous to think that hardly one new idea has come in . . . if it were not that my feelings were as much alive as ever there would be a growing tendency for the mind to barrenness.

And yet the verse Dorothy had never felt able to write in her youth now began, Mary said, to "pour" from her. She was a finer prose writer by far, but there is one poem that has the power to move us as only the Grasmere Journals can. "Thoughts from My Sick-Bed" was written in response to spring flowers, the first of the year, given to Dorothy by visitors. They brought "joy . . . to my *hidden* life, / To consciousness no longer hidden":

> I felt a power unfelt before,
> Controlling weakness, languor, pain;
> It bore me to the terrace walk,
> I trod the hills again:—
>
> No prisoner in this lonely room,
> I *saw* the green Banks of the Wye,
> Recalling thy prophetic words,
> Bard, Brother, Friend from infancy!
>
> No need of motion or of strength,
> Or even of the breathing air:
> I thought of Nature's loveliest scenes;
> And with memory I was there.

No motion has she now: Dorothy is back in the rocky terrain of Lucy once more. But leaving the confines of her mind, she also revisits the lines addressed to her by William half a century earlier, when she had been a part of his inner life rather than imprisoned in her own. Returning to "the green Banks of the Wye," she steps back into "Tintern Abbey," and the "prophetic words" she recalls are these:

> Therefore let the moon
> Shine on thee in thy solitary walk;

And let the misty mountain-winds be free
To blow against thee: and, in after years,
When these wild ecstasies shall be matured
Into a sober pleasure; when thy mind
Shall be a mansion for all lovely forms,
Thy memory be as a dwelling-place
For all sweet sounds and harmonies; oh! then,
If solitude, or fear, or pain, or grief,
Should be thy portion, with what healing thoughts
Of tender joy wilt thou remember me,
And these my exhortations! Nor, perchance—
If I should be where I no more can hear
Thy voice, nor catch from thy wild eyes these gleams
Of past existence, wilt thou then forget
That on the banks of this delightful stream
We stood together.

Dorothy's response to William's final illness in the spring of 1850 left the family baffled. Her dependence on her brother they had believed to be absolute, but as he faded away, she came back into focus. Edward Quillinan reported from the deathbed of the poet:

> Miss W . . . is as much herself as she ever was in her life & has an almost absolute *command* of her own will! Does not make noises; is not all self; thinks of the feelings of others (Mrs. W's for example), is tenderly anxious about her brother; &, in short, but for age & bodily infirmity, is almost *the* Miss Wordsworth we knew in past days.

William Wordsworth died on April 23 and was buried in the southwest corner of Grasmere churchyard, where three of his children and Sara Hutchinson already lay. *The Prelude* was published three months later. Mary outlived William by nine years and Dorothy by four; dependable to the end, she left no one behind to clear up after her, save her two surviving sons. We are told that not once during her marriage was there a cross word between Mary and Dorothy Wordsworth.

Five years after Wordsworth's death, five summers with the length of five long winters, in her bedroom, with John at her side, Dorothy went to what Mary called "her final home." Mary described this last threshold in terms that recall the experience for Dorothy of William's marriage. Her "dear Sister," Mary wrote, was released from "prolonged but *fitful* suffering and some few hours of peaceful and anxious waiting." It was January 1855; over half a century had passed since she had penned the final entry of her Grasmere Journals. For Thomas De Quincey, she had died over fifteen years before. "Farewell, Miss Wordsworth!" he wrote in the conclusion of his essays for *Tait's*, "farewell, impassioned Dorothy!" Outside her window, the laburnum shivered and the pine tree rocked.

A NOTE ON THE PUBLICATION HISTORY OF THE GRASMERE JOURNALS

Parts of the Grasmere Journals were published during Dorothy Wordsworth's lifetime, in Christopher Wordsworth's *Memoirs of William Wordsworth* (Moxon, 1851). Christopher Wordsworth, canon of Westminster and the poet's literary executor, selected those extracts that he hoped would give the reader "a correct idea" of his uncle's pious life at Dove Cottage, and afford him "notices of the occasions on which several of Mr. Wordsworth's poems were composed." The Grasmere Journals later went into the possession of Dorothy's great-nephew Gordon Graham Wordsworth, who bequeathed them to the Wordsworth Museum at Grasmere in 1935. GGW left notes on the names and places mentioned by Dorothy that have proved invaluable to her editors.

Larger extracts from the Grasmere Journals, as well as most of the Alfoxden Journal and the journal kept by Dorothy in Hamburg, were included in William Knight's *Life of William Wordsworth* (Edinburgh, 1889). Eight years later, Professor Knight produced the first "complete" edition of the *Journals of Dorothy Wordsworth* (Macmillan, 1897), notoriously omitting from the text of the Grasmere Journals what he called "numerous trivial details," such as all references to William's and Dorothy's health and to the intimacy between the poet and his sister. Knight described his exclusions as being restricted to those "cases in which the sister wrote, 'To-day I mended William's shirts,' or 'William gathered sticks,' or 'I went in search of eggs,' etc., etc." The first person outside the immediate family circle to read Dorothy's journals, Knight was clearly uncomfortable with what he found. The value of the Grasmere Journals for the reading public, he felt, lay not in the love felt by Dorothy for William but in her "felicitous record of the changes of the seasons and the progress of the year, details as to flower and tree, bird and beast, mountain and lake," and "the flood of light" she was able to cast "on the circumstances under which her brother's poems were composed." Knight's editorial notes explain that the sentences he chose to omit are indicated in the text by asterisks, but this is not always the case. The mention of her headache in Dorothy's first entry, for example, is cut out of the passage so that *arrived at home with a bad head-ach, set some slips of privet,* becomes, in Knight's hands, "arrived at home, set some slips of privet." Nor do asterisks indicate that anything has been cut from Dorothy's description of the exchange of the ring that took place between herself and William on his wedding morning; the three sentences ending *I took it from my forefinger where I had worn it the whole of the night before—he slipped it again onto my finger & blessed me fervently* are simply elided. Knight presumably found the lines already scored over (possibly by the censorious Gordon Wordsworth) when the journals first came into his hands and agreed to overlook what was written there (which it is possible to read with the naked eye). The effect of William Knight's editorial procedure was to present to the public a reverential picture of the laureate's cerebral household.

In 1941, the Wordsworth scholar Ernest de Selincourt produced what still remains the only edition of all the various journals of Dorothy Wordsworth (Macmillan), comprising the Hamburg and Alfoxden journals (1798), the Grasmere Journals (1800–1803), *Recollections of a Tour Made in Scotland* (1803), "Excursion on the Banks of Ullswater" (1805), "Excursion up Scawfell Pike" (1818), "Journal of a Tour on the Continent" (1820), "My Second Tour in Scotland" (1822), and "A Tour in the Isle of Man" (1828). Correcting Knight's omission of "trivial details" from the text, de Selincourt suggested that although "a more beautiful book might doubtless be made by rigorous selection from its contents," the Grasmere Journals' "juxtaposition of entries on such widely different emotional levels . . . stamps the whole as a veritable transcript of real life; and the greater moments are thrown into a stronger relief by their work-a-day setting." De Selincourt did not, however, include the scored-over sentences in Dorothy's account of the morning of October 4, 1802.

The Oxford World's Classics edition of the Grasmere and Alfoxden journals, edited by Helen Darbishire in 1958, was the first unabridged transcription of the four surviving notebooks of the Grasmere Journals, including readings of scored-over words and passages. It was Darbishire who suggested the transcription, which has since become standard, of the erased sentences on the morning of the wedding. But just as readers had not been made aware that passages of Dorothy's prose were omitted in the editions by Knight and de Selincourt, Darbishire incorporated her transcriptions of scored-over words into the main body of the text without letting the reader know that they had been erased in the original manuscript. A revised edition of Darbishire's text was produced in 1971 by Wordsworth's biographer Mary Moorman, in which further words and phrases, which either were illegible in the manuscript or had been erased, were transcribed. Moorman noted when the erasures in the manuscript were by Dorothy herself and when they appeared to be the work of "some hand other than DW's." The editions by Darbishire and Moorman both have attached to them an appendix of poems by Wordsworth referred to in the journals; the implication is that the Grasmere Journals are of interest primarily as a companion to Wordsworth's poetry of the same period.

In 1991, Clarendon Press brought out a fresh transcription of *The Grasmere Journals* edited by Pamela Woof, which offers many different and first-time readings and omits the "companion" poems by Wordsworth. This edition was followed by the revised *Grasmere and Alfoxden Journals* (Oxford World's Classics, 2002), also edited by Pamela Woof, which includes a rereading of the entry for October 4, 1802. Woof suggests that rather than the vital words "& blessed me fervently," what Dorothy Wordsworth actually wrote is "as I blessed the ring softly."

BIBLIOGRAPHIC ESSAY

EDITIONS OF THE GRASMERE JOURNALS

Quotations from the Grasmere Journals are from *The Grasmere and Alfoxden Journals*, edited by Pamela Woof (Oxford World's Classics, 2002), but also consulted were *Journals of Dorothy Wordsworth*, 2 vols., edited by William Knight (Macmillan, 1897); *Journals of Dorothy Wordsworth*, 2 vols., edited by Ernest de Selincourt (Macmillan, 1941); *Journals*, edited by Helen Darbishire (Oxford World's Classics, 1958); *The Journals of Dorothy Wordsworth*, new edition, edited by Mary Moorman (Oxford World's Classics, 1971); *Dorothy Wordsworth's Illustrated Lakeland Journals*, introduced by Rachel Trickett (Collins, 1987); *Selections from the Journals of Dorothy Wordsworth*, edited by Paul Hamilton (Pickering, 1992).

LETTERS

The letters referred to are from the following editions: *Letters of Dorothy Wordsworth*, edited by Alan G. Hill (Clarendon, 1985); *The Early Letters of William and Dorothy Wordsworth, 1787–1805*, edited by Ernest de Selincourt (Oxford University Press, 1935); *De Quincey to Wordsworth: A Biography of a Relationship*, edited by John Emory Jordan (University of California Press, 1962); *The Letters of Mary Wordsworth, 1800–1855*, selected and edited by Mary E. Burton (Clarendon, 1958); *The Letters of William and Dorothy Wordsworth*, 6 vols., edited by Alan G. Hill (Clarendon, 1993); *The Love Letters of William and Mary Wordsworth*, edited by Beth Darlington (Cornell University Press, 1981).

DOROTHY WORDSWORTH'S LIFE

The earliest account of Dorothy Wordsworth to appear is by Thomas De Quincey in his series of articles for *Tait's Edinburgh Magazine*: "Lake Reminiscences, from 1807 to 1830. Nos. I–III—William Wordsworth," January, February, and April 1839; reprinted in *Recollections of the Lakes and the Lake Poets*, edited by David Wright (Penguin, 1970), and more recently in vol. 11 of the Pickering and Chatto *Works of Thomas De Quincey*, general editor Grevel Lindop. De Quincey's essay is to be seen in the light of his having fallen out with the Wordsworths, but despite the mockery behind many of his remarks about the poet himself ("the Wordsworthian legs were certainly not ornamental; and it was really a pity . . . that he had not another pair for evening dress parties"), his picture of Dorothy seems honest to the point of bluntness—he was, after all, not concerned with protecting feelings in the Wordsworth family.

The more dominant version of Dorothy Wordsworth, however, is the tale of docility and devotion to duty best caught in the opening sentence of Collette Clark's edition of the Grasmere Journals, *Home at Grasmere* (Penguin, 1960): "Dorothy Wordsworth was one of those sweet characters whose only life lies in their complete dedication to a man of genius." A similar theme pervades the first full biography, Edmund Lee's *Dorothy Wordsworth: The Story of a Sister's Love* (Clarke, 1886), as well as the chapters on Dorothy in *Some Eminent Women of Our Times* by Mrs. Henry Fawcett (Macmillan, 1889) and *Famous Sisters of Great Men* by Marianne Kirlew (Thomas Nelson & Sons, 1905). Catherine MacDonald Maclean's *Dorothy Wordsworth: The Early Years* (Chatto and Windus, 1932) and Ernest de Selincourt's *Dorothy Wordsworth: A Biography* (Clarendon, 1933; reprinted 1965) continue the tale of joyful selflessness and balance scholarship with sentiment. Catherine MacDonald Maclean's earlier short study, *Dorothy and William Wordsworth* (Cambridge University Press, 1927), provides a more subtle reading of Dorothy's character.

Virginia Woolf captures perfectly the creative interaction between Dorothy and William in "Dorothy Wordsworth," in *The Common Reader*, second series (Hogarth Press, 1932). Elizabeth Hardwick in another important essay, "Amateurs: Dorothy Wordsworth and Jane Carlyle," *New York Review of Books*, November 30, 1972, reprinted in *Seduction and Betrayal: Women and Literature* (Bloomsbury, 2001), questions for the first time since De Quincey whether Dorothy was "happy or unhappy" and notes that her energy "was overwhelming, rather hysterical and engulfing, too great." Elizabeth Gunn's *A Passion for the Particular: Dorothy Wordsworth: A Portrait* (Victor Gollancz, 1981) does not take up any of the points or questions raised by Hardwick but nonetheless provides a good, if truncated, read.

The standard biography is by Robert Gittings and Jo Manton: *Dorothy Wordsworth* (Oxford University Press, 1985). This is a key text for the details of her life and a picture of her times, but Gittings and Manton show a curious absence of analysis in their approach to Dorothy herself, who emerges from their pages as a solid, simple countrywoman about whom there is not much to say. The limitations of their study are described by Norman Fruman in his *Times Literary Supplement* review (June 28, 1985). Fruman expresses surprise at "how little attention is given" by the authors "to Dorothy's erotic feelings and the consequences in so ardent and maternal a person in being deprived not only of a husband and child of her own, but even of acknowledgement of herself as a woman." Because Gittings and Manton avoid exploring the nature of Dorothy's attachment to William, they miss what is "obviously central to an account of her life."

Kathleen Jones in *A Passionate Sisterhood: The Sisters, Wives, and Daughters of the Lake Poets* (Virago, 1998) gives a psychologically rich discussion of Dorothy's responses, examining in detail her interactions with the Hutchinsons, the Coleridges, and the Southeys as well as her relations with William and his children. Dorothy's complexities tend to be dealt with in a more satisfactory way when she is treated as part of a group rather than as an isolated individual, and alongside *A Passionate Sisterhood* there are interesting accounts of her in three highly recommended microhistories: William Heath's *Wordsworth and Coleridge: A Study of Their Literary Relations in 1801 1802* (Oxford University Press, 1970); Richard Matlack's *Poetry of Relationship: The Wordsworths and Coleridge, 1797–1800* (Macmillan, 1997); and John Worthen's often brilliant *The Gang: Coleridge, the Hutchinsons, and the Wordsworths in 1802* (Yale University Press, 2001). Also useful is Amanda Ellis, *Rebels and Conservatives: Dorothy and William Wordsworth and Their Circle* (Indiana University Press, 1967), and Alan Grob, "William and Dorothy: A Case Study in the Hermeneutics of Disparagement," *English Literary History* 65 (Spring 1998).

DOROTHY WORDSWORTH'S WRITING

The most lucid and comprehensive study of Dorothy Wordsworth's prose is *Dorothy Wordsworth, Writer*, by Pamela Woof (Wordsworth Trust, 1988). Woof has written extensively on Dorothy Wordsworth, and her work is the starting point for any researcher. Of particular interest are: "Dorothy Wordsworth's Grasmere Journal: Readings in a Familiar Text," *Wordsworth Circle* (Winter 1989); "Dorothy Wordsworth and the Engendering of Poetry" (in *Wordsworth in Context*, edited by Pauline Fletcher and John Murphy (Bucknell University Press, 1992); "On Editing Dorothy Wordsworth's Grasmere Journals," *Newslet-*

ter, Friends of the Wordsworth Trust, no. 16 (Spring 1992); "Dorothy Wordsworth's Grasmere Journals: The Patterns and Pressures of Composition," in *Romantic Revisions*, edited by Robert Brinkley and Keith Hanley (Cambridge University Press, 1992); "Dorothy Wordsworth in 1802," *Charles Lamb Bulletin*, n.s., 101 (January 1998); "Dorothy Wordsworth: Story-Teller," *Wordsworth Circle* (Spring 2003).

Two of the most perceptive essays on the psychology at work in the Grasmere Journals are Rachel Mayer Brownstein's "Private Life: Dorothy Wordsworth's Journals," *Modern Language Quarterly* 34 (March 1973), and Richard Fadem's "Dorothy Wordsworth: A View from Tintern Abbey," *Wordsworth Circle* (Spring 1978). Brownstein discusses Dorothy as a phenomenological writer who records "insights into the boundaries of sublunary life." Fadem's essay is, among other things, a lesson in how to read the Grasmere Journals: "Her eyes think for her, and what she sees takes the place for her of thoughts. The result is passages of great immediacy but, until we are prepared to read them properly, of a curious emptiness or pointlessness." Other strong discussions are by Alan Lui, "On the Autobiographical Present," *Criticism* 26.2 (1978); A. H. McCormick, "'I shall be beloved—I want no more': Dorothy Wordsworth's Rhetoric and the Appeal to Feeling in the Grasmere Journals," *Philological Quarterly* (1990); and James Holt McGavran, Jr., "Dorothy Wordsworth's Journals—Putting Herself Down," in *The Private Self: Theory and Practice of Women's Autobiographical Writing*, edited by S. Benstock (University of North Carolina Press, 1988). A good review of the later journals is by Carl H. Ketchum, "Dorothy Wordsworth's Journals, 1824–1835," *Wordsworth Circle* (Winter 1978). Margaret Homans has a powerful and provocative chapter on Dorothy Wordsworth's poetry and prose in *Women Writers and Poetic Identity* (Princeton University Press, 1980), and Sarah M. Zimmerman, in *Romanticism, Lyricism, and History* (State University of New York Press, 1999), makes interesting points on her journal writing. Kurt Heinzelman's essay "The Cult of Domesticity: Dorothy and William Wordsworth at Grasmere," in *Romanticism and Feminism*, edited by Anne K. Mellor (Indiana University Press, 1988), is a fascinating account of how the Wordsworths "wrote" themselves into being in Dove Cottage. Susan M. Levin's *Dorothy Wordsworth and Romanticism* (Rutgers, 1987), the only academic book-length study of Dorothy Wordsworth, is important both for her acute analysis of the Grasmere Journals and for her inclusion of the collected poems of Dorothy Wordsworth. Anne K. Mellor's *Romanticism and Feminism* (Indiana University Press, 1988) contains a challenging response to Levin's reading of Dorothy.

For Dorothy Wordsworth in relation to other diarists, I found helpful Margaret Willy, *Three Women Diarists: Celia Fiennes, Dorothy Wordsworth, Katherine*

Mansfield (Longman, 1964); Robert A. Fothergill, *Private Chronicles: A Study of English Diaries* (Oxford University Press, 1974); Harriet Blodgett, *Centuries of Female Days: Englishwomen's Private Diaries* (Alan Sutton, 1989) and *The Englishwoman's Diary* (Fourth Estate, 1992); Felicity Nussbaum, "Toward Conceptualizing Diary," in *Studies in Autobiography*, edited by James Olney (Oxford University Press, 1988); and Judy Simons, *Diaries and Journals of Literary Women from Fanny Burney to Virginia Woolf* (Macmillan, 1990).

DOROTHY'S ILLNESSES

An article in the *British Medical Journal* by Iris I. J. M. Gibson, "Illness of Dorothy Wordsworth" (December 18–25, 1982, p. 1813), put forward the idea that Dorothy suffered from migraines. Gibson suggests that Dorothy's sexual attraction to Coleridge could have contributed to the problem: "It is not so much when Coleridge is actually present that she gets migraine but farewells precipitate attacks." For a more detailed discussion of migraine, I relied on Oliver Sacks, *Migraine: The Evolution of a Common Disorder* (Faber and Faber, 1970), and on Edward Liveing, *On Megrim, Sick-Headache, and Some Allied Disorders: A Contribution to the Pathology of Nerve-Storms* (J. & A. Churchill, 1873). For anorexia, I referred to Joan Brumberg, *Fasting Girls: The Emergence of Anorexia Nervosa as a Modern Disease* (Harvard University Press, 1988), and Rudolph Bell, *Holy Anorexia* (University of Chicago Press, 1985). On Dorothy's trance states in general, there is a study by John Beer, "Coleridge, the Wordsworths, and the State of Trance," *Wordsworth Circle* (Spring 1977). An account of depression similar to the one described by Dorothy in her Grasmere Journals is in Richard Mabey's wonderful *Nature Cure* (Chatto and Windus, 2005). An appendix to Robert Gittings and Jo Manton's *Dorothy Wordsworth* contains a diagnosis, again by Iris I. J. M. Gibson, of Dorothy's later madness, which argues that "Dorothy Wordsworth had senile dementia of the type similar to Alzheimer's disease which is a genetically determined pre-senile dementia." For Dorothy as a sufferer of pseudo-dementia, I found helpful "A Paper on 'Depressive Pseudodementia' or 'Melancholic Dementia': A 19th Century View," by G. E. Berrios in the *Journal of Neurology, Neurosurgery, and Psychiatry* 48 (1985), and Nancy Edwards, "Differentiating the Three D's: Delirium, Dementia, and Depression," *MedSurg Nursing* (December 2003).

SIBLINGS AND INCEST

In 1970, Wordsworth's biographer Mary Moorman gave a lecture, subsequently published as "William and Dorothy Wordsworth" in *Essays by Divers Hands* 37

(1972), in which she argued against the theory put forward by F. W. Bateson in *Wordsworth: A Reinterpretation* (Longman, Green & Co, 1954; 2nd rev. ed., 1956) that Wordsworth and Dorothy were in love. "There is nothing," Moorman argued, "necessarily morbid or dangerous in a brother and sister being deeply—even rapturously—affectionate." In 1974, Molly Lefebure reinforced Bateson's thesis by suggesting in *Samuel Taylor Coleridge: A Bondage of Opium* (Victor Gollancz) that "the picture that emerges from the pages of the Grasmere Journal is one of a woman deeply in love with a man who reciprocates her love to the full but is forced to marry another." The critical response to Lefebure's suggestion can be found on the letters page of the *TLS* between August 9 and December 27, 1974. The exchange, which involved Alethea Hayter and her brother William Hayter, Donald Reiman, Mary Moorman, and Molly Lefebure herself, became less about incest—and still less about Dorothy Wordsworth—than about literary interpretation and the uses of biography. How should Wordsworth's poems be read? Do the Lucy poems have any relation to real feelings? Should biography use the analysis of poetry as source material, and what part should be accorded to sex and sexuality in the reconstruction and representation of a life? An interesting contribution to the incest debate is Donald Reiman, "Poetry of Familiarity: Wordsworth, Dorothy, and Mary Hutchinson," in *The Evidence of the Imagination: Studies of Interactions Between Life and Art in English Romantic Literature*, edited by Donald Reiman, Michael Jaye, and Betty Bennett (New York University Press, 1978).

Sources I have consulted on incestuous relations as either a theme in literature, a cultural taboo, or a social reality are Claude Lévi-Strauss, *The Elementary Structures of Kinship* (Beacon, 1977); Camille Paglia's discussion of what she terms "Romantic incest" in chapters 11, 12, 13, and 17 of *Sexual Personae: Art and Decadence from Nefertiti to Emily Dickinson* (Penguin, 1991); James Twitchell, *Forbidden Partners: The Incest Taboo in Modern Culture* (Columbia University Press, 1987); Ellen Pollak, *Incest and the English Novel, 1648–1814* (Johns Hopkins University Press, 2003); Elizabeth Barnes, ed., *Incest and the Literary Imagination* (University Press of Florida, 2002); Glenda A. Hudson, *Sibling Love and Incest in Jane Austen's Fiction* (Macmillan, 1992); Otto Rank, *The Incest Theme in Literature and Legend* (Johns Hopkins University Press, 1991); and Marc Shell, *The End of Kinship: "Measure for Measure," Incest, and the Ideal of Universal Siblinghood* (Stanford University Press, 1988).

There exists a small but strong body of research on the unconscious dynamics of sibling relationships. Indispensable are Juliet Mitchell's two groundbreaking studies, *Mad Men and Medusas: Reclaiming Hysteria and the Effects of Sibling Relations on the Human Condition* (Penguin, 2000) and *Siblings: Sex and Violence*

(Polity, 2004). Other useful psychoanalytic approaches to sibling relationships are Stephen Bank and Michael Kahn, *The Sibling Bond* (Basic Books, 1982); Prophecy Coles, *The Importance of Sibling Relations in Psychoanalysis* (Karnac, 2003); and Enid Balint, "On Being Empty of Oneself," in *Before I Was I: Psychoanalysis and the Imagination*, edited by Juliet Mitchell and Michael Parsons (Free Association Books, 1993).

A literary and historical approach to siblings can be found in Valerie Sanders's immensely resourceful *The Brother-Sister Culture in Nineteenth-Century Literature: From Austen to Woolf* (Palgrave, 2002), and a remarkable and original study of the drama between William and Dorothy Wordsworth is *Becoming Wordsworthian: A Performative Aesthetics* by Elizabeth Fay (University of Massachusetts Press, 1995).

WILLIAM WORDSWORTH

For contemporary accounts of Wordsworth, there are Thomas De Quincey's essays "Lake Reminiscences, from 1807 to 1830. Nos. I–III—William Wordsworth," *Tait's Edinburgh Magazine*, January, February, and April 1839, reprinted in *Recollections of the Lakes and the Lake Poets*, edited by David Wright (Penguin, 1970); William Hazlitt's essays "My First Acquaintance with Poets," *Liberal*, no. 3 (1823; reprinted by Woodstock Books, 1993), and "Mr. Wordsworth," in *The Spirit of the Age; or, Contemporary Portraits* (Oxford World's Classics, 1904); *Diaries, Reminiscences, and Correspondence of Henry Crabb Robinson*, 3 vols., selected and edited by Thomas Sadler (Macmillan, 1869); Hardwicke Drummond Rawnsley's *Reminiscences of Wordsworth Among the Peasantry of Westmoreland* (Dillon's, 1968); and Coleridge's *Biographia Literaria: or, Biographical Sketches of My Literary Life and Opinions* (Everyman, 1997). A useful collection of reminiscences and biographies can be found in *Lives of the Great Romantics by Their Contemporaries*, vol. 3, edited by Peter Swaab (Pickering, 1996).

Of the recent biographies there is a great deal from which to choose. I found the liveliest portrait of Wordsworth in Kenneth Johnston, *The Hidden Wordsworth: Poet, Lover, Rebel, Spy* (W. W. Norton, 1998), and the most psychologically insightful in Duncan Wu's *Wordsworth: An Inner Life* (Blackwell, 2002). Adam Sisman's *Friendship* (HarperCollins, 2006) provides the best study of the literary and emotional relationship between Wordsworth and Coleridge; Stephen Gill's *William Wordsworth: A Life* (Oxford University Press, 1990) is a masterpiece of erudition, and his later *Wordsworth and the Victorians* (Oxford, 1998) an excellent companion volume on the poet's afterlife; Mary Moorman's two-volume *William Wordsworth: A Biography* (Oxford University Press, 1957) is dated but still valuable; and Juliet Barker's *Wordsworth: A Life* (Penguin, 2000) is both substantial and readable.

Anyone working on Wordsworth is dependent on the work of Mark L. Reed, and I am particularly grateful for his *Wordsworth: The Chronology of the Middle Years, 1800–1815* (Harvard University Press, 1975). Quotations from *Lyrical Ballads* are from *Wordsworth and Coleridge: Lyrical Ballads,* edited by R. L. Brett and A. R. Jones, with a new introduction by Nicholas Roe (Routledge, 2005), and all quotations from Wordsworth's poetry are taken from *William Wordsworth,* edited by Stephen Gill (Oxford University Press, 1984).

On the complexity of the Lucy poems one book looms large: Mark Jones, *The Lucy Poems: A Case Study in Literary Knowledge* (University of Toronto Press, 1995). Also see Richard E. Matlack, "Wordsworth's Lucy Poems in Psychobiographical Context," *PMLA* 93 (1978). Jonathan Wordsworth's reading of Wordsworth's poetry in *The Borders of Vision* (Clarendon, 1982) is witty, insightful, and authoritative. Particularly useful to my purposes were Thomas McFarland, "The Significant Group: Wordsworth's Fears in Solitude," in *Romanticism and the Forms of Ruin: Wordsworth, Coleridge, and the Modalities of Fragmentation* (Princeton University Press, 1981); and John Barrell, "The Uses of Dorothy: The Language of the Sense in *Tintern Abbey,*" in *Poetry, Language, and Politics* (Manchester University Press, 1988).

COLERIDGE

For contemporary accounts of Coleridge, see William Hazlitt's essays "My First Acquaintance with Poets," *Liberal,* no. 3 (1823; reprinted by Woodstock Books, 1993), and "Mr. Coleridge," in *The Spirit of the Age; or, Contemporary Portraits* (Oxford World's Classics, 1904); Thomas De Quincey, "Samuel Taylor Coleridge by the English Opium Eater," *Tait's Edinburgh Magazine,* November 1834 and January 1835, reprinted in *Recollections of the Lakes and the Lake Poets,* edited by David Wright (Penguin, 1970); Joseph Cottle, *Early Recollections* (Longman, Rees and Co., 1837); and *Diary, Reminiscences, and Correspondence of Henry Crabb Robinson,* 3 vols., edited by Thomas Sadler (Macmillan, 1869). For Coleridge on himself, see *Biographia Literaria* (Everyman, 1997) and *The Notebooks of Samuel Taylor Coleridge,* vol. 1, *1794–1804,* edited by Kathleen Coburn (Routledge, 1957; 2002).

Biographies of Coleridge have been written by Rosemary Ashton, *The Life of Samuel Taylor Coleridge: A Critical Biography* (Blackwell, 1996), and Molly Lefebure, *Coleridge: A Bondage of Opium* (Victor Gollancz, 1974), but it is the Coleridge re-created by Richard Holmes in the first volume of his two-volume biography, *Coleridge: Early Visions* (Hodder and Stoughton, 1989), and *Coleridge: Darker Reflections* (HarperCollins, 1998), on whom I depend here. Richard

Holmes's *Coleridge* for the Past Masters series (Oxford University Press, 1982) and his edition of *Samuel Taylor Coleridge, Selected Poems* (Penguin, 1996) are excellent guides to how the poetry should best be read.

GENERAL

For a picture of the Lake District in the late eighteenth and early nineteenth centuries, see Grevel Lindop, *A Literary Guide to the Lake District* (Chatto and Windus, 1993); William Gilpin, *Observations on Cumberland and Westmoreland* (Woodstock Books, 1996); and William Wordsworth, *Guide to the Lakes* (Humphrey Milford, 1926). For sublimity, see Edmund Burke, *A Philosophical Enquiry into the Origin of Our Ideas of the Sublime and Beautiful*, edited by Adam Phillips (Oxford University Press, 1990). Anecdotes of the Wordsworths' lives I found in the *Letters of Elizabeth Gaskell*, edited by J. A. V. Chapple and Arthur Pollard (Manchester University Press, 1997), and *Kilvert's Diary* (Jonathan Cape, 1938). *The Walker's Literary Companion*, edited by Roger Gilbert, Jeffrey Robinson, and Anne Wallace (Breakaway Books, 2000), provided marvelous accounts of the aesthetics of walking, as did Robert MacFarlane's *Mountains of the Mind* (Granta, 2003).

ACKNOWLEDGMENTS

I would like to thank the following: for help and advice, Mark Bostridge, Ophelia Field, Christine Kenyon Jones, Keith Miller, Dr. Ronan MacDonald, Professor Patrick Parrinder, and William St. Clair; for invitations to talk about work in progress, Dr. Jane Jordan, Professor Norma Clarke, Dr. Jane Ridley, Professor Max Saunders, and Dr. Jenny Bourne Taylor; for kindly arranging for me to visit Forncett St. Peter, Ann and Anthony Thwaite and the current owners of the rectory; for reading and commenting on various chapters, Jean Scarlett, James Soderholm, Catherine Taylor, Andrew Wilson, Dr. Anne Wilson, and especially Katie Waldegrave; and, for a last-minute conversation, Grevel Lindop. For his diagnosis of Dorothy's final illness, Ian F. Brockington, professor of psychiatry at Birmingham University; for their enthusiasm and encouragement, my agent, Sarah Lutyens, and my editor, Julian Loose; for their time and help at Dove Cottage, Jeff Cowton, curator at the Wordsworth Trust, and Alex Black, picture librarian at the Wordsworth Trust; for her enduring patience both in Grasmere and in London, Ada Wordsworth. Finally, for her scholarly and stimulating work on Dorothy Wordsworth and for her generosity, my greatest debt of thanks goes to Pamela Woof.

INDEX

Figures in italics indicate captions. "DW," "WW," and "MW" indicate Dorothy, William, and Mary Wordsworth, respectively.

ILLUSTRATION CREDITS

IN TEXT

Pages 26, 31, 78, 203, 209, 234, 240, 260, 269 © Dove Cottage, The Wordsworth Trust.

Page 135 *Scullery, Brathay* (ink on paper) by John Harden (1772–1847) © Abbot Hall Art Gallery, Kendal, Cumbria, U.K./The Bridgeman Art Library.

Page 177 From Walter Hood Fitch, *Illustrations of the British Flora*, 5th revised edition, 1949.

Page 217 From *Land Birds*, 1797, by Thomas Bewick.

Page 275 *Dorothy Wordsworth (1771–1855) in a Wheelchair*, 1842 (ink on paper) by John Harden (1772–1847) © Abbot Hall Art Gallery, Kendal, Cumbria, U.K./The Bridgeman Art Library.

INSERT

1, 2, 3, 4, 5, 7, 8, 9, 10, 12, 14, 15, 16, 17 © Dove Cottage, The Wordsworth Trust.

6 *The Zenith of French Glory; the Pinnacle of Liberty*, James Gillray © www.CartoonStock.com.

11 *Grasmere from the Rydal Road*, 1787, Francis Towne © Birmingham Museums & Art Gallery.

13 *Moonlight, a Landscape with Sheep*, 1831–33, Samuel Palmer © Tate, London, 2007.

18 *Dorothy* by S. Crosthwaite. Courtesy of Rydal Mount House, Ambleside, Cumbria.